SOC Mastery: The Complete Blueprint for Building, Operating, and Scaling Modern Security Operations Centers

A practical guide for designing enterprise-grade SOCs, engineering secure architectures, deploying tool stacks, tuning detections, running incident response, and leading elite analyst teams.

Garrett Music

A special thanks to my wife Rebekah for her support and inspiration

---

This book is a work of nonfiction. All examples, case studies, and descriptions of security operations are presented for educational purposes. Any resemblance to actual organizations, systems, or incidents is either coincidental or used with permission.

Printed in the United States of America.
First Edition, 2025.

ISBN: 979-8-9988141-9-8

Table of Contents

Foreword

Security Operations Centers are often described as the "nerve center" of an organization's cybersecurity strategy. In practice, however, this description vastly understates what a SOC truly is, and what it must become to be effective. A SOC is not a room full of screens. It is not a collection of tools. It is not even a single team or function. A SOC is a living system, shaped by engineering discipline, operational design, communication, leadership, and an organization's willingness to continuously adapt to an adversary that never stops evolving.

Organizations that succeed with a SOC understand that cybersecurity is not static. Threat actors change tactics faster than policies change approval cycles. Environments shift constantly from cloud migrations, SaaS adoption, identity sprawl, remote work and each change reshapes the attack surface. A SOC exists to bring order to that chaos, translating raw telemetry into clarity and decisive action. When done well, it becomes a stabilizing force for the business. When done poorly, it becomes an expensive noise generator that erodes trust and burns out its people. Too many SOCs are built backwards. Tools are purchased first, dashboards are stood up quickly, alerts begin flowing and only then does the organization realize there is no shared understanding of what action looks like, who owns decisions, or how success is measured. Analysts drown in alerts. Leadership sees cost without value. Incidents escalate late or not at all. Eventually, confidence in the SOC erodes, even though the failures were structural, not human.

This book was written to address that gap.

A modern SOC must be engineered, not improvised. It requires deliberate design of workflows, service boundaries, escalation paths, tuning cycles, and communication models before a single alert reaches an analyst. It requires alignment between technology and process, between humans and automation, and between security and the broader business. Most importantly, it requires discipline, the discipline to tune relentlessly, to measure honestly, and to evolve continuously.

The reality of today's threat landscape is unforgiving. Attackers automate. They reuse infrastructure. They exploit misconfigurations, identity weaknesses, and operational blind spots rather than novel exploits. The SOC's task is not to chase every alert, rather it is to identify signals in noise fast enough to protect the organization without exhausting the people doing the work. That balance cannot be achieved through tooling alone.

This book is not concerned with theory in isolation. It is a blueprint. It is written for practitioners who build SOCs, lead SOCs, operate within them, or sell them as services. It focuses on *how* SOCs actually function day to day and how alerts should flow, how incidents should be handled, how analysts should be trained, and how leadership should measure effectiveness without distorting behavior.

Most importantly, it treats the SOC as a system that must be learned. Every investigation teaches something. Every false positive is feedback. Every incident is an opportunity to improve detection, response, and resilience. SOCs that survive are not the ones with the most tools, they are the ones that institutionalize learning faster than their adversaries evolve.

Why SOCs Fail

SOCs do not typically fail because of lack of talent or technology. They fail because the foundation wasn't built correctly from the start. It starts and ends with engineering. Building a solid SOC foundation and then monitoring KPIs for continuous improvement.

They collect logs without understanding them.

A SIEM full of noise is not visibility therefore it's blindness disguised as data which leads to spikes in false positive alerts and therefore alert fatigue among analysts. As a SOC leader it is imperative to be aware of this, as many in my experience will trade a finely tuned alerting environment for an abundance of alert types and data ingestion under the assumption this makes their SOC more robust and advanced. This is a dangerous assumption. While it is important to have diversity in alert types, keeping the noise down and tuning out false positives to the lowest level possible is key. This increases the chances of true positive alerts being investigated and reduces the amount of time spent in triage thus increasing overall response time and SOC effectiveness.

They deploy tools without designing processes.

EDR, SOAR, SIEM, TIPs. None of these matter if workflows and playbooks aren't defined, documented, and maintained. They assume that implementing a SIEM or signing with an EDR vendor instantly creates capability. In reality, deploying technology before defining processes is the fastest way to create a dysfunctional, noisy, and ineffective SOC.

SOPs Always Come First

A SOC must be built around SOPs (Standard Operating Procedures) not tools. SOPs are the blueprint. Tools are only the equipment used to execute that blueprint. Without SOPs, tools become expensive noise generators that analysts have no consistent, mature, or repeatable method for managing. A SIEM can only automate what you tell it to. A SOAR can only orchestrate what you've documented. An EDR can only support workflows you've clearly defined. This is why the strongest SOCs design process first, technology second.

A proper SOC doesn't begin with log ingestion or tool integration it begins with:

Defined workflows

What happens when an alert fires?
Who handles it?
What should they check?
When should it be escalated?
When is it resolved?

Documented playbooks

Step-by-step procedures for every alert type.
Repeatable actions that ensure consistency.
Criteria for true vs false positives.

Escalation paths

Who gets called, when, and for what reason.
How severity is determined.
Time-bound criteria for SLAs.

Roles and responsibilities

What Tier 1 does.
What Tier 2 does.
What the IR lead owns.
What the SOC Manager approves.

SLA definitions

Response times.
Containment commitments.
Internal vs external expectations.

Once this foundation is set, then the SOC leadership selects and deploys tools to support those SOPs. It should never be the other way around. Think of the Software Development Lifecycle (SDLC), what comes first? Requirements, think of the SOP in this light and you'll be thinking like a leader.

Why Tools Without SOPs Fail

Let's make this extremely clear:

- A SIEM without defined workflows becomes a flood of meaningless logs.
- A SOAR without documented playbooks becomes an unused automation engine.
- An EDR without escalation criteria becomes a source of confusion instead of protection.
- A TIP without enrichment workflows becomes a dashboard nobody opens.

- Tools do not create structure, they only amplify whatever structure exists. If the structure is chaos, the tools only amplify chaos.

SOP-Driven SOC Design

A mature SOC follows this hierarchy:

a. *SOPs & Processes: Define what needs to be done.*

b. *Workflows & Playbooks: Define how it needs to be done.*

c. *Tool Selection: Choose the platform that best carries out the above.*

d. *Tool Configuration: Tune the tools to match the documented process.*

e. *Automation: Build SOAR playbooks based on the SOPs already in place.*

f. *Continuous Improvement: Update SOPs as threats evolve.*

This is how elite SOCs operate. Start with the process and understand the requirements. Build the SOC from the documentation and requirements outward. Only then should leadership layer on technology and redundancy.

Why SOCs Succeed

The SOCs that thrive and truly protect organizations, impress clients, and run like elite teams share a common theme:

Intentional engineering: *They know why each log source matters, what each tool contributes, and how data flows from ingestion → analysis → action.*

Clear and documented processes: *Every alert type has a workflow, every escalation path is known, every SLA is measurable.*

Effective use of automation: *They use SOAR platforms, enrichment APIs, and playbooks to remove analyst guesswork and accelerate decision-making.*

Continuous detection tuning: *They tune rules weekly, evaluate false positives, and relentlessly iterate.*

Analysts share findings, run mock IRs, debrief incidents, and speak confidently to both technical and non-technical audiences. They cross train in other areas such as engineering and threat hunting as well as IR to the lowest tier analyst. This is a key point as many SOCs and MSSPs fail to nurture inexperienced and newer analysts.

They don't wait for detections to trigger,

they search for the quiet, subtle, and behavioral indicators attackers rely on. I've spent hours of downtime personally in the SOC when the alert boards were calm and took a deep dive into SentinelOne's deepvis or Crowdstrike and sifted through noise and uncovered malicious activity that had serious consequences for clients, this is how a SOC analyst can be proactive in defending, by seeking out the bad things living in the environment that never triggered an alert. Most importantly, successful SOCs understand that security is not a product, it's a practice. It is something you build, operate, refine, and evolve every single day.

What You Will Learn in This Book

This book is designed to be the complete, end-to-end blueprint for building, operating, and scaling a modern SOC, whether you are an analyst, an engineer, a manager, a business owner, or an MSSP founder.

By the time you finish, you will understand:

- How to design SOC architecture from the ground up

- How SIEM, SOAR, EDR, and TIP platforms actually work
- How to deploy tools and onboard data sources
- How to write and tune detections
- How to automate enrichment using VirusTotal, AbuseIPDB, GreyNoise and other APIs
- How to run SOC operations day-to-day
- How to conduct incident response, threat hunting, and malware analysis
- How to identify false positives vs true positives
- How to manage client bridge calls with calm and authority
- How to measure SOC success using SLAs, KPIs, and reporting
- How to build a scalable SOC offering for an MSSP or enterprise environment

How to Apply This Immediately

Whether you are trying to break into cybersecurity, level up your SOC career, or build your own SOC practice, this book gives you a roadmap you can apply from day one.

- Analysts can use it to sharpen triage, investigation, and detection skills.
- Engineers can use it to architect more resilient, scalable environments.
- SOC managers can use it to improve processes, elevate training, and drive performance.
- Business owners and MSSP founders can use it to launch or refine a profitable SOC offering.

No matter your role, this book will give you the clarity, structure, and proven frameworks needed to operate a truly successful SOC one that protects, performs, and scales.

SECTION I
FOUNDATIONS OF A MODERN SOC

Chapter 1

What a SOC Actually Is (and Isn't)

A Security Operations Center (SOC) is often misrepresented as purely a team, a room, or a collection of cybersecurity tools. In reality, a SOC is none of those things by itself. A SOC is a function, a discipline, and a framework for protecting an organization through continuous monitoring, detection, analysis, response, and improvement.

A SOC is the central nervous system of cybersecurity operations and like any nervous system, it must be intentional, organized, and connected. This chapter lays the foundation for understanding what a SOC truly is, how it should operate, and how it matures over time.

The Purpose of a Security Operations Center

At its core, the SOC exists for one reason; To protect the organization by identifying, investigating, and responding to threats as quickly and effectively as possible. Everything else: tools, people, dashboards and budgets is in service of that mission.

A SOC's purpose can be summarized by four strategic pillars:

1. Visibility

Without visibility, security cannot exist. The SOC's first mission is to ensure that every meaningful event across the environment from network traffic to authentication, endpoint behavior, identity changes, cloud activity, and more is all captured, monitored, and understood.

2. Detection

Detection is the science of identifying suspicious or malicious activity among millions of legitimate events. The SOC uses detections, correlation rules, machine learning models (if applicable), and behavioral analytics to surface threats quickly and with minimal noise.

3. Response

A detection means nothing without action. The SOC coordinates containment, eradication, and recovery efforts from isolating endpoints to resetting credentials, disabling accounts, blocking IPs, and engaging the incident response team.

4. Improvement

A SOC is never "finished." Every incident is a lesson. Every false positive is a tuning opportunity. Every detection rule can be refined. Every analyst can be trained. Every process can be improved. A SOC should evolve weekly, not yearly or even quarterly.

SOC Maturity Models

Not all SOCs are equal. SOCs evolve through maturity levels that reflect their visibility, capabilities, automation, and institutional discipline. Two models are most commonly referenced: the Capability Maturity

Model (CMM) and the SOC-CMM model, but regardless of the framework, SOC maturity generally progresses through the following stages:

Level 0 Nonexistent / Siloed Security

- No SOC.
- Log data exists but is not monitored.
- No formal detections or response processes.

Level 1 Basic SOC

- Manual monitoring.
- Analysts react to alerts as they appear.
- Processes are inconsistent or tribal knowledge.
- Limited visibility.
- High alert fatigue.

Level 2 Structured SOC

- Documented SOPs and workflows exist.
- Analysts follow defined triage steps.
- Improved visibility across endpoints and identity.
- Basic SIEM use cases implemented.
- Regular tuning cycles begin.

Level 3 Proactive SOC

- Threat hunting introduced.
- Playbooks developed for common alerts.
- SOAR automation implemented.
- Detection engineering becomes a discipline.
- Regular reporting and KPI tracking.
- Cloud telemetry incorporated.

Level 4 Optimized SOC

- Fully mature processes.

- High automation for enrichment and containment.
- Predictive and behavioral detections.
- Cross-team collaboration (IT, GRC, IR, DevOps).
- Budget and operations scaled effectively.
- Analysts are highly trained and focused on high-value tasks.

Level 5 Intelligence-Driven SOC

- Threat intel deeply integrated.
- Adversary profiling and proactive defense.
- Custom detection content.
- Real-time enrichment APIs.
- Red/purple team alignment.
- SOC becomes a strategic business asset.

A goal of this book is to help readers understand how to move from Level 1 to Level 4, the operating range of well-run enterprise and MSSP SOCs.

MSSP vs In-House SOC

Not all SOCs operate under the same business model. Two dominant frameworks exist: in-house SOCs and MSSP SOCs. Each has strengths, limitations, and strategic implications.

In-House SOC

Strengths

- Full environmental context
- High control over architecture and tooling
- Alignment with business objectives
- Ability to integrate deeply with IT, DevOps, and cloud teams
- Direct access to executive stakeholders

Challenges

- Higher cost
- Hiring and retaining staff
- Limited 24/7 capability unless heavily resourced
- May lack specialized expertise (malware, forensics, threat intel)

An in-house SOC is ideal for large enterprises with sensitive data or regulatory requirements.

MSSP SOC (Managed Security Service Provider)

Strengths

- Lower cost for clients
- Built-in 24/7 monitoring
- Established playbooks, tools, and workflows
- Scalable operations

- Broad exposure to multiple client environments
- Specialized analysts (IR, threat hunting, detection engineering)

Challenges

- Limited visibility into client internal processes
- Varying client architectures create complexity
- Must balance scale and customization
- Requires strong communication and reporting
- Must maintain strict SLAs across many tenants

MSSPs excel at providing SOC capability to small and mid-sized businesses or augmenting enterprise SOCs.

Key SOC Functions and Services

A modern SOC performs a wide range of responsibilities that revolve around one mission: defend the organization. These responsibilities include:

1. Monitoring & Detection

- SIEM log monitoring
- EDR/XDR alert triage
- Cloud security monitoring
- Identity security monitoring
- Network traffic analysis

This is the "eyes-on-glass" function many people commonly associate with SOC work.

2. Incident Response

- Containment

- Eradication
- Recovery
- Forensics and evidence gathering
- Coordination with business stakeholders
- Post-incident analysis
- Root cause identification

IR is where true SOC maturity becomes visible.

3. Threat Hunting

- Hypothesis-driven investigations
- Behavioral and anomaly-based searches
- Proactive pursuit of dormant attackers
- Hunting for TTPs aligned to MITRE ATT&CK
- Baseline establishment and deviation analysis

Threat hunting separates proactive SOCs from reactive ones.

4. Detection Engineering

- Building and tuning SIEM rules
- Writing YARA and Sigma rules
- Creating correlation logic
- Reducing false positives
- Increasing detection fidelity

Without detection engineering, SOCs drown in noise.

5. Vulnerability & Exposure Analysis

- Identifying weak configurations
- Integrating vulnerability scanners
- Monitoring exposed assets
- Feeding findings into detection logic

This function often overlaps with GRC and IT security teams.

6. Threat Intelligence Enrichment

- Leveraging TI feeds
- VirusTotal, AbuseIPDB, GreyNoise API enrichment
- Domain, IP, URL reputation
- Actor attribution (optional but valuable)

Threat intel elevates investigations.

7. Reporting & Compliance

- Executive summaries
- KPI and SLA reports
- Compliance documentation (PCI, HIPAA, etc.)
- Daily, weekly, and monthly reporting cycles

Reports demonstrate SOC value to stakeholders and clients.

Core SOC Workflows

Every Security Operations Center regardless of size, tooling, or maturity operates on a foundation of core workflows that make security operations consistent, repeatable, and measurable. These workflows align closely with frameworks such as NIST 800-61 (Computer Security Incident Handling Guide), NIST CSF, and MITRE ATT&CK, which help ensure that SOC processes remain structured, defensible, and adaptable as threats evolve. Each workflow supports the others, creating a cyclical ecosystem where monitoring feeds investigations, investigations feed response, response feeds tuning, and tuning improves monitoring. When executed properly, these workflows transform raw telemetry into intelligence and intelligence into action. Below is a detailed overview of each workflow, how to conduct it, and best practices for operational excellence.

Monitoring & Triage

Monitoring and triage form the front line of SOC operations. This workflow begins with alert ingestion from SIEM, EDR, IDS/IPS, cloud security platforms, or custom log sources. Once alerts arrive, analysts perform initial analysis by reviewing event details, timestamps, correlated logs, and enrichment sources such as VirusTotal, AbuseIPDB, internal asset inventories, and threat intelligence feeds. The goal at this stage is to quickly determine whether the activity is benign, suspicious, or malicious. Effective classification is rooted in both context such as user behavior, asset criticality, and recent changes and in detection engineering logic that maps to MITRE ATT&CK techniques.

To implement strong triage, SOCs must establish Standard Operating Procedures (SOPs) that define how analysts classify alerts and what constitutes a valid escalation. Documentation is essential; every alert should have clear notes describing what was observed, why the determination was made, and what data sources were consulted. Escalation to higher tiers occurs only when additional expertise or authority is required, ensuring efficient use of analyst time. The best SOCs also incorporate enrichment and tagging automatically within the SIEM so analysts spend more time analyzing and less time searching. This workflow is ultimately where noise is filtered out and genuine threats are surfaced; without disciplined triage, the SOC collapses under alert fatigue.

Best practices:
– Enforce strict triage SLAs to maintain rapid detection.
– Require documented reasoning for every classification decision.
– Use automation for routine enrichment (whois lookups, hash lookups, geo-IP, etc.).
– Map alerts to ATT&CK techniques to guide investigations.
– Maintain an up-to-date asset inventory to contextualize alerts.

Incident Response Workflow

Incident response (IR) is the SOC's most visible and high-impact capability. Once a threat is confirmed, which is to say, once triage determines activity is malicious the SOC transitions into IR following the structure recommended in NIST 800-61. The first priority is containment: isolating infected endpoints, disabling compromised accounts, blocking malicious IPs, or halting lateral movement. After containment, analysts identify the scope by determining which systems, users, or data paths were affected. This often involves log correlation, endpoint forensics, memory analysis, or packet capture review.

Eradication follows once analysts understand what the attacker did. This may include removing malware, deleting persistence mechanisms, closing exploited vulnerabilities, or resetting credentials. Recovery then restores affected systems to normal operations, ideally using clean backups or reimaged endpoints. Communication with leadership is critical throughout the process to ensure alignment on risk, business impact, and required actions. After the incident is resolved, the SOC documents lessons learned, captures what went well or poorly, and updates playbooks and detection logic to prevent recurrence.

To implement this effectively, a SOC must have predefined IR playbooks mapped to common attack types such as ransomware, credential theft, phishing, and C2 activity. These playbooks standardize decision-making and ensure consistency across analysts.

Lets review containment, eradication and recovery in depth.

Containment, eradication, and recovery form the tactical heart of incident response, representing the moment when the SOC moves from analysis into direct action. These phases require more than theoretical knowledge, they demand a deep understanding of how operating systems behave, where forensic evidence originates, and how attackers establish persistence. Effective execution of these steps determines how quickly an organization returns to a healthy state and whether an attacker can regain access after being removed.

Containment

Containment is the immediate effort to stop the attacker's activity and prevent further damage. When the SOC confirms malicious behavior, whether through EDR telemetry, correlated alerts in the SIEM, suspicious authentication patterns, or anomalous process execution, the first priority is to prevent lateral movement and data exfiltration while avoiding unnecessary operational disruption. Signals that trigger containment often originate from process creation events, unusual network connections, file modifications, registry changes, privilege escalation attempts, or known Indicators of Compromise (IOCs). These signals come from endpoint monitoring tools, Windows Event Logs, Sysmon, Linux audit logs, network firewalls, cloud telemetry, and third-party threat intelligence feeds.

In practice, containment often begins with isolating a compromised host using EDR tooling, cutting it off from the network while maintaining analyst access for investigation. At the same time, any compromised user accounts are disabled, sessions terminated, and MFA resets initiated. Network controls are tightened by blocking malicious IP addresses or domains and disabling attacker-controlled services or scheduled tasks. Short-term containment aims to freeze the attack in place, while long-term containment focuses on preventing re-entry by patching vulnerabilities, correcting misconfigurations, tightening firewall rules, and ensuring the attacker has no remaining access points.

Eradication

Eradication begins once containment is stable. This phase focuses on removing every malicious file, script, registry key, persistence mechanism, credential artifact, unauthorized account, or backdoor left by the attacker. Analysts rely heavily on forensic data collected during investigation process trees, command-line arguments, loaded DLLs (dynamic link library), network connections, scheduled tasks, and registry modifications, logged and observed, to identify what must be eliminated.

In Windows environments, eradication requires inspecting common persistence locations. Analysts review directories frequently abused by malware such as \APPDATA\, \PROGRAMDATA\, \TEMP\, and user profile paths. The Windows Registry is a major focus; attackers commonly create persistence in keys such as Run, RunOnce, Winlogon\Userinit, and Services. Tools like Sysinternals (system internals) Autoruns, RegEdit (registry editor), and PowerShell commands help locate and remove these entries. DLL persistence and hijacking require checking for unsigned, suspicious, or misplaced libraries within System32, SysWOW64 (system windows on windows), or application directories. Malicious services are identified by reviewing service configurations, startup types, and associated binaries, then removed using Service Control Manager commands or PowerShell. Scheduled tasks created through Task Scheduler, schtasks.exe, or PowerShell are inspected for malicious triggers or payloads and deleted.

Linux eradication follows similar principles but targets different locations and mechanisms. Persistence often appears in systemd (system daemon) service files under /etc/systemd/system/, cron jobs, shell initialization files such as .bashrc or .profile, or scripts placed in /tmp or /var/tmp. Analysts use tools like ps aux, lsof, netstat, ss, auditd, and file integrity monitoring systems to identify malicious processes, connections, or modified binaries. Rootkits are detected through specialized tools such as chkrootkit or rkhunter, and unauthorized SSH (Secure Shell) keys or modified configurations are carefully reviewed and removed.

Across both platforms, eradication must be thorough; even a single overlooked persistence mechanism can allow an attacker to return with full privileges.

Recovery

Recovery focuses on restoring the environment to a trustworthy, fully operational state. This phase begins only when analysts are confident that no active threat remains. Recovery includes reimaging compromised systems, restoring data from known-clean backups, rotating credentials, enforcing MFA, and applying patches or configuration changes that close the original attack vector. It also involves validating system integrity, running full EDR scans, verifying file hashes, checking for abnormal network behavior, and reviewing logs to confirm normal operational patterns have resumed.

The SOC coordinates closely with IT and leadership during this phase because recovery often impacts production services. Any system that was deeply compromised, especially domain controllers, authentication servers, or systems involved in lateral movement may need to be rebuilt entirely. Recovery also includes strengthening the environment by implementing lessons learned: new detection rules, updated firewall policies, hardened configurations, or improved monitoring coverage.

Finally, the SOC compiles a detailed post-incident report documenting the attack timeline, affected systems, root cause, containment actions, eradication steps, and long-term recovery tasks. This not only satisfies audit and compliance requirements but also feeds future detection engineering and prevention strategies.

Figure 3: Recovery Lifecycle Overview

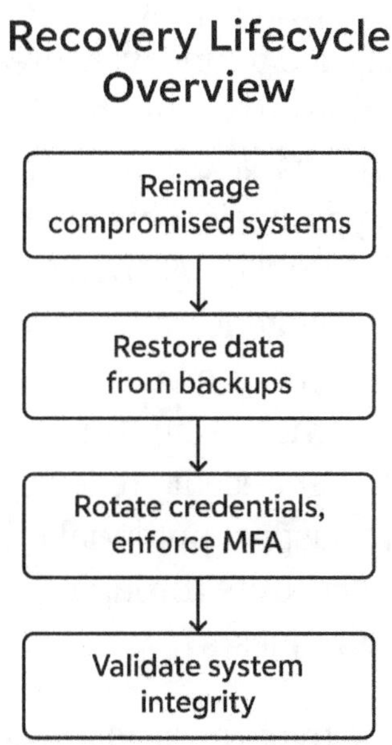

Best practices:
– *Use isolation capabilities within EDR solutions for rapid containment.*
– *Maintain a communication plan defining who is informed at each IR stage.*
– *Perform root-cause analysis (RCA) to determine how the incident began.*
– *Document every containment or eradication action with timestamps.*
– *Feed every incident into tuning and threat hunting cycles.*

Threat Hunting Workflow

Threat hunting is the SOC's proactive capability, designed to uncover threats that existing detections have missed. Unlike monitoring, which reacts to alerts, hunting starts with a hypothesis. This hypothesis is usually based on MITRE ATT&CK techniques, recent threat intelligence, anomalies observed in the environment, or known gaps in logging or visibility. For example, a hunting hypothesis might state: "Given recent credential theft campaigns, we suspect potential misuse of compromised accounts through abnormal Kerberos ticket requests."

Once the hypothesis is set, analysts identify the relevant data sources such as authentication logs, DNS logs, network flows, EDR telemetry, or PowerShell logs. They query the environment using SIEM queries, EDR search functions, or threat hunting platforms to look for patterns or anomalies. Any suspicious findings are investigated in depth, including endpoint inspection or cross-correlation with threat intelligence. All findings, whether malicious or benign, must be documented because this documentation becomes the foundation for future hunts.

The final step is detection improvement. If a hunt uncovers activity that was previously undetected, the SOC creates new detection rules, updates filters, or tunes existing logic. Threat hunting feeds detection engineering, making the SOC progressively stronger and more resistant to advanced threats.

Best practices:

– *Conduct hunts on a regular cadence (weekly, biweekly, or monthly).*

– *Base hunts on MITRE ATT&CK to ensure coverage of known adversary behaviors.*

– *Document hypotheses, methodology, findings, and recommendations.*

– *Turn every valid finding into a new detection use case.*

– *Use hunts to validate and strengthen EDR and SIEM visibility.*

Reporting Workflow

Reporting is the mechanism through which the SOC demonstrates value, transparency, and impact. Reports may be daily, weekly, or monthly, depending on the organization's needs. These reports summarize alerts, incidents, trends, and operational metrics such as mean time to detect (MTTD), mean time to respond (MTTR), SLA adherence, and reductions in false positives. Reports also identify emerging risks, provide recommendations for improving security posture, and highlight any recurring patterns in incidents or alert types.

Implementing an effective reporting workflow requires consistency in format and meaningful metrics that reflect actual SOC outcomes rather than vanity statistics. Reports should speak the language of stakeholders: technical details for IT, risk-based insights for leadership, and compliance-relevant information for auditors. Reports are also an essential historical record that helps the SOC track progress over time, justify budget or staffing increases, and validate operational maturity.

Best practices:
– Align reporting with NIST CSF categories (Identify, Protect, Detect, Respond, Recover).
– Incorporate trend analysis to show improvements or emerging issues.

– Track SLA performance transparently.
– Present data visually when possible (graphs, heat maps, ATT&CK matrices).
– Provide actionable, prioritized recommendations, not just raw data.

Tuning & Continuous Improvement

Tuning and continuous improvement ensure the SOC remains effective and avoids collapse under the weight of false positives. This workflow begins with reviewing false positive alerts, analyzing their root cause, and adjusting detection logic or thresholds. Rules may need refinement based on behavior baselines, new threat intelligence, or lessons learned from recent investigations. Continuous improvement also includes implementing new detections, revising SOPs and playbooks, and improving automation based on analyst feedback.

This workflow ties directly into frameworks like MITRE ATT&CK for coverage mapping and NIST CSF for aligning improvements with broader security strategy. A SOC that consistently tunes becomes more accurate, more efficient, and more capable of handling advanced threats. Conversely, a SOC that fails to tune accumulates noise, wastes analyst time, and eventually becomes ineffective.

In addition to refining detections and updating playbooks, tuning and continuous improvement also depend heavily on measuring and improving key performance indicators (KPIs) and service-level agreements (SLAs). These metrics provide an objective lens through which SOC performance can be evaluated. KPIs typically include operational measures such as time-to-triage (TTT), mean time to detect (MTTD), mean time to respond (MTTR), alert closure rates, false-positive ratios, incident recurrence, and threat hunt efficiency. SLAs, on the other hand, define the guaranteed performance expectations between the SOC and its stakeholders, for example, "High-severity alerts must be triaged within 15 minutes," or "Incident reports must be delivered within 24 hours of closure." Both KPIs and SLAs must be tracked continuously, ideally through automated dashboards in SIEM, SOAR, or ticketing systems.

To effectively track these metrics, a SOC should implement a ticketing workflow where every alert, investigation, and incident is time-stamped at each step of its lifecycle. Tools like Sentinel, Splunk, Elastic, ServiceNow, or custom SOC dashboards can automatically calculate averages and deviations.
Time-to-triage, for example, is measured from the moment an alert is generated to the moment an analyst classifies it. MTTD tracks the time between the attacker's first observable action

and the SOC's detection, while MTTR measures from detection to full eradication or containment. When these metrics trend downward, it signals increasing SOC agility and efficiency; when they trend upward, it often indicates understaffing, alert fatigue, poorly tuned rules, or tooling gaps.

Improving KPIs and SLAs comes down to two primary factors: reducing noise and speeding up analyst action. This means tuning out false positives, enriching alerts automatically, refining detection logic, and ensuring SOPs guide analysts clearly and consistently. Improved SLAs often require better automation such as automated containment triggers or auto-triage enrichment as well as structured escalation pathways that eliminate bottlenecks. Leadership should review KPI and SLA reports regularly, identify trends, and convert them into actionable tuning tasks or process adjustments. Ultimately, metrics are not just numbers; they are the pulse of the SOC. When measured honestly, reviewed regularly, and used to drive iterative improvements, they become one of the strongest indicators of SOC maturity.

Best practices:

– *Schedule regular tuning sessions weekly for*

small SOCs, daily for large ones.
– Maintain a detection engineering backlog and prioritize high-impact improvements.
– Use ATT&CK mapping to identify detection gaps.
– Incorporate feedback from IR, threat hunting, and monitoring teams.
– Continuously update SOPs, playbooks, and runbooks as tools and processes evolve.

A SOC that neglects these workflows becomes stagnant and overwhelmed. A SOC that masters them becomes resilient, scalable, and operationally unstoppable.

A SOC is not a tool. It is not a dashboard. It is not a Tier 1 analyst looking at alerts in isolation. A SOC is a system, an interconnected, documented, disciplined system of people, processes, technology, working toward continuous improvement. Understanding this foundation will shape how every other chapter in this book is approached, built, and applied.

Chapter 2

SOC Organizational Structure

A Security Operations Center succeeds or fails based on its organizational structure and the clarity with which responsibilities, workflows, and escalation paths are defined. Technology alone cannot compensate for poorly structured teams or undefined processes. A mature SOC is intentionally designed, with each role serving a distinct function within a broader operational system. This chapter describes, in detailed and practical terms, how to build such a structure from staffing tiers to training programs, shift models, hiring techniques, and performance measurements.

Understanding SOC Roles and Responsibilities

A modern SOC is usually built around a three-tiered analyst structure supported by specialized roles such as threat hunters, detection engineers, an IR lead, and a SOC manager. Each role contributes uniquely to holistic detection, response, and continuous improvement.

Tier 1 analysts form the front line of the SOC. They spend most of their time performing alert monitoring, triage, and initial enrichment. Their job is to identify whether an alert is benign, suspicious, or malicious using investigative techniques guided by SOPs and playbooks. Tier 1 analysts are not expected to have advanced forensics skills but must excel at pattern recognition, disciplined documentation, and following standardized workflows. The best Tier 1 hires demonstrate curiosity, coachability, and the ability to learn structured processes quickly. Training usually begins with tool familiarization, step-by-step triage simulations, and crash courses on Windows, Linux, cloud logs, and common attack techniques.

Tier 2 analysts perform deeper investigations and validate escalating threats. When Tier 1 identifies activity that requires more context, Tier 2 takes over. They gather evidence, pivot across telemetry sources such as EDR, Sysmon logs, cloud audit trails, and network data, and determine the scope and nature of a threat. They often engage directly with IT teams during active incidents and initiate containment steps using EDR isolation, SOAR blocking actions, credential resets, or firewall modifications. Tier 2 analysts must be able to form investigative hypotheses, test them, and present findings clearly.

Tier 3 analysts act as subject-matter experts in complex incidents. They uncover lateral movement, persistence mechanisms, or stealthy command execution. They may reverse engineer malware, perform disk forensics, or help determine whether a threat actor achieved long-term persistence. They also propose new detections, guide tuning efforts, and mentor lower tiers. Tier 3 analysts are the calm center of the storm during major incidents and often act as technical leads.

The SOC Manager oversees the entire operation. This role ensures the SOC meets SLAs, manages staffing and shift schedules, maintains SOPs and playbooks, and ensures operational consistency. The SOC Manager is responsible for daily standups, weekly escalation reviews, and continuous improvement initiatives. They also serve as the escalation point for unresolved operational issues and ensure analysts receive ongoing training.

The IR Lead coordinates high-severity incidents and ensures containment, eradication, and recovery efforts match organizational priorities. This person manages communication with executives, legal, HR, or external partners and maintains the IR plan according to standards such as NIST 800-61r2.

Threat Hunters operate proactively rather than reactively. They create hypotheses based on attacker TTPs, threat intelligence reports, or observed anomalies, then search the environment for evidence of stealthy compromise. When they uncover suspicious behavior, they collaborate with detection engineers to turn their findings into new detection rules.

Detection Engineers design and maintain the SOC's detection and alerting mechanisms. They understand logging pipelines, event schemas, SIEM normalization, EDR telemetry, and SOAR automation. They create correlation rules, reduce false positives, adjust thresholds, and deploy new detection content aligned with frameworks such as MITRE ATT&CK.

Shift Models: Structuring Coverage for a Modern SOC

Choosing the correct shift model affects analyst well-being, SLA compliance, and SOC maturity. A 24/7 shift model is common for MSSPs or global enterprises that require real-time monitoring. Analysts work in fixed or rotating eight-hour, ten-hour, or twelve-hour schedules, ensuring continuous coverage. Although this structure is effective, it requires careful workload balancing to prevent burnout. A follow-the-sun model distributes SOC teams across multiple time zones, eliminating overnight work and supporting higher analyst morale, but it requires strong handoff procedures and consistent SOPs to maintain cohesion. Hybrid models combine staffed core hours with after-hours on-call escalation, which works well for mid-sized organizations with lower alert volumes.

Hiring for the SOC: How to Recruit the Right People

Successful SOC hiring focuses on aptitude and mindset as much as experience. Instead of relying exclusively on degree requirements, organizations should prioritize candidates with demonstrated curiosity, analytical thinking, and strong documentation skills. Practical assessments outperform interviews alone. For Tier 1, candidates can be evaluated through simulated alert triage scenarios, basic investigation exercises, or simple query challenges in KQL or SPL. Tier 2 and Tier 3 candidates may be tested with log-correlation tasks, small malware samples, or root-cause analysis exercises.

Communication is another essential skill, especially for roles that interact with clients or leadership. For MSSPs, analysts must be able to explain technical findings to non-technical customers. The hiring process should include writing tests or mock ticket write-ups to ensure candidates can produce clear, concise documentation.

Training and Career Progression

A SOC that does not train cannot improve. A structured 30-day onboarding program introduces analysts to the SOC's toolset, SOPs, ticketing standards, and detection technologies. Hands-on labs with real telemetry help analysts quickly learn the difference between normal and anomalous behavior. Ongoing training includes weekly threat intel briefings, regular red-versus-blue simulations, and quarterly tabletop exercises. Many SOCs support certifications such as Security+, CySA+, GCIH, GCIA, or Azure Security certs to help analysts grow professionally.

Career progression typically follows a path from Tier 1 to Tier 2 to Tier 3, with branching specializations such as IR, detection engineering, or threat hunting. This internal mobility reduces burnout and turnover to major SOC challenges.

KPIs for SOC Teams

SOC performance is measured using a combination of KPIs that reflect speed, accuracy, noise levels, and operational maturity. The mean time to triage (MTTT) captures how quickly analysts evaluate new alerts. Mean time to contain (MTTC) measures how rapidly threats are neutralized. Mean time to respond or recover (MTTR) reflects the time between detection and full resolution. False-positive rate and detection coverage measure the quality of SOC detection engineering.

These metrics can be tracked using SIEM dashboards, SOAR workflow timestamps, or ticketing system analytics. KPIs improve when the SOC tunes alerts, reduces unnecessary noise, expands visibility, and improves automation. Regular review cycles allow the SOC Manager to identify bottlenecks and set improvement goals.

SECTION II

ENGINEERING & DESIGNING THE SOC

Chapter 3

SOC Architecture & Infrastructure Blueprint

A Security Operations Center is only as effective as the architecture that supports it. The infrastructure behind a SOC determines the visibility analysts have, the speed at which data can be processed, how long logs can be retained, and how defensible the environment is during an incident. SOC architecture is a blend of networking, systems engineering, cloud design, and security engineering brought together to support continuous monitoring and rapid response. Whether a SOC is deployed on-premises, in the cloud, or in a hybrid model, the same foundational principles apply: reliable log ingestion, secure data storage, scalable compute resources, resilient network segmentation, and compliance alignment. This chapter provides a full blueprint for building or upgrading a SOC environment with a step-by-step explanation of each architectural component.

SOC Deployment Models: On-Prem, Cloud, and Hybrid

A SOC can operate in one of three broad architectural models, each designed around an organization's scale, regulatory environment, and technical maturity. On-premises SOC environments offer tight control and are often preferred in highly regulated industries such as federal agencies or healthcare providers. In on-prem deployments, all log collectors, SIEM infrastructure, packet capture appliances, and case-management platforms reside inside the organization's physical data centers. The primary benefit is full data sovereignty and tight integration with legacy systems. However, teams must manage their own hardware lifecycle, storage expansion, and scalability planning.

Cloud-based SOCs leverage platforms such as Microsoft Sentinel, Google Chronicle, or Elastic Cloud to handle ingestion, correlation, analytics, and storage. This model drastically reduces operational overhead while enabling nearly unlimited scale. Cloud-native SOCs benefit from elastic compute during peak alert storms and enjoy stronger disaster recovery characteristics because logs exist redundantly across multiple regions. The challenge arises when ingesting logs from internal systems behind firewalls, which requires secure collectors, VPN tunnels, or private endpoints.

Most modern enterprises choose a hybrid SOC model, combining on-prem collectors with cloud analytics pipelines. This allows full visibility into internal traffic while leveraging the cloud for correlation, enrichment, long-term retention, and threat intelligence. Hybrid SOCs are especially powerful for organizations that cannot move certain datasets off-prem but still want cloud scalability.

Log Ingestion Pipelines

At the core of every SOC is the log ingestion pipeline, a structured system that receives data from endpoints, servers, cloud services, network devices, and security tools, then reliably transfers it into a centralized analytics platform. A well-designed pipeline must be fault-tolerant, support high throughput, and ensure integrity of every event.

The ingestion process typically begins with agents or collectors deployed across the environment. On Windows and Linux systems, these may be OS-native logging mechanisms (e.g., Windows Event Forwarding, Sysmon, auditd, journald), or dedicated agents from EDR and SIEM vendors. Network-based logs often originate from firewalls, routers, load balancers, and intrusion detection systems. These feed into a message broker or collector tier, such as Kafka,

Logstash, Fluentd, nxlog, or a vendor-provided forwarder.

Next, data is normalized and enriched. Normalization converts logs into structured fields using schemas such as the Elastic Common Schema (ECS) or Open Cybersecurity Schema Framework (OCSF). Enrichment layers may add threat intelligence tags, geolocation information, host metadata, or correlation identifiers. Once processed, logs are forwarded into the SIEM for indexing and correlation.

A strong SOC pipeline must incorporate buffering so logs are not lost during outages. Queues such as Kafka or cloud equivalents (e.g., Azure Event Hub, AWS Kinesis) ensure durable, distributed log delivery. Another best practice is schema validation, which prevents malformed logs from breaking analytics rules.

Storage and Retention Strategy

The SOC's storage architecture determines how long data can be analyzed, how quickly it can be searched, and how much it costs to retain security-relevant events. Most compliance frameworks require specific retention periods for example:

- PCI-DSS mandates at least 1 year of log retention, with 3 months immediately available.

- HIPAA commonly requires 6 years of security logs depending on interpretation.
- SOX requires retention of records relevant to financial auditing for 7 years.

Retention is typically divided into tiers. **Hot storage-indexed, high-performance disk** is used for the most recent weeks or months of data, allowing analysts to query it quickly during active investigations. Warm storage offers slower, cheaper access for older logs. Cold storage, such as archive tiers in cloud platforms, stores logs inexpensively for long periods but requires time to rehydrate or restore before analysis.

On-prem SOCs must plan storage clusters carefully, accounting for ingestion volume, compression ratios, and expected growth. Cloud SOCs can leverage automated lifecycle policies to move data from hot to cold tiers without manual intervention. Best practice dictates that the SOC monitors indexing latency, hot storage disk usage, and ingestion lag to prevent performance degradation.

A critical operational step is validating log integrity. Hashing, blockchain-based immutability systems, or cloud-native immutability locks ensure that logs cannot be altered, vital for regulatory and legal defensibility.

Compliance Requirements and Architectural Impact

Regulatory frameworks heavily shape SOC architecture. PCI-DSS, for example, requires strict segmentation between cardholder data environments (CDE) and monitoring systems. All log transfers must use encrypted channels, and system access must be audited. HIPAA emphasizes access controls, encryption at rest, and monitoring of protected health information. FedRAMP imposes even stricter controls, including FIPS-validated cryptography, multi-region redundancy, continuous monitoring dashboards (CONMON), and strict incident reporting timelines.

Compliance also affects where the SIEM can be hosted. FedRAMP High, for example, limits organizations to approved sovereign clouds. PCI may restrict how logs are moved out of the cardholder environment. SOX requires ensuring logs related to financial systems remain fully auditable.

Architecturally, the SOC must implement:

- strict role-based access control (RBAC)
- multi-factor authentication
- encrypted log transport (TLS 1.2+)
- immutable storage for audit trails
- evidence collection workflows
- documented change management

Compliance should be treated not as a burden but as a roadmap to mature architecture. Strong governance results in more reliable investigations and defensible security controls.

Network Segmentation and Secure SOC Network Design

A secure SOC environment depends on robust network segmentation. Analysts cannot effectively defend a network if the monitoring infrastructure is exposed or reachable by the very threats it monitors. A mature SOC isolates its own systems, data stores, and administrative tools inside a SOC enclave, a restricted network segment, accessible only to SOC personnel and monitored with heightened scrutiny.

The SOC enclave typically houses SIEM servers, SOAR tooling, threat-intelligence platforms, packet capture appliances, case management systems, and forensic analysis workstations. Access to the enclave is restricted through firewall rules, jump servers, privileged access management (PAM), and VPN tunnels with device certificates. The enclave should have no direct inbound internet exposure and must enforce egress filtering, allowing only connections required for threat intelligence feeds or cloud SIEM connectors.

For production networks, segmentation prevents lateral movement. Critical assets like domain controllers, databases, and industrial systems are placed in separate network zones with tightly controlled access pathways. Log collectors inside each zone communicate with the SOC using encrypted, authenticated channels protected by firewall rules that only allow outbound transfers to designated collector endpoints.

Best practice also includes deploying out-of-band forensic networks for imaging systems, performing malware analysis, and transferring evidence. This ensures investigations cannot be disrupted by adversary activity in the production environment.

Chapter 4

SIEM Engineering & Data Pipeline Design

A Security Information and Event Management (SIEM) platform is the analytical engine of the SOC. It ingests events from across the enterprise, correlates hostile behaviors, surfaces anomalies, and presents analysts with actionable insights. SIEMs have evolved from simple log aggregators into cloud-scale analytics platforms with threat intelligence integration, machine learning capabilities, and automated response functions. Engineering a SIEM requires thoughtful design choices, selecting the correct platform, building reliable ingestion pipelines, structuring normalized data, and developing high-quality detections. A well-designed SIEM becomes the SOC's single source of truth; a poorly configured one becomes a noisy data dump. This chapter provides a full blueprint for evaluating, deploying, and optimizing SIEM technology.

Selecting a SIEM

Choosing a SIEM is a strategic decision that affects the entire SOC architecture. Organizations should evaluate a SIEM not only by its features, but by how well it aligns with the enterprise's size, architecture, compliance obligations, and staffing capabilities. Cloud-native platforms such as Microsoft Sentinel, Google Chronicle, and Elastic Cloud offer near-infinite scalability, quick onboarding, and low infrastructure maintenance, making them ideal for hybrid or distributed organizations. On-premise SIEMs like Splunk Enterprise or QRadar appeal to heavily regulated environments requiring tight control of storage, data sovereignty, or air-gapped operations.

The evaluation process should test ingestion throughput, query performance under load, ease of onboarding new log sources, correlation rule flexibility, and the maturity of automated enrichment. It is equally important to examine cost predictability cloud SIEMs often charge by data volume, while on-prem SIEMs incur hardware and licensing costs. A proof-of-concept deployment is recommended before full adoption; this allows SOC engineers to ingest production logs, write test detections, and validate performance expectations. Governance and compliance should also influence the decision: PCI, HIPAA, CJIS, and FedRAMP environments often mandate specific encryption, retention, and access control capabilities.

Log Onboarding

Once a SIEM is selected, onboarding logs is the most labor-intensive and foundational engineering task. Each log sourcewhether endpoint telemetry, cloud audit logs, firewall events, DNS queries, or identity systems must be configured to securely and reliably forward data. Log onboarding begins with identifying business-critical systems and prioritizing high-value telemetry such as endpoint detection and response (EDR), identity logs (Active Directory, Azure AD), firewall traffic, and critical infrastructure servers. Each source must have forwarding agents installed or syslog connectors configured with TLS encryption to prevent tampering in transit.

Successful onboarding involves validating event volume, checking for dropped messages, ensuring timestamps are synchronized (via NTP), and confirming that all logs contain unique identifiers such as hostnames or asset IDs. Engineers should also confirm that privileged logs, domain controller events, VPN authentication logs, or privileged access activity are protected from tampering by limiting local log retention permissions.

Best practice requires maintaining a "Log Source Onboarding SOP" documenting prerequisites, access requirements, configuration scripts, verification steps, and rollback instructions. Once installed, logs must be tested using scenario-based validation: generating failed logins, firewall blocks, PowerShell commands, or file modifications to confirm the SIEM receives expected telemetry.

Parsing, Normalization, and Enrichment

Raw logs are difficult for analysts and detection rules to interpret. Parsing breaks logs into structured fields. Normalization standardizes those fields across log types. Enrichment enhances the events with context. Together, these processes form the analytics foundation of the SIEM pipeline.

Parsing typically occurs through custom parsing rules, regular expressions, Grok patterns, XML/JSON extractors, or vendor-specific ingestion modules. Normalization applies a consistent schema such as Elastic Common Schema (ECS), Open Cybersecurity Schema Framework (OCSF), or

Splunk Common Information Model (CIM). Proper normalization allows detections to work across different technologies. e.g. a rule for "authentication failure" should match Windows, Linux, VPN, and Okta logs without separate queries.

Enrichment adds value by appending threat intelligence indicators, geolocation, asset metadata (owner, business unit, criticality rating), vulnerability data (CVSS score), or identity-based attributes (MFA status, privileged role). This transforms events from raw data into fully contextualized security telemetry. Enrichment should be automated through lookup tables, TI feeds, CMDB integrations, or SOAR workflows.

Engineers must continuously validate parsed fields using field-checks in dashboards and automatically alert on parsing failures or schema drift. Normalization accuracy directly impacts detection accuracy; therefore, schema governance must be a formal SOC engineering responsibility.

Common Log Sources and What They Provide

Every SOC should prioritize telemetry sources based on visibility, detection value, and investigative utility. Endpoint logs (Windows event logs, Sysmon, Linux auditd), for example, provide granular insight into process creation, registry changes, file modifications, persistence mechanisms, and kernel-level activity. Identity logsfrom Active Directory, Azure AD, Okta, or Duoreveal authentication attempts, privilege escalation, MFA bypass attempts, and lateral movement behaviors.

Network and firewall logs capture east-west and north-south traffic, blocked connections, command-and-control attempts, and port scanning. DNS logs record domain queries, allowing detection of DGAs (domain generation algorithms), tunneling, or beaconing. Cloud platform logs (AWS CloudTrail, Azure Activity Logs, GCP Audit Logs) surface misconfigurations, privilege misuse, and anomalous service creation. Email security logs show phishing attempts, malicious file attachments, and impersonation. Application logs provide insight into API misuse, business logic abuse, or data exfiltration.

Selecting the right sources requires mapping logs to use cases. For example, detecting ransomware requires file modification events, EDR telemetry, and authentication logs. Detecting insider threats requires identity logs, proxy logs, DLP alerts, and database query logs.

Building Use Cases

Use case development is the process of defining what threats the SOC must detect and creating the correlation logic to surface them. Use cases should align with the organization's threat model, business priorities, MITRE ATT&CK techniques, and regulatory requirements. A mature SOC maintains a use case catalog describing each detection: its purpose, data sources, logic, severity, false-positive risks, and required enrichment.

Use cases often fall into several categories: identity misuse, privilege escalation, lateral movement, persistence, malware execution, data exfiltration, cloud misconfiguration, and business fraud. Each use case begins with a hypothesis such as "an attacker who compromises a workstation may attempt to steal domain credentials." Engineers then define required data sources (EDR, Windows logs, VPN logs), write correlation queries, test against real data, and tune for minimal false positives.

Use cases must be reviewed periodically to reflect new attacker behaviors. High-quality use cases include automated response actions, isolating endpoints, disabling accounts, updating firewall rules or at minimum alert templates that guide Tier 1 analysts through triage steps.

Detection Engineering Lifecycle

The detection engineering lifecycle governs how rules are created, tested, deployed, tuned, and retired. It ensures detections are reliable, measurable, and aligned with evolving threats. The lifecycle begins with visibility analysis and engineers must first confirm they have adequate telemetry to detect a given technique. Next, they design detection logic using SIEM query languages, correlation rules, machine learning models, or behavioral analytics.

Each detection must go through lab testing using simulated attacks (Atomic Red Team, Caldera, manual adversary emulation) and then move into a monitored "gray" environment where false positives can be measured. Once deployed into production, detections must be continuously tuned based on real analyst feedback and statistical performance metrics. Detections should include metadata: MITRE ATT&CK technique IDs, severity level, impacted business processes, and escalation requirements. Engineers must also retire outdated detections that no longer provide value or have been replaced by more accurate behavioral models.

Best practice dictates maintaining a Detection Engineering SOP, a dedicated detection repository, and a versioning system so that changes can be audited. The detection lifecycle forms the feedback loop between threat hunting, incident response, and continuous tuning. SIEM engineering is the discipline that transforms logs into intelligence and noise into actionable signals. By selecting the correct platform, carefully onboarding telemetry, structuring data through parsing and normalization, developing use-case-driven detections, and following a disciplined engineering lifecycle, the SOC gains deep visibility and fast response capability. This chapter provides the "how-to" blueprint required to build and maintain a world-class SIEM ecosystem.

Chapter 5

SOAR Implementation & Automation Workflows

Security Orchestration, Automation, and Response (SOAR) platforms extend the SOC's capabilities by automating repetitive tasks, orchestrating multi-tool actions, and enforcing consistent response processes. A SOAR is not a replacement for analysts, it is a force multiplier. Its value lies in reducing investigation time, lowering analyst fatigue, improving SLA performance, and ensuring that incidents are handled the same way every time. A well-implemented SOAR transforms the SOC from a reactive environment into a proactive, high-speed operational machine.

A SOAR platform integrates with SIEMs, EDRs, identity systems, threat intelligence tools, and ticketing platforms to execute workflows called playbooks. These playbooks automate triage, enrichment, containment, reporting, and cross-team communication. SOAR systems typically rely on API integrations, webhooks, OAuth tokens, and service accounts to interact with other applications. An operational SOAR instance requires engineering discipline: credential management, role-based access control, error handling, versioning of playbooks, and strict testing procedures before deployment.

What a SOAR Is and How It Works

A SOAR platform serves as the orchestration and automation engine at the center of modern SOC operations. While the SIEM is responsible for collecting, correlating, and alerting on telemetry, the SOAR transforms those alerts into structured, repeatable workflows that reduce manual effort and accelerate decision-making. When the SIEM generates an alert, it sends the event payload to the SOAR, typically through an API, webhook, or built-in connector. The SOAR receives this alert, classifies it, and determines which playbook should execute based on alert type, severity, tags, or metadata embedded within the alert. This mapping capability ensures that every alert type follows a predefined, consistent workflow rather than relying on individual analyst interpretation.

A SOAR playbook is essentially a codified set of investigative actions that reflect the SOC's Standard Operating Procedures. Once a playbook is triggered, the SOAR begins executing a series of automated steps such as querying threat intelligence sources, extracting contextual data, pulling host details from EDR, retrieving user authentication history from an identity provider, or collecting network telemetry from firewalls. These actions happen within seconds, long before an analyst even opens the alert. As the playbook progresses, data gathered from multiple tools is normalized and consolidated into a single coherent investigation page, allowing analysts to interpret the findings without manually pivoting across several dashboards.

SOAR playbooks can operate in different modes depending on organizational risk tolerance, maturity, and the sensitivity of the action being taken. In fully automated mode, the SOAR performs every step without human involvement including containment actions like isolating a host or disabling a compromised account. This model is ideal for commodity threats, brute-force attacks, known malware signatures, and other situations where automation poses minimal operational risk. In semi-automated mode, the SOAR performs all enrichment tasks automatically but pauses for human approval when reaching high-impact actions such as network blocks, user lockouts, or device quarantines. This hybrid approach balances speed with oversight, ensuring human validation during critical steps. In manual-assist mode, the SOAR acts primarily as a data aggregator and workflow organizer collecting and presenting all relevant information so analysts can make informed decisions quickly, without performing redundant manual lookups.

The true power of SOAR lies in orchestration. A single alert may require information from firewalls, EDR tools, cloud identity systems, DNS logs, threat intelligence repositories, vulnerability scanners, messaging platforms, and ticketing systems. Without a SOAR, analysts must pivot across these tools one by one, copy-pasting data and mentally stitching together context. With SOAR orchestration, as soon as the alert arrives, the platform can execute dozens of API calls in parallel, gather enrichment from every relevant system, evaluate the results against defined logic, and present a complete investigation package within seconds. This orchestration collapses time-to-triage dramatically, from minutes or hours to mere seconds and ensures that the SOC operates with consistency, precision, and repeatability. Beyond enrichment, a SOAR also enforces workflow discipline. It ensures that certain alerts always trigger specific notifications, that escalation paths are followed correctly, and that evidence is collected and logged in a standardized way. The SOAR also creates audit trails documenting every automated and human action taken during the incident, which supports compliance, forensic investigation, and quality assurance. In mature environments, SOAR platforms become the operational backbone of the SOC, centralizing decision logic, standardizing responses, enabling scalable automation, and freeing analysts from repetitive, low-value tasks so they can focus on true investigative work.

Creating Playbooks for Common Threats

Playbook creation requires careful planning. Every playbook must be grounded in documented SOPs, mapped to MITRE ATT&CK techniques, and aligned with response policies. The development process begins by identifying high-frequency alerts such as phishing emails, malware detections, suspicious authentications, and brute-force activity. For each alert type, engineers convert the human SOP into a machine-executable workflow. For instance, a malware alert playbook might retrieve EDR process trees, gather hash information, submit the hash to VirusTotal, check outbound connections, isolate the host if the hash is malicious, and generate a structured report. A phishing playbook might extract sender information, check domain reputation, analyze the message headers, detonate attachments in a sandbox, and block the sender domain automatically.

Playbooks must be modular broken into reusable components such as "get host info," "lookup IP reputation," or "disable user account." Modularization accelerates development and reduces maintenance overhead. Each playbook must include decision branches so it can handle benign events gracefully, escalate suspicious ones, or act aggressively when high-confidence threats are detected.

Automated Triage Workflows

Automated triage allows the SOAR to replicate the initial steps a Tier 1 analyst would normally take. This includes collecting process arguments, authenticating users, checking login patterns, retrieving device health, analyzing related historical alerts, and extracting file metadata. With triage automated, Tier 1 analysts review only the *decision-ready* results. For example, when the SIEM reports "Multiple Failed Logins Followed by Success," the SOAR might automatically verify whether the login was from a known location, whether MFA was enabled, the user's normal login hours, whether their password was recently changed, and if similar events occurred on other machines. Within seconds, the SOAR gives a confidence score such as "Likely Legitimate," "Suspicious," or "High Risk: Confirmed Compromise."

By standardizing triage, the SOC reduces the variance between analysts and ensures alerts are handled with consistent quality. Automated triage also drastically reduces Mean Time to Detect (MTTD).

Auto-Enrichment Using API Keys

SOAR systems rely heavily on external enrichment sources to validate the maliciousness of IPs, hashes, files, emails, and domains. Most enrichment steps occur through API calls using securely stored API keys. These must be kept in encrypted storage within the SOAR's secret vault and rotated regularly. Below is how each enrichment source is used.

VirusTotal

VirusTotal provides hash lookups, file reputation scoring, sandbox behavior analysis, and domain/IP insights. SOAR playbooks typically query:

- File hash reputation
- Sandbox analysis reports
- Community comments
- First-seen dates

If VirusTotal returns a malicious score above a predefined threshold, the SOAR can automatically isolate the endpoint.

AbuseIPDB

AbuseIPDB is used to evaluate IP addresses associated with brute force, spam, scanning, or malicious activity. The SOAR can:

- Query IP reputation
- Retrieve abuse types
- Check hit frequency
- Flag persistent attackers

This is especially effective for automated firewall block playbooks.

GreyNoise

GreyNoise differentiates between targeted malicious activity and "internet background noise." With GreyNoise, the SOAR can determine:

- Whether an IP is a known harmless scanner
- Whether it is part of a benign botnet

- Whether it has targeted activity specific to the organization

GreyNoise drastically reduces false positives.

IPQualityScore

IPQS specializes in:

- Fraud scoring
- Proxy/VPN detection
- TOR exit node identification
- Bot activity

This is invaluable for identity-based playbooks such as "Impossible Travel" or "Suspicious Account Sign-In."

Auto-Containment

Auto containment is one of the most powerful yet potentially risky capabilities available within a SOAR platform. It allows the system to take direct defensive actions without waiting for human intervention, which can drastically reduce the time an attacker has to operate inside the environment. However, because these actions directly impact users and systems, auto containment must be designed with strict safeguards, clear decision logic, and continuous oversight. Containment actions may include isolating a host from the network, disabling a user account, stopping a malicious process, blocking an external address, quarantining an email message, or restricting access to a critical application. Each of these actions carries operational impact, which means they must only occur when the SOAR has strong evidence that malicious activity is truly present. Effective auto containment begins with confidence scoring. The SOAR should never perform a disruptive action based on a single signal. Instead, it must gather multiple corroborating data points that indicate a real threat. These may include process lineage from the endpoint detection tool, threat intelligence confirmation, abnormal identity behavior, and a match to known adversary techniques. Only when these indicators align should the SOAR consider an automated containment action. Even then, many SOCs choose to insert an optional analyst approval step for sensitive actions involving user accounts, production servers, or devices that support critical business functions.

Before isolating a device, for example, the SOAR may perform a series of automated checks. It might verify whether the system belongs to a critical business function such as finance, medical support, manufacturing control, or identity provider operations. It may confirm that the device is a workstation rather than a server that hosts applications or authentication services. It may query multiple intelligence sources to validate that a file or process involved in the alert is truly malicious and not a false positive. It may also review related behavior such as repeated failed logins, unauthorized remote execution, or suspicious network traffic that supports the conclusion of an active threat.

Operational communication is also essential. Auto containment must always notify the IT team, SOC leadership, and system owners immediately so that teams understand why a system or user was impacted. Nothing damages trust faster than an application going offline without explanation. When communication is built into the workflow, auto containment becomes a coordinated defensive measure rather than an unexpected disruption.

In a disciplined SOC, auto containment is introduced gradually. The SOC first deploys it in observer mode where all actions are simulated but not executed. This allows engineers to test logic, reduce false positives, and confirm that each containment path behaves as expected. Once the SOC builds confidence through repeated testing and operational validation, auto containment moves into limited production use with clearly defined rules, restricted scope, and regular review cycles. When implemented with maturity and caution, auto containment becomes one of the most impactful components of modern security operations. It allows the SOC to act faster than any human team can respond and ensures that dangerous threats are contained immediately, even during off hours or peak alert periods. At the same time, auto containment reinforces the principle that automation is most powerful when it is controlled, deliberate, evidence driven, and fully aligned with business needs.

Error Handling and Rollback Logic

A mature SOAR workflow is not defined only by its ability to perform correct actions but also by its ability to handle failure gracefully. Automation is powerful, but without proper safeguards it can amplify mistakes at machine speed. This is why every SOAR design must include strong error management and thoughtful rollback steps that protect the environment from unintended consequences. The goal is not perfection. The goal is resilience.

When an action fails, the entire workflow should not collapse. Instead, the SOAR must recover, retry, and adapt with minimal disruption to the SOC or the organization.

Automation errors often originate from unpredictable external systems. An API may be unavailable, an authentication token may expire, a firewall may reject an update, or an identity provider may throttle requests. When the SOAR encounters these issues, the workflow should never halt abruptly. Instead, it should retry the request using an approach such as exponential backoff, where the system waits slightly longer between each retry. This avoids unnecessary strain on external services and gives temporary issues time to resolve. Clear error messages and structured logging allow analysts to understand the exact point of failure without digging through raw code or tool output. There will be times when incorrect actions occur despite these protections. A SOAR might disable a legitimate user account during a noisy login event, or it might isolate an endpoint that hosts a critical business application. These actions cannot always be prevented entirely, which is why rollback logic must be built into the workflow from the beginning. A well designed SOAR can reverse its own actions. It can restore an account to an active state, remove an incorrectly applied firewall block rule, unisolate an endpoint that was mistakenly quarantined, or return a legitimate email message that was sent to quarantine during aggressive filtering. These corrective steps allow the SOC to recover from errors without lengthy manual work.

Rollback does not always need to occur immediately. There are situations where the SOC wants containment to remain in place temporarily while analysis continues. For this reason, rollback can be triggered automatically after a certain timeout or manually by an analyst through a dedicated rollback console. An analyst should always be able to see which actions the SOAR performed, which assets were affected, and what options exist to reverse or adjust those actions. This not only helps during live response but also builds trust between analysts and automation. Version controlled playbooks add another important layer of protection. Every change to a playbook should be tracked, reviewed, and logged. When a failure occurs, the SOC must be able to trace exactly which version of the playbook executed and what logic was present at the time. Execution logs reveal each step taken by the SOAR, each decision branch, each external call, and each response from integrated systems. This level of transparency is essential for audit readiness, compliance obligations, and general accountability. Robust error handling and rollback design ensures that automation remains a force multiplier rather than a source of risk. The goal is confidence.

Analysts must trust that when the SOAR acts, it acts safely, and when something goes wrong, it can be undone cleanly. Mature SOAR workflows reflect this philosophy, transforming automation into a controlled, reliable, and resilient part of security operations.

SOAR platforms empower SOC teams to operate faster, more efficiently, and with greater consistency. By automating enrichment, triage, and containment, the SOC reduces alert fatigue and accelerates response. Properly engineered playbooks, enriched with external intelligence, controlled with safe-guards, and supported by error-handling mechanisms, turn the SOAR into a central operational engine of the cybersecurity program. This chapter provides the full blueprint for designing, implementing, and scaling SOAR automation in any environment.

Chapter 6

Ticketing System & Alert Workflow Engineering

A Security Operations Center becomes operationally effective only when its alert workflows are structured, predictable, and tightly integrated across the entire detection and response stack. In many organizations, alerts begin in the SIEM, pass to automation via SOAR, and culminate in a ticketing or case-management platform where analysts perform investigation and documentation. Figure 1 in this chapter illustrates the recommended alert flow: logs enter the SIEM, detections trigger SOAR playbooks, and the resulting actions create or update tickets in a unified queue. This layered architecture is not optional; it is the backbone that maintains accountability, auditability, and repeatable incident response across the SOC.

Designing an Integrated SIEM → SOAR → Ticketing Pipeline

Integrating a SIEM, a SOAR platform, and a ticketing system is one of the most important architectural decisions a SOC will ever make. These systems must work together with precision, consistency, and predictable logic. When integrated properly they create a powerful and efficient security response pipeline that reduces human workload, improves alert fidelity, and shortens both detection and response times. When integrated poorly they create the opposite effect. Alerts become fragmented across consoles, analysts lose context as they pivot between systems, and automation becomes unreliable. Effective integration demands intentional sequencing so that each component is assigned responsibilities that align with its strengths. No single tool should be overloaded with duties it was not designed to perform.

The SIEM serves as the analytical foundation of the SOC. It ingests logs from every monitored asset, normalizes the data into structured formats, correlates activity across sources, and applies detection logic such as behavioral analytics, anomaly detection, pattern matching, and correlation searches. The SIEM is the authoritative detection engine and the original source of truth for any alert that the SOC will investigate. A common mistake among inexperienced SOCs is to use the SOAR platform to perform detection or use the ticketing system as the primary triage interface. This turns the workflow inside out and creates confusion about where alerts originate, how they are enriched, and where investigation begins. The guiding principle is simple. Detection belongs inside the SIEM. Investigation support and automation belong inside the SOAR. Case tracking and documentation belong inside the ticketing system.

When a detection rule inside the SIEM fires, the SIEM immediately hands off the alert to the SOAR layer. This handoff usually occurs through webhooks, alert forwarding configurations, or API driven exports. At this moment the alert is nothing more than a data object with fields that may be incomplete or unclear. The SOAR platform performs the transformation required to turn a raw alert into an enriched and fully contextualized investigation. This process often begins with basic normalization of fields so that enrichment steps can rely on predictable structure. The SOAR then extracts relevant artifacts such as IP addresses, domains, user names, host names, file hashes, and command strings. These artifacts are sent simultaneously to a wide range of enrichment sources including threat intelligence platforms, reputation scoring systems, endpoint telemetry queries, identity provider logs, and internal asset inventories.

During enrichment the SOAR also applies its own internal logic. It may conduct pattern recognition on command line arguments, identify geographic locations of external addresses, evaluate whether a user account shows signs of credential compromise, or determine whether endpoint processes follow known malicious sequences. These automation steps elevate the fidelity of the alert and replace the repetitive research tasks that traditionally consume analyst time. Enrichment also improves accuracy. An alert that appears severe in the SIEM may be downgraded after the SOAR determines the activity is associated with a known trusted process or expected administrative behavior. Conversely, an alert may be upgraded if enrichment reveals coordinated suspicious behavior across multiple systems.

Severity calculation inside the SOAR represents another crucial element of integration. Severity should not be static. It should be informed by a blend of detection type, contextual data, relationships to historical incidents, user or asset sensitivity, and additional indicators that emerge during enrichment. The SOAR applies predefined logic to evaluate all of these factors and assign an accurate severity level. Only after severity has been evaluated should the alert progress to the next stage. If the alert does not require human intervention because the automated decision logic confidently resolves it as benign, the workflow ends without involving the ticketing system. This approach prevents unnecessary noise from reaching analysts and significantly reduces response fatigue. When the SOAR workflow reaches a decision point that does require human review, the next step is case creation inside the ticketing system. The SOAR pushes the enriched alert into the system through dedicated connectors or API calls. At this point the ticket contains a complete investigation ready record. It includes enrichment details, summary notes, threat intelligence context, preliminary severity, asset information, and recommended next steps. The ticket is no longer a simple alert notification. It is a structured case file that equips the analyst to move immediately into investigative mode without spending time on data gathering.

This approach preserves each tool's strengths and ensures that the SOC pipeline is predictable and efficient. The SIEM focuses entirely on detection and correlation. The SOAR focuses on enrichment, orchestration, and intelligent automation. The ticketing system focuses on workflow, communication, documentation, and compliance. Together they form a unified and scalable architecture for modern security operations.

Designing Service Level Agreements (SLAs)

SLAs govern the responsiveness and accountability of the SOC and must be written with precision. A well-structured SLA defines the expected maximum time to triage an alert, the maximum investigation window before a ticket must be escalated, and the expected communication windows with stakeholders. For example, a critical alert SLA may require acknowledgement within 15 minutes, initial triage within 30 minutes, and full investigation within 4 hours. SLAs must also reflect staffing models; a 24/7 SOC can support aggressive SLAs, whereas a business-hours SOC must adjust accordingly.

Writing SLAs begins with understanding average daily alert volume, analyst capacity, automation coverage levels, and false-positive rates. Once baselines are established, target response times can be calculated realistically. Figure 3 demonstrates a typical SLA matrix covering severity categories from informational to critical. Organizations should review SLAs quarterly to ensure they align with actual SOC performance and automation maturity.

Escalation Guidelines and Multi-Tier Handoff

Escalation guidelines define exactly when and how an alert transitions from Tier 1 to Tier 2, Tier 2 to Tier 3, or to Incident Response. These guidelines must be explicit, not left to analyst discretion, to ensure consistent outcomes. Tier 1 analysts are generally responsible for initial triage, enrichment review, basic correlation, and determining whether activity is expected, benign, or suspicious. If the alert requires deeper log correlation across data sources, malware analysis, threat attribution, or requires administrative access, Tier 1 escalates to Tier 2. Tier 2 investigates complex events, creates containment recommendations, and may escalate to Tier 3 if reverse engineering, forensic imaging, or advanced IR expertise is required.

Escalation should occur based on predefined conditions such as incomplete triage after a set period, detection of lateral movement, indicators of compromise linked to known APT groups, or discovery of privilege escalation. Figure 4 provides a visual escalation ladder showing exactly when each tier becomes responsible. The key to success is precision: escalations must document what has already been done, what evidence is attached, and what investigative gaps remain. This prevents rework and ensures a smooth transfer of responsibility.

Real-World Ticket Flow Examples

In a mature SOC environment the lifecycle of a ticket reflects the discipline, structure, and clarity of the entire security program. A well designed workflow ensures that analysts do not waste time gathering basic information and instead begin each investigation with context that has already been enriched automatically. A typical ticket originates in the SOAR platform, which receives an alert from the SIEM and immediately triggers the appropriate playbook. Before the analyst ever touches the ticket, the SOAR has already performed the initial research tasks. It gathers IP reputation scores, identifies the geographic location of external connections, retrieves associated user information, queries endpoint security tools for process activity, and attaches asset details such as system role, operating system version, and recent authentication activity. When the case appears inside the ticketing system it is already structured, annotated, and ready for investigation.

The ticket description should always begin with clarity. It lists the SIEM rule that fired, the data source that triggered the alert, and a precise timestamp. Many SOCs also include a short narrative summary written by the SOAR playbook that explains why this activity was considered suspicious and what evidence contributed to that assessment. This allows Tier 1 analysts to quickly understand the nature of the alert before they begin validation. The first responsibility of an analyst is simple but essential. They must confirm that the alert represents meaningful activity. They check authentication logs to see if the user behavior aligns with historical patterns. They review endpoint telemetry to determine whether a process started in a legitimate context. They verify whether the network connection came from an expected service or a known administrative workflow. If the analyst determines the activity is benign, they document the reasoning behind that conclusion and close the ticket. Proper documentation ensures the SOC can tune future detections to eliminate redundant noise.

More complicated cases follow a very different path. Consider a scenario where the SIEM detects suspicious PowerShell execution that includes encoded commands. The SOAR playbook already extracted the command string, decoded it if possible, and attached process lineage information from the endpoint. The Tier 1 analyst now examines the decoded command, the parent process, the user who ran it, and recent behavior on the host. They look for indicators that separate administrative scripts from malicious ones, such as unusual obfuscation, attempts to reach unknown external addresses, or the creation of persistence mechanisms. When early analysis reveals possible malicious intent, the analyst escalates the case to Tier 2.

Tier 2 analysts take the investigation deeper. They may pull full process execution graphs from the EDR, retrieve the memory image of the running process, or run yara rules to search for adversary tradecraft signatures. If file artifacts were created, they look for known malware families using hash lookups or sandbox detonation outputs. They examine whether the system attempted authentication events outside normal hours or whether lateral movement markers appear inside logs. The goal of Tier 2 is not merely to determine whether the activity was malicious, but to understand its nature, scope, and potential impact across the environment. Throughout this workflow the SOAR platform may intervene automatically when a predefined level of confidence is reached. If the enrichment strongly suggests that the activity is harmful, the SOAR may isolate the endpoint to prevent further spread. In identity related cases the SOAR may temporarily disable the user account or force a password reset, depending on the rules established during design. These actions always produce entries inside the ticket so that analysts can see exactly what the SOAR executed and at what time. Automated actions significantly reduce the window of opportunity for attackers, especially in ransomware precursor events.

A full example of this process can be seen in a ransomware precursor investigation. The SIEM detects unusual command line activity associated with native Windows tools often abused by adversaries. The SOAR enriches the activity, discovers network connections to a rare external address, evaluates threat intelligence scores that classify this address as infrastructure used by a known ransomware group, and automatically raises the severity of the alert. Tier 1 confirms the suspicious behavior and escalates the case. Tier 2 identifies additional activity such as credential harvesting attempts or the placement of suspicious scheduled tasks. Containment steps are executed. The endpoint is isolated, the account is disabled, and lateral movement possibilities are reviewed. Final remediation includes patching the vulnerability used for initial access, resetting credentials, cleaning residual artifacts, and updating detection logic to capture future variants of the same behavior.

The complete ticket reflects every stage of this journey. It includes the original detection, the automated enrichment steps, the Tier 1 findings, the Tier 2 investigations, the containment and eradication actions performed by the SOAR or analysts, and the closing recommendations for the client or internal IT teams. This ticket does not merely document an incident. It documents the maturity of the entire SOC, demonstrating how detection, automation, analysis, containment, and communication come together to form a coherent and effective security response.

Internal Runbooks and Operational Processes

Runbooks form the backbone of disciplined SOC operations. They ensure that every analyst, regardless of experience level or shift assignment, performs investigations in a consistent and predictable manner. A runbook is essentially the operating manual for a specific detection or class of incidents. It removes guesswork, reduces variability, and ensures that no critical step is overlooked during periods of stress or high alert volume. When a detection use case triggers an alert, analysts should be able to open the corresponding runbook and immediately see a clear sequence of actions that guide them from triage through closure. Each runbook begins by defining the scope of the alert. It explains why the detection exists, what behavior it is meant to identify, and what risks it represents from the perspective of adversary tradecraft. The next section outlines triage steps, which usually include quick validation checks such as confirming process ancestry, reviewing authentication context, or comparing suspicious activity against known false-positive patterns. Runbooks should provide sample queries for the SIEM, search filters for endpoint tools, and a list of required log sources. These references save analysts time and reinforce institutional knowledge by documenting the fastest path to clarity.

Beyond triage, runbooks include a detailed chain of investigative actions. These actions guide analysts in determining whether the activity is malicious, benign, or inconclusive. For example, a runbook for suspicious PowerShell behavior will instruct analysts to examine decoded command strings, review parent processes, check the user account's recent authentication history, and inspect network connections created during execution. It will also clarify which enrichment steps are performed automatically by the SOAR system so analysts do not duplicate those tasks. Clear separation between automated actions and analyst responsibilities ensures smooth collaboration between human and automated components.

Containment logic is a critical section of every runbook. It explains under what conditions an account may be disabled, an endpoint isolated, or a process terminated. Containment conditions should be specific and risk based. Runbooks must clearly state which actions require analyst approval and which steps may be executed automatically by SOAR. In mature environments, containment workflows also include instructions for coordinating with IT teams, system owners, and business leadership to prevent surprises when critical systems are temporarily disrupted. This coordination protects business operations while allowing security teams to act decisively during incidents.

Escalation criteria are another essential component. Runbooks define the exact conditions that warrant escalation to Tier 2, Tier 3, the incident response team, or the on-call manager. These criteria should be objective and tied to observable indicators such as lateral movement markers, privilege misuse, confirmed communication with known malicious infrastructure, or the creation of persistence mechanisms. Escalation paths must be documented thoroughly to ensure rapid handoff when time is critical.

Operational processes surrounding runbooks are equally important. SOCs must have strict rules governing how tickets are tagged, organized, and documented. Every ticket should reflect the investigative steps taken, the evidence collected, the decisions made, and the reasoning behind those decisions. Evidence such as process trees, decoded scripts, screenshots, packet captures, and SIEM query results must be attached directly to the case so future analysts or auditors can reconstruct what occurred. This documentation not only ensures accuracy but also strengthens the SOC's legal and compliance posture. Some workflows require tickets to trigger automatic sub-tasks. If an incident requires forensic imaging, the ticketing system should immediately generate a task for the forensics team with clear instructions and deadlines. If an account is disabled due to compromise, automatic notifications should be sent to IT service management, identity administrators, and human resources. These automated follow-up processes ensure that actions taken by security do not create operational gaps elsewhere in the organization.

Runbooks also govern communication. They specify how analysts record conversations with system owners, how escalation messages are structured, and how incident summaries must be formatted before closure. Consistent communication practices reduce confusion and provide stakeholders with reliable clarity during stressful situations. When runbooks are followed rigorously, SOCs gain stability and predictability even during chaotic events. Runbooks must evolve. They are living documents that require review after every major incident, new detection, or false-positive tuning cycle. A stale runbook is worse than no runbook because it creates a false sense of confidence. Regular review cycles and version control ensure runbooks always reflect current tooling, current threats, and current best practices.

SECTION III
DEPLOYMENT PHASE

Chapter 7

Building & Launching the SOC

Launching a Security Operations Center is a major strategic initiative, one that blends cybersecurity engineering, project management, executive coordination, infrastructure design, staff development, and continuous improvement. Many organizations underestimate this phase, believing that the SOC emerges as soon as tools are installed or analysts are hired. In reality, a successful SOC launch is a phased, deliberate process that can take several months when done correctly.

Building a SOC is comparable to building a critical piece of infrastructure: a hospital, a fire department, or an air traffic control tower. The underlying architecture must be strong. The workflows must be consistent. The staff must be trained. The detections must be tested. The technology must be tuned. And the entire system must be piloted in controlled conditions before being put into full production. This chapter offers a comprehensive, structured approach for launching a SOCfrom the early project-planning stages through tool integration, detection deployment, soft-launch testing, and tuning periods.

Project Planning: Preparing the Foundation

A SOC project begins long before the first tool is deployed or the first analyst is hired. The planning stage is the foundation on which every operational, technical, and procedural decision will rest. It is both a security design exercise and a project management initiative, because a SOC is not merely a collection of tools. It is a cross functional program that requires the coordination of people, processes, technology, and governance structures. Effective planning therefore demands alignment with senior leadership, because the SOC ultimately influences nearly every operational and business domain: IT operations, security architecture, legal, human resources, risk management, compliance, and sometimes the board or external auditors.

A key project management principle in this stage is scope definition. The organization must determine the mission of the SOC, the operating model, the boundaries of responsibility, and the measurable outcomes that will define success. Without a clearly defined scope, a SOC will drift toward reactive firefighting, chasing alerts without a strategic framework. Planning requires identifying what the SOC is expected to detect, how it will respond, which assets it will monitor, and how it will interact with other teams during incidents. The SOC must also define what it will not do. Scope creep in SOC design leads to budget overruns, staffing shortages, and systemic operational stress.

A second project management principle is stakeholder alignment. A SOC cannot operate successfully if IT operations and security architecture do not support the mission. For example, a SOC that needs specific logs for detection cannot function if those logs require approvals from reluctant system owners. Planning must identify all affected groups and clearly articulate how responsibilities will be shared. This includes who approves containment actions, who receives escalations, who owns identity systems, who manages cloud infrastructure, and who handles post-incident recovery. Establishing these boundaries early reduces friction later and provides the SOC with predictable workflows. The planning phase also requires early prioritization. Organizations must identify their crown jewel systems, critical business processes, revenue producing applications, and high risk assets. A SOC that attempts to monitor everything equally will monitor nothing effectively. Instead, detection and response priorities should map directly to business risk. These priorities guide selection of telemetry sources, staffing decisions, escalation procedures, and response protocols. They also influence budget allocations because high value assets require higher fidelity monitoring.

During this stage the SOC team develops the detection scope based on a formal threat model. This ensures the SOC is built to defend against realistic adversary behaviors rather than vague general risk. The threat model informs what telemetry is required, what analytics must be implemented, and where enrichment or correlation will be necessary. It also influences the SOC's choice of SIEM and SOAR platforms since each technology has strengths and limitations that affect detection engineering. A critical project management artifact created during planning is the SOC charter. The charter states the mission, guiding principles, authorities, responsibilities, and constraints of the SOC. It formalizes the operating structure and ensures leadership understands what the SOC will deliver. The charter also outlines communication expectations, escalation rules, and reporting obligations. When disagreements arise later, the charter provides the authoritative reference that protects the SOC from misalignment or shifting expectations.

Governance standards are also defined in this phase. The SOC must establish how detections will be authored and reviewed, how runbooks will be maintained, how access will be controlled, and how the SOC will interface with enterprise change management processes. Governance defines how documentation is versioned, how metrics are collected, and how audits will be managed. Without these standards, the SOC quickly becomes inconsistent, tribal, and dependent on unwritten knowledge. Planning also includes the design of reporting frameworks. These frameworks outline how the SOC will communicate with leadership, how often reports will be delivered, which metrics will be tracked, and how success will be measured. A SOC that does not report effectively will always struggle for budget because leadership cannot assess its value. Defining reporting structures early ensures that when operations begin, performance data flows naturally into established communication channels. Project planning sets the stage for phased implementation. A SOC cannot be built all at once. Project management principles encourage phased rollouts, milestone tracking, risk registers, dependency mapping, and resource allocation. These allow leadership to see progress, anticipate obstacles, and allocate funding responsibly. By blending cybersecurity strategy with disciplined project management, the SOC begins on stable footing and avoids the common pitfalls that plague rushed or ad hoc deployments.

Building the Deployment Checklist

Once the planning phase concludes and the SOC's mission, scope, and governance structure are established, the next step is to translate the strategy into a structured deployment checklist. This checklist is not a simple collection of technical errands. It is a foundational project management artifact that ensures all prerequisites are satisfied before the SOC accepts its first live alert. A SOC cannot operate effectively if even one component is missing. Therefore, the deployment checklist functions as both a roadmap and a quality assurance framework that validates operational readiness across infrastructure, processes, people, and governance.

From a technical perspective, the checklist begins with infrastructure provisioning. This includes establishing the SOC enclave, configuring secure network segmentation, allocating storage tiers for log retention, and provisioning cloud tenants if the SOC will operate in a hybrid or cloud native environment. SIEM environments must be created with ingestion pipelines, parsing rules, log connectors, and baseline correlation logic. Similarly, the SOAR platform requires orchestration engines, playbook libraries, API integrations, and secrets management configured before any automation can safely run. The ticketing system, which becomes the operational spine of the SOC, must be configured with workflows, ticket states, SLA timers, assignment groups, escalation paths, and audit logging. Access control systems must be aligned to the SOC's segregation of duties, ensuring analysts have what they need without exceeding least privilege boundaries. Identity provider integration also appears early in the checklist because authentication, logging, and user context are core to many detections.

A comprehensive checklist extends beyond infrastructure and into the operational design of the SOC. The deployment phase requires that all necessary documentation be drafted, reviewed, and approved. This includes standard operating procedures, triage guidelines, evidence handling processes, escalation flows, and communication templates for major incident announcements. Runbooks for primary detections must be fully authored and tested long before the SOC begins receiving alerts. These documents ensure analysts respond consistently and that incident workflows align with governance expectations and regulatory obligations.

Training preparation forms another major component of the deployment checklist. Tier 1 analysts require instruction in triage fundamentals, SIEM search techniques, and ticketing workflows. Tier 2 and Tier 3 analysts need deeper training in investigation methodologies, playbook design, memory analysis, and adversary emulation. The SOC manager must receive leadership training focused on metrics review, SLA compliance, performance monitoring, and bridge call leadership. Without structured role based training, even the most well designed SOC will suffer from inconsistent execution and operational drift.

Endpoint readiness is also essential. Before launch, the organization must deploy agents such as EDR, log forwarders, cloud sensors, and vulnerability scanners across the environment. The deployment checklist validates coverage, confirms health, and verifies that telemetry is flowing into the SIEM without gaps. A SOC built on incomplete telemetry cannot function, so this step is one of the final before the readiness review. The deployment checklist includes validation tasks that confirm everything works in concert. Test alerts are generated to evaluate detection logic. SOAR playbooks are run in simulation mode to ensure correct data flows and decision branching. Ticket creation is tested from initial alert through closure. Escalation workflows are exercised with mock incidents. The checklist concludes only when leadership can demonstrate that the SOC is ready from every angle: technically, procedurally, and operationally. By treating the deployment checklist as a structured project management document rather than a technical reference, organizations ensure that the SOC launches with maturity and discipline instead of improvisation. It becomes the authoritative artifact that signals when the SOC can safely transition from planning to execution.

Tool Integrations: Connecting the SOC Ecosystem

A modern SOC only functions when its tools operate as a unified system rather than a collection of isolated technologies. Integration is the process that transforms separate platforms into a cohesive operational ecosystem. This process begins by establishing secure communication channels between all critical components, typically through tightly scoped service accounts, encrypted application program interfaces, and vetted connectors. Properly designed integrations allow data to move reliably from where events occur to where decisions are made and ultimately to where responses are executed. At the center of this ecosystem is the SIEM. It acts as the aggregation and correlation engine, collecting logs from servers, endpoints, cloud services, network appliances, authentication systems, and business applications. The SIEM normalizes these logs into consistent schemas, enriches them with metadata, applies detection logic, and surfaces notable events. Without full integration of log sources, the SIEM cannot produce high quality detections. Therefore, engineers must validate ingestion and parsing for every log type during integration to ensure visibility and accuracy.

Once the SIEM identifies suspicious activity, it hands the alert off to the SOAR platform. The SOAR acts as the automation and orchestration layer. It gathers enrichment from threat intelligence platforms, pulls endpoint context from the EDR system, queries identity providers to verify user attributes, and correlates this information into a unified investigation record. With each enrichment request, the SOAR draws on external sources such as reputation services, malware databases, cloud audit logs, and internal asset inventories. These operations must operate seamlessly so that analysts receive complete context without manual pivoting across tools.

The EDR platform must also integrate directly with the SIEM and SOAR. It provides deep behavioral telemetry such as parent and child processes, command line arguments, registry interaction, network connections, driver loads, and in-memory indicators. More importantly, it enables response actions including endpoint isolation, process termination, and remediation steps. These actions are typically executed through the SOAR rather than requiring analysts to log in to the EDR portal. This integration shortens time-to-containment and simplifies operational workflow.

Identity solutions including Active Directory, Azure AD, Okta, or other identity platforms supply the authentication data required for credential compromise detection. They also support response actions such as disabling compromised accounts or enforcing conditional access policies. Integrating identity systems ensures that authentication logs flow into the SIEM, that high risk identity events contribute to correlation logic, and that automated actions can be executed cleanly during incidents.

Firewalls, proxy appliances, cloud platforms, and vulnerability scanners must also be incorporated into the ecosystem. Firewalls provide perimeter visibility, application control events, and response capabilities such as blocking malicious addresses. Proxy appliances reveal outbound web activity relevant to command and control channels, data exfiltration, or credential phishing. Vulnerability scanners supply context for prioritizing risk. Cloud platforms contribute audit logs, configuration drift alerts, and access events that are essential for cloud security monitoring.

However, integration is not achieved simply by activating connectors. Engineers must perform extensive validation. This includes confirming log integrity, ensuring that event fields map correctly to required schemas, verifying timestamp accuracy, and validating that enrichment sources return correct data. Simulated malicious events are used to test the entire detection and response flow: from ingestion through correlation, from alert creation through enrichment, and from automated escalation through containment and ticket creation. The goal is to prove that every component in the pipeline can communicate reliably under realistic conditions.

A fully integrated SOC toolset behaves like a single coordinated system rather than a collection of separate applications. When integration is done correctly, analysts can move from detection to investigation and ultimately to containment with minimal friction. More importantly, the SOC becomes resilient, efficient, and capable of responding to threats at machine speed rather than human speed. This integration work, often invisible to stakeholders, is one of the most critical foundations of a successful SOC.

Use Case Deployment Schedule: Phasing in Detections

One of the most critical tasks during SOC launch is deploying use cases in a controlled, staged schedule. Attempting to activate all detection rules at once leads to noise, alert fatigue, and operational chaos. Instead, SOCs should deploy use cases in phases aligned with business risks and visibility readiness.

The first phase typically focuses on foundational detections: authentication anomalies, privilege escalations, suspicious PowerShell or bash activity, malware execution, endpoint behavior anomalies, and basic network scanning indicators. These detections rely on mandatory telemetry sources such as EDR,

Windows security logs, cloud identity logs, and firewall events. Once analysts are comfortable handling core detections, the SOC adds more advanced use cases dealing with lateral movement, persistence, exfiltration patterns, cloud-specific threats, and application-layer behaviors.

Each use case undergoes a full lifecycle: designing the detection logic, testing it with lab simulations, deploying it in "gray" mode to monitor false-positive behavior, and finally pushing it to production. Engineers must work closely with Tier 1 and Tier 2 analysts to tune thresholds, refine queries, and adjust enrichment logic based on real-world behavior. A good use case deployment schedule spans several weeks or months rather than days.

Soft Launch vs. Hard Launch Models

Launching a SOC is not simply a technical milestone. It is an organizational change event that affects analysts, engineers, IT operations, business units, and often external partners. Because of this, the method chosen to begin live operations has a significant impact on early success. In practice, organizations rely on two primary launch models: the hard launch and the soft launch. Each model carries benefits and risks, but they differ dramatically in operational maturity, readiness, and tolerance for early failure.

A hard launch is an immediate transition into full operations. The moment the SOC goes live, every alert is real, every ticket is active, and analysts are responsible for triage, investigation, containment, and communication. Full service level agreements take effect at the same moment, meaning response timelines, escalation paths, and reporting requirements become contractually binding from day one. Hard launches are usually chosen when regulatory deadlines, audit findings, or executive mandates demand rapid deployment. Although this approach creates a sense of urgency, it carries substantial risk. Detections may not be fully tuned for the environment, automation may not be tested under real-world load, analysts may be unfamiliar with workflow expectations, and cross-team procedures may still be in early development. A hard launch often exposes gaps that were not visible during laboratory testing, sometimes resulting in alert overload, misclassification, or response delays. In short, a hard launch prioritizes speed over stability and should only be used when the organization has no flexibility in timelines.

A soft launch takes the opposite approach. Instead of activating the entire SOC at once, the organization gradually introduces live monitoring, beginning with a carefully selected subset of use cases. These initial use cases are typically high-confidence detections such as malware outbreaks, command and control beaconing, suspicious PowerShell execution, or critical identity events. During this early phase, the SOC operates without binding service level agreements. Analysts and engineers use the soft launch period to study alert volumes, tune rules, test enrichment workflows, and validate containment steps. This controlled expansion allows the SOC to build competence and confidence before assuming full operational responsibility. A distinguishing feature of the soft launch is the use of shadow mode. During shadow mode, Tier 1 analysts practice triage and documentation, but senior engineers or SOC leadership are responsible for completing investigations and taking any response actions. Analysts gain hands-on experience with real alerts without the pressure of immediate accountability. This mentorship-driven model accelerates skill development, exposes analysts to the full alert lifecycle, and reveals gaps in training or documentation. The soft launch also provides a unique opportunity to test processes across organizational boundaries. For example, analysts may practice communicating with IT support teams to validate workflows for account resets, endpoint isolation, firewall updates, or log retrieval. This ensures that when incidents occur at scale, cross-team coordination is smooth rather than chaotic. Additional scenarios such as after-hours escalation, communication templates, and emergency containment procedures can also be tested in controlled conditions.

As the soft launch progresses, additional use cases are added, alert routing becomes more complex, and automated playbooks begin to take on greater responsibility. Eventually, once alert volumes stabilize, detection tuning reaches acceptable quality, and analysts demonstrate consistent performance, the SOC transitions out of soft launch status. Only at this point should service level agreements begin. By the time the SOC reaches full operational readiness, the team has already navigated real alerts, refined internal processes, and established confidence in the toolchain.

In practice, the soft launch model is almost always superior. It transforms the SOC deployment from a single event into a guided maturation process. It reduces operational risk, improves detection accuracy, strengthens training, and establishes strong coordination pathways across the organization. Most importantly, it ensures that when critical incidents occur, the SOC is prepared not just theoretically but operationally.

Tuning Period Strategies

The tuning period is the most important stage of a SOC launch, and ironically, it is also the most commonly neglected. When a new SOC begins receiving live telemetry, every detection rule that appeared well engineered during testing suddenly meets the complexity of real users, real systems, and real business processes. Even the strongest correlation logic will produce noise until it is aligned with the environment's normal operations. This period transforms the SOC from a theoretical design to a practical operational system. Tuning begins the moment the SOC receives its first live alerts. Analysts must immediately start documenting the behavior that triggered each alert, the context surrounding it, and the reason the alert was or was not malicious. This documentation drives the entire tuning process. It reveals legitimate administrative actions that resemble attacks, legacy applications that behave unpredictably, automation tasks that mimic lateral movement, and user habits that trigger authentication anomalies. Without structured feedback from analysts, tuning is blind and relies on guesswork instead of evidence.

Effective tuning requires active collaboration between analysts and detection engineers. Analysts serve as the eyes and ears of the SOC because they are the first to encounter noise. They must describe false positives clearly, consistently, and with context, such as whether an alert originated from a scheduled task, a trusted application, or user behavior that is predictable rather than suspicious. Detection engineers then review these patterns, examine multiple alerts across tenants or business units, and adjust rules to reduce noise while protecting fidelity. This continuous dialogue prevents rules from being disabled prematurely or left unchanged simply because no one understood their purpose.

The tuning period typically spans sixty to one hundred twenty days. This timeline varies based on environment size, detection sophistication, identity complexity, cloud usage, and endpoint diversity. During the first thirty days, alert volumes are often high and unpredictable. This is normal. It reflects the fact that detections were built in a vacuum before the SOC understood what normal activity looks like. As tuning progresses, noise decreases and true positives become easier to identify. By sixty days, a well managed SOC begins to stabilize. By ninety days, the SOC should have a solid understanding of its environment and clear prioritization of detections that require ongoing refinement.

Tuning is not just about reducing alerts. It also involves strengthening detections. Rules that fire too often may lack enrichment, such as user risk scoring, device trust level, asset classification, or threat intelligence context. Adding enrichment can transform a noisy rule into a high certainty detection. For example, instead of alerting on all PowerShell usage, the SOC may enrich the event with parent process data, command line flags, script block logging, and user identity risk indicators. The result is fewer alerts but more accurate ones. Tuning also requires careful decisions about allowlists. Allowlisting should never become a shortcut that bypasses proper detection engineering. Every allowlist entry must be documented and justified. It must also be reviewed regularly, because what is legitimate today may become malicious tomorrow. A trusted domain may become compromised, an internal script may be rewritten with insecure behavior, or an application owner may leave the organization. Poorly managed allowlists create blind spots and undermine SOC accountability.

Retiring legacy rules is another essential tuning activity. Many initial detections are inherited from vendor templates or old SOCs and no longer reflect useful signals. If a behavior-based rule supersedes several atomic detections, the older rules should be removed. This prevents duplication, reduces alert fatigue, and clarifies investigative flow. Similarly, if a rule has not fired for months and no longer aligns with current threat models, it may be removed or rewritten.

The tuning period also involves expanding the detection landscape. As analysts encounter new threats or suspicious patterns, detection engineers can convert these real-world observations into new use cases. For example, if analysts frequently investigate suspicious PowerShell commands that involve encoded payloads, engineers may create detections for unusual encoding activity or for PowerShell processes spawned by non-administrative applications. This ensures the detection portfolio grows with the environment and remains relevant. Tuning marks the transition from "theoretical SOC design" to "real operational SOC performance." During tuning, analysts gain confidence, engineers refine pipelines, and leadership gains clarity on expected alert volumes and response behavior. When tuning is neglected, alert fatigue becomes inevitable, causing missed incidents, slow triage, and analyst burnout. When tuning is executed correctly, the SOC evolves into a precise, efficient, and scalable operational capability capable of supporting the business with accuracy and confidence.

Building and launching a SOC is a transformational effort that requires engineering precision, disciplined project management, mature documentation, gradual deployment, and sustained tuning. This chapter offers the blueprint for executing each stage successfully from planning to tool integration, detection deployment, controlled soft launches, and fully tuned operations. By following this structured approach, organizations ensure their SOC is stable, reliable, effective, and ready to protect the environment from day one.

Chapter 8

Monitoring Strategy & Telemetry Coverage

Monitoring is the operational heartbeat of a SOC. Every alert, every investigation, every containment decision originates from the quality of telemetry available to the analysts. A detection pipeline cannot outperform the visibility beneath it; even the best SIEM or SOAR will fail if it is fed incomplete or low-fidelity data. Monitoring strategy is far more than turning on log sources, it is the discipline of knowing which telemetry matters the most, validating that it is collected reliably, structuring how analysts review it, and building dashboards that allow immediate situational awareness. This chapter defines what "complete visibility" truly means and provides a blueprint for creating a monitoring program that is both comprehensive and operationally manageable.

What "Complete Visibility" Actually Means

Complete visibility is one of the most misunderstood concepts in SOC design. Many organizations assume it means collecting every log from every system without discrimination. That assumption is not only incorrect, it is dangerous. Collecting all available logs creates massive ingestion bills, increases noise, slows detections, and overwhelms analysts with data that provides little or no investigative value. True complete visibility is not about quantity. It is about relevance, depth, and alignment with attacker behaviors.

Complete visibility begins with collecting the telemetry that exposes the stages of an attack across the entire cyber kill chain. A SOC must see where attackers probe, where they authenticate, where they move laterally, where they execute commands, and where they attempt persistence or data exfiltration. This requires targeted log collection from five core domains: endpoints, identity systems, network traffic, cloud environments, and business critical applications. Endpoint visibility includes behavior rich telemetry such as process creation events, command line arguments, registry modifications, PowerShell script block logging, and kernel level monitoring through platforms such as EDR or Sysmon. This is where many attacks begin and where lateral movement becomes visible. Identity visibility requires auditing authentication events, conditional access decisions, multi factor authentication outcomes, privilege escalations, and directory changes. Identity is now the primary attack surface in most organizations, so these logs are indispensable for spotting credential theft and misuse.

Network visibility fills another critical gap. Even in a zero trust model, attackers generate traffic that reveals intent. Proxy logs, DNS queries, firewall flows, and intrusion prevention alerts allow the SOC to correlate endpoint behavior with external destinations and internal traversal. Without this, a compromised host can beacon or exfiltrate undetected. Cloud visibility is equally essential, because modern infrastructure relies heavily on cloud providers and SaaS platforms. API level logs, resource creation and deletion events, role assignments, configuration changes, and cross tenant interactions must be monitored continuously. Attackers frequently exploit weak cloud audit trails, so cloud logging must be intentional and complete, not default or ad hoc.

Application visibility ties monitoring back to the business itself. Critical systems, such as payment processing platforms, medical record systems, manufacturing control systems, or financial databases, generate unique logs that reveal misuse or compromise. Complete visibility ensures that the SOC understands which applications matter most to organizational mission and that their telemetry is collected, parsed, and monitored.

Achieving complete visibility requires more than selecting the right log sources. It depends on accuracy and fidelity. Logs must be timestamped correctly, especially when spanning multiple systems and geographic regions. Engineers must validate that clocks are synchronized and that time drift does not break correlation logic. Logs must also be parsed correctly so that key fields such as user identity, IP address, command line, device name, or action type are extracted cleanly. A log that arrives unparsed has little operational value to a SIEM or SOAR. The SOC cannot investigate what the SIEM cannot understand.

Correlation is another requirement for complete visibility. Logs from endpoints, identity systems, cloud platforms, and networks must come together in a unified schema that enables analysts to move seamlessly across domains. Without correlation, an attacker may appear as four different entities in four different log sources. Normalization frameworks such as ECS, CIM, or OCSF provide the structural foundation for this unified view.

Enrichment elevates raw telemetry to operational intelligence. Complete visibility means associating logs with contextual attributes such as asset classification, user role, geo location, threat intelligence, vulnerability status, and behavioral baselines. A login from an unusual location looks very different when the account belongs to a privileged administrator rather than a guest user. Enrichment allows detections to incorporate this nuance.

True complete visibility requires ongoing validation. Logging does not remain static. Agents break, configurations drift, cloud providers modify schema, and network paths fail. Critical systems may silently stop forwarding logs and no one notices until an incident occurs. A mature SOC performs regular visibility audits using dashboards or automated health checks that confirm log ingestion health, parsing consistency, and schema alignment. These audits ensure that complete visibility is not a one time achievement but a sustained operational discipline. Complete visibility means that the SOC can detect, investigate, and understand an attacker's full lifecycle without guesswork. It means the right logs are collected, enriched, normalized, correlated, and validated continuously. It means the SOC has no silent gaps where adversaries can hide. This is not maximal logging but intentional logging, engineered for clarity, depth, and defensive power.

Prioritizing Critical Log Sources

A mature monitoring strategy begins by prioritizing the telemetry that provides the greatest detection value. Endpoint logs remain the crown jewel; attackers interact with endpoints at every stageinitial access, persistence, privilege escalation, lateral movement, and exfiltration. EDR telemetry is therefore non-negotiable, as it captures process behavior, parent-child relationships, command-line arguments, file modifications, injected threads, and malicious indicators.

Identity logs are equally important. Active Directory logs reveal password spray attacks, anomalous authentication attempts, privilege assignments, Kerberos ticket anomalies, and account misuse. Azure AD, Okta, or other cloud identity provider logs extend this visibility into remote and SaaS environments. Identity data sits at the intersection of user access and attacker progression, making it essential.

Network logs from firewalls, proxies, and DNS resolvers provide insight into command-and-control activity, domain fronting, tunneling, and malware beaconing. Cloud platform logsAWS CloudTrail, Azure Activity Logs, GCP Audit Logscapture API misuse, privilege escalations, and configuration drift that attackers exploit when breaching cloud workloads.

Operationally, prioritizing log sources requires mapping them to use cases. For example:

- To detect ransomware, the SOC prioritizes file modification logs, process creation, suspicious scripting engines, and SMB traffic.

- To detect account compromise, the SOC prioritizes identity logs, geolocation patterns, device trust logs, and login anomalies.

- To detect exfiltration, the SOC prioritizes proxy logs, egress patterns, cloud storage events, and DLP telemetry.

Alert Noise Management

Alert noise is the silent killer of SOC performance. It does not arrive dramatically or announce itself as a crisis. Instead, it accumulates day after day until analysts are buried beneath alerts that have no real investigative value. High noise levels increase triage time, dilute analyst attention, hide real incidents in a sea of false alarms, and accelerate burnout across the team. Left unmanaged, noise transforms even a well staffed SOC into a reactive, overwhelmed operation. Effective noise management is not about disabling alerts. It is about engineering clarity through deliberate tuning, intelligent correlation, and automated enrichment.

Noise management begins with the recognition that every alert should represent a decision, not just an event. A SIEM rule should fire only when there is meaningful evidence of potential malicious activity. Vendors often ship detections that are intentionally broad to ensure coverage across many environments. While valuable as starting points, these rules must be customized. A detection designed for a global enterprise will not behave properly in a small business environment, and vice versa. Rules that flag “Multiple Failed Logins” must account for service accounts, legacy systems, or applications that retry authentication. Similarly, a detection for "PowerShell Execution" should not alert every time PowerShell runs. Instead, it should focus on suspicious command line patterns, encoded scripts, unusual parent processes, or unexpected user contexts.

Noise management requires thoughtful tuning of thresholds and correlation logic. Threshold-based rules must reflect actual baseline activity. For example, a threshold of five failed logins in one minute may be appropriate in one environment but ineffective in another where automated scanners routinely trigger authentication retries. Correlation rules can consolidate related activity into a single alert, such as grouping a sequence of suspicious events into one case rather than generating multiple independent alerts. This approach reduces analyst workload and improves context by presenting the full chain of behavior at once. Enrichment is at the core of effective noise reduction. The SOAR platform performs automated triage before an analyst ever sees the alert. This includes reputation checks for IP addresses and hashes, device context analysis from EDR platforms, user risk scoring from identity systems, and comparisons against behavioral baselines. Enrichment transforms a raw alert into a contextualized event with clear next steps. In many SOCs, automated enrichment and filtering reduce alert volume by sixty to eighty percent. This allows analysts to dedicate their time to genuinely suspicious behavior rather than sifting through a mountain of benign noise.

Noise management also depends on collaboration between roles. Analysts are the first to identify false positives because they interact with alerts directly. Their observations must be documented in a structured, consistent manner: what triggered the alert, why it was benign, and what pattern indicates it should not fire again. Detection engineers then review these patterns, identify common root causes, and implement improvements to rule logic or enrichment workflows. This feedback loop must be continuous and measurable. A rule that consistently produces false positives is not merely annoying; it is a detection engineering failure that must be corrected.

Metrics support effective noise management. SOCs should routinely measure alerts per analyst per shift, false positive rates by rule, detection conversion rates, and mean time to triage. When noise levels rise, the SOC must investigate whether new log sources, recent configuration changes, increased user activity, or detection drift are responsible. Regular noise audits ensure that detection logic evolves alongside the environment. Noise management is a strategic engineering discipline, not a reactive task. It requires continuous refinement, strong communication between analysts and engineers, and a commitment to designing detections that prioritize clarity over quantity. A quiet SOC is not a weak SOC. It is a mature SOC where every alert matters.

Daily and Weekly Monitoring Routines

Security Operations Centers function best when anchored by disciplined, repeatable routines. These routines give structure to the work, ensure situational awareness, and prevent operational drift during periods of high alert volume or crisis. A SOC without well defined daily and weekly rhythms will inevitably fall into reactive mode, losing visibility into ingestion health, detection fidelity, and the overall threat landscape. Mature SOCs therefore implement routines that balance immediate operational needs with strategic oversight and continuous improvement.

Daily monitoring routines form the backbone of SOC readiness. The first task of every shift is a review of the alert queue, ensuring that no critical or high severity alerts have aged beyond acceptable thresholds. Analysts should check for new incidents generated by the SIEM or SOAR and validate that auto enrichment completed successfully. A parallel check of ingestion health dashboards confirms whether all critical log sources continue to send data. Even a brief ingestion outage can create dangerous blind spots, so verifying log flow is just as important as reviewing alerts. This includes confirming that EDR agents report active status, that cloud connectors are operating properly, and that identity logs from systems such as Active Directory or Azure AD are flowing without delay.

A comprehensive daily routine also includes reviewing the health of automation systems. Analysts must confirm that playbooks executed correctly overnight, that API keys have not expired, and that enrichment pipelines are functioning. Unexpected failures in automation can create artificial triage bottlenecks or result in alerts lacking necessary context. Reviewing threat intelligence updates is another essential daily practice. Analysts should scan for new advisories related to ransomware campaigns, emerging vulnerabilities, phishing infrastructure, or changes in adversary behavior. Daily intelligence reviews help analysts understand whether recent activity in their environment aligns with global trends.

Shift handoffs are an often underestimated but critical part of daily SOC operations. Each shift should begin with a review of ongoing investigations, pending escalations, active incidents requiring monitoring, and any containment measures currently in effect. Documentation should be structured, precise, and housed in the ticketing system rather than informal chats or verbal summaries. A strong shift handoff prevents duplicated effort, missed investigative steps, and loss of context when incidents span multiple shifts. Analysts must clearly note what has been completed, what remains outstanding, and what the next steps should be.

Weekly monitoring routines expand beyond operational tasks and focus on deeper analysis and continuous improvement. Weekly trend reviews provide insight into detection performance, alert volume changes, and unusual activity patterns. Analysts and engineers should evaluate false positive trends, documenting common causes and identifying detections that require tuning. Weekly reviews are also the appropriate time to examine SIEM performance, reindexing requirements, query optimization needs, and storage utilization patterns.

Backlog management is another important weekly task. Complex investigations sometimes accumulate in Tier Two or Tier Three queues, requiring prioritization discussions. Weekly meetings help ensure that no significant case remains dormant without a clear investigative direction. Weekly case review sessions allow analysts to present challenging alerts or unusual findings. These sessions serve as practical training, improving analytical rigor, investigative creativity, and cross team knowledge sharing. Weekly routines should also include reviewing key performance indicators. Metrics such as time to triage, time to notify, false positive rates, enrichment success rates, SOAR automation success, and mean time to detect reveal whether SOC operations are improving or declining. These metrics guide managerial decisions, training priorities, and resource allocation. Daily and weekly routines create a structured operational rhythm that protects the SOC from chaos. Even during major incidents, these routines ensure that ingestion health remains monitored, detections continue to evolve, and analyst workloads remain balanced. Consistent routines transform the SOC from a reactive alert factory into a disciplined, high reliability security organization.

Using Dashboards Effectively

SIEM dashboards serve as the operational cockpit of the SOC. When designed correctly, they provide instant situational awareness, highlight emerging threats, and guide analysts toward the areas most in need of attention. When designed poorly, they bury analysts in noise, display vanity metrics that add no value, and obscure the very insights the SOC depends on. Effective dashboards are purposeful and audience specific. They are not collections of charts, but instruments engineered to answer precise operational questions.

Dashboards for Tier One analysts should prioritize real time visibility. Their primary responsibility is rapid triage, so their dashboards must display new alerts as they arrive, highlight high severity detections, and provide summaries of endpoint activity, authentication anomalies, and critical network events. Trendlines are especially valuable for Tier One, because they reveal deviations from normal volume patterns. A sudden spike in failed logins, unusual outbound connections, or rapid file modifications may indicate active attack behavior. Because Tier One analysts require clarity, not complexity, their dashboards must remain clean, minimal, and focused exclusively on front line monitoring.

Dashboards for Tier Two analysts are more investigative in nature. These analysts pivot across multiple log sources, so their dashboards should display correlated timelines, behavioral summaries, and multi source event relationships. Visualizations such as lateral movement maps, user behavior baselines, cloud

API modification histories, and identity correlation charts help Tier Two analysts identify patterns that span systems and domains. These dashboards must support investigative depth, allowing analysts to quickly pivot into queries or drill into event detail when correlations suggest suspicious behavior.

SOC managers require a completely different perspective. Their dashboards must focus on operational health rather than technical detection data. Queue size, SLA compliance, analyst workload distribution, alert aging, shift performance, and backlog trends appear prominently in managerial dashboards. These displays help managers identify resource constraints, workload imbalances, and early warning signs of fatigue or staffing gaps. A well designed managerial dashboard prevents operational bottlenecks long before they become crises. Detection engineers also rely heavily on dashboards, but theirs must be precision instruments. Engineer dashboards display rule performance metrics, including false positive rates, conversion ratios, firing frequency, and suppression history. They also highlight ingestion delays, schema drift, parsing failures, field extraction errors, and enrichment anomalies. These dashboards reveal where detections require tuning, where log sources are misconfigured, and where engineering attention must be directed to sustain SOC accuracy and efficiency.

Regardless of the audience, dashboards must remain lean and intentional. A common pitfall is creating dashboards that attempt to show everything at once. Overloaded dashboards confuse analysts and hide the key indicators that matter. Each dashboard should answer a specific operational question. For Tier One, the question is "What requires immediate attention right now?" For Tier Two, the question is "What patterns reveal the deeper story behind existing alerts?" For managers, the question is "Is the SOC performing efficiently and meeting commitments?" For detection engineers, the question is "Are our detections and pipelines functioning as intended?"

Dashboards should evolve continuously. As detection logic matures, new threats emerge, and organizational priorities change, dashboards must be revisited and refined. Metrics that once served a purpose may become irrelevant. Others may appear due to new use cases or newly integrated log sources. A mature SOC regularly evaluates dashboard effectiveness and removes any chart or widget that does not directly support decision making. Dashboards are not decoration; they are operational tools. Their purpose is fast comprehension, clarity, and action. A SOC that designs dashboards intentionally will understand its environment at a glance, respond to incidents faster, and maintain far greater operational stability than one overwhelmed by visual noise.

Monitoring strategy and telemetry coverage form the core of SOC effectiveness. Without complete visibility, properly prioritized logs, disciplined routines, noise management, and intelligent dashboards, the SOC becomes reactive rather than proactive. This chapter provides the blueprint needed to build a monitoring program that is rigorous, high-performing, and aligned with modern detection and response demands. With this foundation, analysts can operate confidently and reliably in even the most complex environments.

SECTION IV ONGOING OPERATIONS

Chapter 9

Analyst Training: How to Read Alerts & Find the Signal in the Noise

A SOC analyst's greatest skill is the ability to interpret alerts accurately and quickly. The modern security environment is noisy and littered with false positives, benign process executions, routine authentication anomalies, and non-critical system events. Beneath that noise, however, lie the subtle traces of real compromise. High performers in SOC operations develop a disciplined, structured approach to reading alerts, understanding context, interpreting behavioral signals, and forming investigative hypotheses. This chapter provides the operational blueprint for training analysts to cut through ambiguity and find the signal in the noise.

Anatomy of an Alert

Mastering the anatomy of an alert is one of the most critical skills in SOC operations. Alerts are the starting point for nearly every investigation. They define what the analyst sees first, what questions they ask next, and how quickly they understand the potential risk. Yet many junior analysts treat alerts as shallow notifications titles to be read, buttons to be clicked, and tickets to be closed. This mindset is the root of slow investigations, missed incidents, and constant escalation. Elite SOCs understand that alerts are structured messages carrying multiple layers of meaning. To interpret them correctly, analysts must break them down into fundamental components before taking action.

Every alert, regardless of the SIEM, EDR, or SOAR platform that generates it, contains four essential elements: the trigger logic, the observed behavior, the contextual metadata, and the recommended next steps. These components form the "alert DNA" and determine whether an analyst can extract the right insight quickly. Analysts who understand this structure begin an investigation with clarity. Those who do not often spiral into guesswork, unnecessary queries, and wasted triage cycles.

The first and most important component is the trigger logic. Trigger logic describes why the alert fired. It reveals the exact conditions that caused the detection to activate. This may be a correlation rule, a behavioral anomaly, a threshold condition, a machine learning detection, or a signature match. Analysts must always start by reading the detection criteria.

Too often, analysts assume the alert name describes the full intent. It rarely does. A rule labeled “Suspicious PowerShell Usage” could detect obfuscated commands, encoded payloads, unsigned modules, or even benign administrative tasks. Without reading the logic, the analyst cannot know which. The trigger logic provides the investigative frame of reference. It answers the question: *What did the detection engine believe was suspicious enough to surface?* If an analyst does not understand this, they are no longer investigating the alert, they are merely reacting to it.

The second component is the observed behavior. This is the actual activity that occurred in the environment and was captured by logs or endpoint telemetry. It may include process creation events, file execution, registry modification, scheduled task creation, authentication attempts, network connections, cloud API calls, privilege escalations, or lateral movement behavior. Thorough analysts extract key fields from this behavior to reconstruct what happened. They look at process paths, parent-child relationships, command line arguments, user accounts, source and destination IPs, port numbers, authentication methods, device names, and timestamps. They piece together a narrative: *Which entity acted? What did it do? What was the system trying to accomplish?* This step is essential because some detections fire on benign behavior that mimics malicious patterns. Only understanding the behavior itself can reveal whether the activity is harmful or harmless.

The third component is contextual metadata. Context transforms an otherwise basic alert into actionable intelligence. Metadata enriches the event with attributes such as device criticality, user role, previous risk scores, known vulnerabilities, threat intelligence verdicts, organizational grouping, and historical patterns. For example, a failed login from a privileged administrator is not the same as a failed login from an intern's workstation. A suspicious network connection originating from a domain controller carries completely different significance than the same event originating from a kiosk machine. Threat intelligence metadata may classify an external IP as a known scanner, a command and control endpoint, a ransomware distribution node, or a benign research crawler. Analysts who ignore this context risk treating all alerts equally which is a catastrophic mistake. Context allows analysts to prioritize rapidly, exclude false leads, and understand the broader risk landscape surrounding the event.

The final component of an alert is the recommended next steps. In a mature SOC, these steps are provided either through detection documentation, embedded alert guidance, or automated SOAR playbooks that populate triage procedures directly into the analyst's interface. Recommended steps may include validating user activity, checking EDR telemetry for additional processes, reviewing authentication logs, isolating a device, resetting credentials, querying cloud audit trails, or escalating the event to a higher tier. These recommendations act as investigative guardrails, especially for junior analysts. They ensure that basic triage steps are never missed and that alerts follow a consistent investigative path. They also improve speed, because analysts do not need to reinvent investigative workflows every time a rule fires.

When analysts learn to dissect alerts into these structural components, something transformative happens. Investigation becomes faster, cleaner, and more focused. Analysts begin to see patterns across alerts, identify recurring false positives, and understand detection gaps. They approach each alert with an informed hypothesis, rather than blind curiosity. They begin thinking like engineers, not clerks.

The SOCs that struggle the most are the ones that train analysts to read alert titles and click "Close" or "Escalate." Those that excel train analysts to think in terms of alert anatomy: *Why did this trigger, what exactly happened, what context surrounds it, and what are the prescribed next actions?* This mindset separates a reactive SOC from a strategic one. Elite analysts do not simply respond to alerts; they interpret them.

Mastering the anatomy of an alert is the foundation upon which all advanced SOC skills are built. It is the difference between shallow triage and deep understanding. It is the difference between missed incidents and timely detection. And ultimately, it is the difference between an overwhelmed SOC and a high performance security operation capable of defending an organization at scale.

How to Quickly Identify False Positives

False positives consume enormous amounts of analyst time. The ability to instantly recognize them separates junior analysts from seasoned professionals. A false positive is rarely identified by a single field; instead, analysts must look at a combination of behavioral context, asset information, and user activity patterns.

The fastest way to evaluate a potential false positive is to ask: *Does the event make sense for the asset, the user, and the time?* If the alert is for a domain administrator performing a known patching procedure, or a service account launching a scheduled maintenance task, it may be expected behavior. Analysts must also check whether the command or behavior has been seen regularly on that machine or userSOAR enrichment and SIEM history searches make this much faster.

Device criticality helps identify false positives as well. A developer workstation running compilation tools may generate many command-line events that look suspicious in other contexts but are entirely normal for that role. Service accounts will often trigger repetitive authentication events that benignly resemble brute-force patterns. When reviewing network alerts, internal scanning tools or vulnerability assessment systems frequently generate noise that resembles attacker reconnaissance.

False positives usually share patterns: repeated benign events, common system processes, predictable timing, known automation routines, or events matching acceptance patterns identified during tuning. Analysts must develop familiarity with the environment so they can recognize expected behavior instantly.

Behavioral Indicators of True Positives

While false positives tend to follow predictable, repetitive, and often mundane patterns, true positives contain behavioral characteristics that rarely, if ever, appear in normal operational activity. These characteristics form the “signature” of real attacker activity even when no explicit indicators of compromise are present. Behavioral detection is the foundation of modern SOC work. Analysts who learn to recognize these patterns instinctively become exponentially faster, more accurate, and more confident in identifying genuine threats. True positive analysis is not the art of spotting noise, but the discipline of observing deviations from how systems, identities, and applications behave under legitimate conditions.

One of the strongest behavioral indicators is abnormal process lineage. Every operating system has predictable parent child relationships for common activities. Attackers break these patterns constantly because malicious actions rarely follow the same pathways as legitimate workflows. For example, a trusted application like Outlook or Chrome spawning PowerShell is not typical user behavior. A WMI provider invoking cmd.exe with encoded arguments, or a script host such as wscript.exe launching rundll32.exe, is equally suspicious. These sequences immediately compel deeper investigation because legitimate administrative tasks almost never follow these indirect routes. Process lineage tells a story about intent. When the story does not make sense, compromise becomes a likely explanation.

Credential misuse is another hallmark of true positive behavior. Identity is the new battleground, and attackers almost always begin with stolen or weakened credentials. Behavioral indicators include authentication from previously unseen locations, especially those outside expected geographic patterns; sudden privilege escalations with no administrative justification; multiple failed authentication attempts followed by a successful one; and authenticating at improbable times, such as during off hours or while the user is confirmed inactive. Even subtle identity anomalies, such as service accounts performing interactive logins, or privileged accounts logging into endpoints rather than servers, strongly suggest attacker activity. Unlike endpoint anomalies, identity-based anomalies rarely arise from normal operations. They are disproportionately reliable indicators of compromise.

Command line behavior is another rich source of truth. Attackers often rely on encoded or obfuscated commands to hide malicious functionality. Command lines containing base sixty four encoded strings, long unintelligible character sequences, or suspicious combinations of flags immediately warrant scrutiny. Commands referencing temporary directories, unusual file paths, or staging areas for payload delivery often appear during true compromises. Tools such as PsExec, net.exe, sc.exe, wmic, and reg.exe appear frequently during both legitimate operations and attacks. What makes them suspicious is context: who ran them, how they were run, and what preceded or followed them. Attackers rarely take the time to blend perfectly into normal administrative habits. Small deviations expose their presence.

Network anomalies provide another layer of confirmation. True positives often involve repeated outbound connections to extremely rare domains, connections using ports not typically associated with business operations, or beaconing activity that follows rhythmic intervals. Beaconing is especially important, because legitimate software rarely communicates with such precise repetition. Sudden increases in outbound volume, encrypted traffic to untrusted destinations, or the creation of unauthorized tunnels all signal malicious intent. These behaviors are difficult to explain through normal business processes, making them reliable indicators.

In cloud environments, attackers exhibit similarly predictable deviations. The unexpected creation of new API keys, unusual IAM role assumptions, large scale permission modifications, unapproved resource deployments, or mass data exfiltration to object storage services all point toward compromise. Cloud architectures allow for high visibility when configured correctly, and attackers tend to leave clear footprints when manipulating identity or resource configurations.

One defining characteristic of true positives is that they rarely occur in isolation. Attack behavior almost always generates a constellation of anomalies across multiple domains such as identity, endpoint, network, and cloud. A suspicious command line on its own may not be enough to confirm compromise. But combine it with abnormal identity access, strange process lineage, and unusual network traffic, and the picture becomes unmistakable. Attackers must complete several steps to progress toward their objectives, and each step leaves a detectable trace if the SOC knows how to interpret it.

Elite analysts recognize that true positives follow patterns because adversaries, no matter how skilled, must obey the constraints of the systems they target. They must authenticate, execute code, move laterally, persist, and communicate. Each action introduces variance from legitimate behavior. Analysts who train themselves to see that variance develop an instinct for detecting real threats long before they escalate into incidents. This instinct is not innate; it is cultivated by repeatedly studying behavioral signals, comparing them against baselines, and cross referencing them with known attacker techniques.

Understanding true positive behavior is one of the highest value skills in SOC mastery. It empowers analysts to distinguish noise from danger, act decisively, and detect real compromises before catastrophic damage occurs.

Understanding Event Sequences

Individual events rarely tell the complete story of an incident. Analysts must learn to interpret event sequences as the chain of attacker actions occurring before, during, and after the alert. Timelines provide the context needed to understand intent and distinguish benign anomalies from true threats. Analysts should always examine what happened one minute before, five minutes before, thirty minutes before, and one hour after the alert in question. This reveals patterns such as failed authentications prior to a successful login, suspicious file downloads preceding command execution, or lateral movement attempts following credential misuse.

A sequence-based investigation transforms an isolated alert into a meaningful narrative. For example, a "Suspicious PowerShell Command" is not simply a single alert but potentially the midpoint of a ten-step attack chain. By reviewing the events leading up to and following the execution, analysts may uncover initial access, credential harvesting, privilege escalation, and reconnaissance events that dramatically change the severity and required response. The alert becomes a doorway into understanding the broader operation, allowing analysts to assess attacker progression and determine whether immediate containment is necessary.

Event sequence analysis is also critical for identifying the scope and depth of compromise. By examining whether multiple hosts, identities, or cloud resources were involved, analysts can determine whether the attack is isolated or systemic. This insight enables prioritization; early-stage activity such as reconnaissance can be contained quickly, whereas later-stage activity such as lateral movement or exfiltration demands urgent escalation. Sequences also allow analysts to predict attacker intent, as adversaries often follow recognizable behavioral patterns across identity, endpoint, network, and cloud layers.

Timeline thinking must become instinctive. Analysts should automatically pivot through authentication logs, endpoint telemetry, network flows, cloud audit logs, and previous alerts from the same user or host. This multi-log correlation forms a holistic understanding of the incident. When analysts adopt this mindset, they stop treating alerts as individual items and begin viewing them as interconnected steps in a broader attack narrative. This shift marks the transition from basic triage to true investigative mastery.

Understanding sequences reveals not only what happened but why it happened and how far the attacker progressed. It is one of the strongest tools for distinguishing noise from meaningful threat activity and is essential for both rapid containment and long-term detection refinement.

Common Attack Patterns

Attackers tend to reuse patterns because these patterns are reliable. SOC analysts become far more effective when trained to recognize the "shape" of an attack. Most intrusions follow common frameworks such as the MITRE ATT&CK, Cyber Kill Chain, or cloud-native variants. Attackers typically begin with initial access (phishing, credential theft, vulnerable services), followed by execution (PowerShell, bash, macros), persistence (registry run keys, scheduled tasks, systemd services), privilege escalation, lateral movement, and finally exfiltration or sabotage.

Analysts should be trained to recognize these patterns immediately: phishing leading to credential usage, credential usage leading to lateral movement, lateral movement leading to privilege escalation, and privilege escalation leading to data theft or ransomware deployment. Once familiar with these progressions, analysts begin to anticipate what the attacker will do next.

By teaching analysts to understand patterns rather than isolated alerts, the SOC transforms tactical responders into strategic defenders capable of seeing the broader attack campaign.

MITRE ATT&CK Mapping

MITRE ATTACK mapping is one of the most important disciplines in modern detection engineering and analyst development. It provides a universal framework for describing adversary behavior across all stages of an intrusion. Without this structure, analysts rely on isolated descriptions of activity that lack broader context. With ATTACK mapping, every alert and every investigative finding becomes part of a well defined and globally recognized behavioral model. Each ATTACK entry includes a specific technique that describes how an adversary performed an action and a broader tactic that explains why the action was taken. This allows analysts to move beyond technical symptoms and understand the strategic purpose of the activity they are seeing.

Mapping alerts to ATTACK techniques enables analysts to identify exactly where in the attack chain the activity belongs. For instance, a PowerShell execution alert may map to technique T1059 dot zero zero one which is part of the Execution tactic. By identifying the tactic, the analyst recognizes immediately that the alert occurred after the adversary had already obtained a foothold and is now attempting to run commands or code. If that same alert shows signs of credential manipulation, the analyst may also map activity to technique T1003 dot zero zero one which belongs to the Credential Access tactic. This dual mapping illustrates that the adversary may be advancing from simple execution to account compromise, which significantly raises the urgency of the investigation.

ATTACK mapping also helps analysts anticipate what is likely to occur next. Techniques rarely occur in isolation. Execution events often precede privilege escalation attempts. Credential theft is usually followed by lateral movement. Persistence actions may surface after initial compromise. When analysts map a detection correctly, they gain predictive insight. They can look for related behaviors and proactively examine surrounding logs rather than waiting for additional alerts to fire. This predictive capability transforms the investigation from reactive triage into forward leaning threat analysis.

Another major value of ATTACK mapping is its ability to support trend identification across longer time frames. If multiple alerts over several days or weeks consistently map to the same tactic, it may indicate that the organization is experiencing focused targeting or that a specific technique is being abused repeatedly. For example, repeated mapping to the Initial Access tactic may suggest misconfigurations on externally facing assets or a phishing campaign underway. Repeated mapping to the Privilege Escalation tactic may highlight weaknesses in identity governance. These insights drive threat hunting, root cause analysis, and strategic detection engineering rather than ad hoc incident response.

ATTACK mapping also improves documentation quality and communication. When analysts write case notes or escalations using ATTACK terminology, investigations become more consistent, structured, and easily interpretable by senior responders, auditors, and leadership. Incident reports that reference ATTACK techniques provide clarity about adversary capability, sophistication, and tradecraft. They also support cross team collaboration because everyone can reference the same framework without ambiguity.

Over time, ATTACK mapping becomes a mindset rather than a mechanical task. Analysts begin to automatically associate observed behaviors with technique categories. They develop intuition for attacker objectives and typical attack patterns. This reduces cognitive load during active investigations and enhances the accuracy of triage decisions. A SOC that consistently maps detections to ATTACK techniques gains both tactical clarity and strategic awareness, allowing it to detect, understand, and disrupt adversary actions with far greater effectiveness.

The ability to distinguish meaningful alerts from background noise is the defining skill of a SOC analyst. Through structured training focused on alert anatomy, false-positive recognition, behavioral indicators, event sequence analysis, attack-pattern literacy, and ATT&CK mapping, analysts develop the intuition and investigative discipline required for high-performance cybersecurity operations. This chapter establishes the foundation for that training, enabling the SOC to elevate its detection quality, reduce triage time, and strengthen its defensive posture.

Chapter 10

Incident Response (IR) for SOC Analysts

Incident Response is the highest-pressure, highest-impact function of a SOC. While detections and monitoring identify threats, IR is where security teams *stop attacks, remove adversaries, and restore normal operations.* Effective IR requires discipline, procedural rigor, cross-team communication, and a deep understanding of attacker behavior. For SOC analysts, IR is not a theoretical exercise; it is a daily responsibility that requires the ability to triage quickly, investigate accurately, escalate appropriately, contain confidently, and document thoroughly.

This chapter provides the complete blueprint for how SOC analysts conduct incident response using NIST standards, operational best practices, and real-world techniques.

The NIST IR Lifecycle

The NIST Special Publication 800 61, titled the Computer Security Incident Handling Guide, defines incident response not as a single action but as a structured lifecycle with four interconnected phases. These phases are Preparation, Detection and Analysis, Containment Eradication and Recovery, and Post Incident Activity. Together, they create a continuous improvement cycle that strengthens the organization's ability to respond to threats with discipline, clarity, and repeatability. Although Security Operations Center analysts often spend the majority of their time in the Detection and Analysis phase, understanding the entire lifecycle allows them to recognize how their work fits into broader organizational resilience.

The first phase, Preparation, is the most important and often the most underestimated. Preparation occurs long before any adversary activity is detected. It includes building clear incident response plans, establishing communication channels, training analysts, defining escalation paths, provisioning tooling, establishing asset inventories, and deploying logging infrastructure. Preparation also includes conducting tabletop exercises, rehearsing communication strategies, and ensuring that all stakeholders understand their roles during an incident. A well prepared environment enables analysts to respond confidently and effectively when malicious activity appears. Without preparation, even a minor event can escalate into a major incident simply because teams are disorganized or tools are not ready.

The second phase, Detection and Analysis, is the operational center of most Security Operations Centers. Analysts validate alerts, differentiate false positives from true security events, classify the severity of activity, and determine whether the organization is experiencing a genuine incident. This phase requires strong analytical skills, familiarity with attacker behavior, and mastery of investigative techniques. Analysts review logs, correlate events, search for related indicators, and reconstruct timelines to build contextual understanding. The goal of this phase is not only to detect malicious actions but also to understand the scope and intent of the activity. During this stage the decision to escalate an event from an alert to a confirmed incident is made, which shapes the actions that follow.

The third phase, Containment Eradication and Recovery, involves actively stopping the adversary, eliminating their presence, and restoring normal operations. Containment strategies vary depending on the incident. Temporary containment may isolate a compromised host or block a malicious IP address to prevent additional damage. Long term containment may involve segmentation, password resets, or modifications to authentication mechanisms. Eradication focuses on removing malicious artifacts, closing exploited vulnerabilities, and eliminating unauthorized access paths. Recovery activities include restoring systems from backups, validating the integrity of affected assets, reintroducing systems into production, and monitoring for signs of reinfection. This phase requires coordination across multiple teams, including information technology operations, network administrators, cloud engineers, and executive leadership. Effective containment and recovery depend on the preparatory work completed earlier in the lifecycle.

The final phase, Post Incident Activity, transforms incidents into long term improvements. It involves conducting lessons learned meetings, documenting findings, updating detection rules, enhancing playbooks, improving controls, and refining incident response plans. Post incident reviews are not optional. They provide essential insight into what succeeded, what failed, and what must be changed to prevent recurrence. Mature teams treat this phase as a critical component of operational growth rather than an administrative formality. The improvements generated during this phase strengthen the Preparation phase, completing the cycle and enhancing readiness for future incidents.

Understanding the NIST Incident Response Lifecycle gives analysts a holistic view of their role and responsibilities. Investigations are not isolated tasks. They are part of a structured approach that spans preparation, detection, containment, restoration, and continuous refinement. Mastery of this lifecycle allows analysts to see the bigger picture. It helps them understand how their triage work influences recovery efforts, how containment decisions affect business continuity, and how post incident insights shape future detection engineering. In this model, incident response is not a reactive discipline but a continuous improvement loop that strengthens the organization every time an event occurs.

How to Conduct a Triage

Triage is the initial decision making moment in incident response and often the single most important step in determining whether an organization maintains control of a situation or allows an attacker to advance. The purpose of triage is not to perform a complete investigation, nor is it to gather every available piece of evidence. Instead, triage aims to quickly and accurately classify an alert into one of three categories: benign behavior, suspicious activity requiring deeper review, or confirmed malicious action. This classification allows the Security Operations Center to allocate time and resources effectively, ensuring that true threats receive immediate attention while normal activity is dismissed without unnecessary effort. A disciplined triage process begins with the most fundamental question: Is the alert based on a real event. Analysts must first validate the authenticity of the event itself. This involves reviewing the raw log entry, confirming that timestamps are accurate, verifying that host names and user accounts exist within the environment, and ensuring that no parsing errors or duplicated logs created a misleading signal. This validation prevents the Security Operations Center from wasting time on phantom alerts that arise from misconfigured agents, malformed logs, or test activity.

Once authenticity is confirmed, the analyst must examine the alert through the lens of environmental context. Context separates meaningful signals from routine behavior. Analysts must ask whether the user involved normally performs administrative functions, whether the device has a history of scripting activity, whether the service account frequently authenticates across multiple servers, or whether the network destination is consistent with the system's normal communication patterns. Without contextual awareness, even harmless events can appear threatening. Conversely, familiarity with normal patterns allows subtle deviations to stand out.

After establishing context, analysts proceed to enrichment. Enrichment is the rapid gathering of additional data points that clarify intent. This includes checking file hashes against threat intelligence sources, retrieving IP reputation scores, reviewing domain age and hosting patterns, examining recent authentication attempts by the same user, and validating whether the device involved currently exhibits high risk signals within the endpoint detection and response platform. Enrichment transforms an isolated alert into a multidimensional picture of what is actually happening.

During triage, analysts must also consider whether the behavior aligns with known attacker techniques. Unexpected scripting, encoded commands, unusual parent child process relationships, privilege escalation, or connections to rare external destinations all increase suspicion. At the same time, analysts must avoid overreacting to harmless noise, such as system updates, configuration management tools, or normal administrative activity. The skill of triage lies in recognizing the difference quickly and reliably.

A successful triage concludes with a clear decision. If evidence strongly indicates normal or expected activity, the alert may be closed as benign with documented justification. If uncertainty remains, or if multiple anomalous factors are present, the alert should be escalated for deeper investigation by a higher tier analyst. If malicious intent is reasonably certain, the analyst must immediately classify the event as an incident and initiate containment procedures in accordance with the organizations response protocols.

At its core, triage is about balancing speed with accuracy. Analysts must work efficiently while maintaining disciplined analytical standards. Mastery of triage reduces time to detect, prevents alert backlogs, and ensures that real incidents receive rapid and focused attention. It is the foundation upon which all effective Security Operations Center operations are built.

Running Investigations

Once triage classifies an alert as suspicious, the work transitions into a formal investigation. This phase is far more comprehensive and methodical than triage. An investigation aims to reconstruct the full narrative of an event by analyzing logs, endpoint telemetry, network activity, cloud audit trails, identity events, and any related historical signals. While triage answers the question of whether deeper review is needed, the investigation answers the questions of what happened, how it happened, and how far the attacker progressed. The goal is not only to determine whether the activity is malicious but to understand its origin, scope, impact, and potential continuation.

Investigations begin with a focus on chronology. Analysts must build a timeline that includes events leading up to the alert, the moment of detection, and any activity occurring afterward. This timeline is the backbone of the investigative narrative. It reveals whether the suspicious behavior is an isolated anomaly or part of a broader chain of actions. For example, a suspicious PowerShell execution becomes far more concerning when preceded by an unusual login, followed by a credential access attempt, and then by lateral movement activity. Without a chronological view, investigators risk missing patterns that expose the attackers true objectives.

Once the timeline structure is in place, analysts pivot into relevant data sources. The SIEM provides log based insights across the environment. Endpoint detection platforms provide detailed process trees, parent and child relationships, kernel events, script execution details, and memory behavior. Authentication logs reveal unusual access patterns, geolocation anomalies, or sudden privilege changes. Network data enables the analyst to trace outbound connections, detect command and control patterns, identify data staging, or observe beaconing intervals. Cloud environments contribute audit logs showing resource changes, new token generation, unexpected role assumptions, or unauthorized configuration modifications. Each data source contributes a different part of the investigative mosaic.

A central investigative task is understanding process lineage. Attackers frequently hijack legitimate system utilities, but they often do so in sequences that do not occur during normal operations. For example, a web browser spawning Command Prompt, or a Microsoft Office document spawning PowerShell, is rarely legitimate. Analysts inspect the entire process tree to determine whether child processes were launched unexpectedly, whether command line parameters were obfuscated, and whether binaries were unsigned or unusual for the device. Another essential investigative focus is the presence of privilege escalation or lateral movement attempts. If an attacker successfully elevates privileges, the threat becomes significantly more urgent, as elevated permissions open the door to persistence creation, domain wide compromise, and data exfiltration. Investigators therefore review whether privilege changes occurred shortly before or after the suspicious activity. Similarly, analysts examine authentication logs and network traffic for evidence of lateral movement activities such as remote command execution, remote registry access, administrative share access, or credential reuse across servers.

In cloud environments, investigations must assess whether unauthorized API calls occurred, whether service accounts behaved unusually, or whether new keys or tokens were generated without proper change control. Attackers who compromise cloud resources can rapidly escalate privileges or gain access to sensitive data through automated services, making cloud specific investigation skills essential for modern Security Operations Centers.

Throughout the investigation, analysts continuously test hypotheses. For example, if an analyst believes credential theft occurred, they must search for supporting evidence in authentication logs, memory artifacts, or suspicious tooling. If they suspect malware execution, they must retrieve file hashes, review binary behavior, and correlate findings with threat intelligence sources. If they suspect an external exploit, they must identify vulnerable services, review inbound access logs, and determine whether exploitation attempts match known patterns.

An investigation is considered successful when the analyst can clearly articulate the five core investigative outcomes. First, what exactly happened. Second, how it happened including root cause, whether through phishing, social engineering, credential compromise, exposed public services, vulnerable software, or insider misuse. Third, how far the attacker progressed, which defines the scope. Fourth, what the attacker attempted to achieve. Finally, whether the attacker remains present or retains any foothold in the environment.

Only with these questions answered can the SOC make informed decisions about containment. Effective containment requires precision. Without a correct understanding of the attackers methods and reach, containment may fail, allowing the threat to persist or spread. Likewise, incomplete investigations lead to premature or overly aggressive containment actions that may disrupt business unnecessarily. Investigations are the disciplined pursuit of truth. They transform an alert from a blinking indicator into a complete, evidence backed story that guides response, communicates risk, and ultimately protects the organization. A SOC that excels in investigations possesses one of the most important capabilities in modern cybersecurity: the ability to understand attacker behavior deeply, accurately, and with confidence.

Escalation Criteria

Escalation is necessary when the incident exceeds the authority, capability, or expertise of the current analyst tier. Clear escalation criteria prevent delays and ensure incidents are handled by the right people at the right time.

Escalation typically occurs when an investigation uncovers:

- confirmed credential theft
- malware execution with persistence
- lateral movement or evidence of internal reconnaissance
- privilege escalation to administrator or root
- suspicious actions on critical systems such as domain controllers
- ransomware behavior (file encryption

patterns, shadow copy deletion)
- cloud resource manipulation such as role assumption or API key creation

SOC Tier 1 analysts escalate findings to Tier 2 when complex log correlation, host forensics, or advanced threat analysis is required. Tier 2 escalates to Tier 3 or IR leads when containment actions could disrupt business operations or when attacker activity appears part of an advanced campaign.

Containment Strategies

Containment is the art of stopping attacker activity without causing unnecessary business disruption. SOC analysts must weigh urgency against operational impact. Containment may be immediate or delayed if premature action would alert the attacker or interrupt critical systems.

There are two types of containment:

Short-term containment focuses on preventing further spread. This may involve isolating endpoints using EDR tools, blocking malicious IP addresses at firewalls, disabling compromised accounts, killing malicious processes, or quarantining suspicious email messages.

Long-term containment addresses underlying weaknesses such as patching vulnerable systems, resetting passwords across affected accounts, restricting lateral movement paths, tightening segmentation, or disabling misconfigured cloud access policies.

Containment must be coordinated with IT teams, business owners, and sometimes legal or HR especially when the incident involves insider activity or sensitive data.

Evidence Collection

Evidence collection is one of the most critical phases of incident response, and it is often the area where SOCs unintentionally undermine their own investigations. The ability to determine the root cause of an intrusion, assess its scope, reconstruct attacker behavior, and prove findings to regulators or legal authorities depends entirely on the quality and integrity of the evidence preserved. Collecting evidence is not merely a technical action but a forensic discipline grounded in accuracy, consistency, and legal defensibility. A SOC that mishandles evidence risks losing visibility into the attack, misdiagnosing the threat, or compromising the organization's ability to pursue legal or regulatory remedies.

A foundational principle of evidence collection is the chain of custody, the documented, unbroken record of who collected, accessed, transferred, stored, or analyzed an artifact. Every piece of evidence must be identified, hashed, dated, and preserved in a manner that prevents tampering or accidental modification. Hashing, typically performed with SHA-256, ensures that any change to an artifact becomes detectable and allows investigators, auditors, and courts to trust the integrity of the data. The importance of chain-of-custody discipline cannot be overstated; even technically perfect evidence loses value if its handling cannot be verified.

Collecting high-quality evidence requires using approved tools and methodologies. In Windows environments, tools such as Sysinternals, KAPE, FTK Imager, and Velociraptor help analysts acquire registry artifacts, event logs, scheduled tasks, process information, memory dumps, and disk artifacts without altering the underlying system. Registry hives, autorun locations, AmCache and ShimCache entries, PowerShell transcripts, and Sysmon logs often hold the most revealing forensic clues. Event logs, particularly Security, System, and PowerShell Operational logs, help reconstruct authentication events, service installations, and script executions. During malware incidents or suspected credential theft, capturing memory becomes critical because malicious code, injected processes, and credential material may exist exclusively in RAM.

Linux forensics follow similar principles but involve different artifacts. Analysts typically extract shell histories, SSH key configurations, authentication logs, systemd journal entries, cron jobs, and startup script modifications. Because attackers often tamper with command histories or logs, analysts must correlate local evidence with centralized telemetry such as SIEM queries, EDR data, or remote logging platforms. Memory acquisition on Linux, often performed using LiME, is sensitive and must be executed carefully to avoid altering the running system. Startup scripts, modified binaries, malicious cron tasks, and unauthorized SSH keys frequently reveal persistence or privilege escalation techniques.

Network-level evidence provides additional clarity across both Windows and Linux environments. Firewall logs, DNS queries, NetFlow data, and packet captures may show command-and-control communications, lateral movement indicators, or exfiltration attempts. Analysts must collect this data as early as possible in the investigation since network buffers rotate quickly and critical logs may be overwritten. For all evidence typesdisk, memory, network, log data, screenshots, or extracted artifacts, preservation must occur in tamper-proof storage, accompanied by cryptographic hashes and appropriate documentation. Throughout the process, analysts must minimize their impact on the affected system. Every action taken on a compromised endpoint changes its state. Running antivirus scans, killing processes, opening files, or even navigating directories can alter metadata and invalidate timestamps. Analysts must therefore follow strict procedures: collect volatile memory before shutting down a system, gather logs before restarting services, use read-only tools, and avoid interacting with suspicious binaries directly. When in doubt, the safest action is often to isolate the system and perform acquisition from a forensic workstation or through a remote collection tool designed for live response.

Different SOC tiers contribute uniquely to evidence collection. Tier 1 analysts typically preserve screenshots, extract SIEM event data, and gather preliminary observations without modifying the endpoint. Tier 2 analysts perform structured acquisition using forensic tools, retrieving logs, event data, and file samples while preserving integrity. They build timelines and begin correlating telemetry. Tier 3 analysts and IR leads conduct full forensic acquisition including memory dumps, disk images, root cause analysis, and deep-dive artifact reconstruction and ensure that all evidence follows chain-of-custody requirements. The IR lead additionally validates that evidence aligns with broader legal, regulatory, or compliance obligations, such as HIPAA, PCI, SOX, GDPR, or state breach statutes.

Ultimately, evidence collection is not simply about gathering as much information as possible, it is about collecting the *right* information, in the *right* order, using the *right* techniques, and preserving it in a way that maintains forensic integrity. A SOC that masters evidence collection gains the ability to understand exactly what happened during an intrusion, why it happened, and how to prevent it in the future. A SOC that neglects evidence collection loses the truth of the incident before the investigation even begins.

Host Isolation

Host isolation is one of the most decisive and effective defensive actions available to a SOC, particularly in environments supported by modern EDR platforms. Isolation severs a compromised endpoint's ability to communicate across the network, cutting off command-and-control (C2) channels, preventing lateral movement, halting data exfiltration, and immediately reducing the attacker's operational freedom. Unlike a traditional network quarantine, EDR-based isolation typically preserves remote forensic access, allowing analysts to investigate safely without risking further spread. Because of this dual benefit, containment without losing visibility isolation often represents the pivotal moment when an active intrusion shifts from attacker-driven to defender-driven control.

Before isolating a system, however, analysts must carefully evaluate the operational impact. Not all hosts are equal, and isolating the wrong system at the wrong time can cause widespread business disruption. Domain controllers, core application servers, point-of-sale systems, medical equipment, and multi-user systems require heightened scrutiny before quarantine. An EDR isolation on a domain controller, for example, may inadvertently break authentication across the enterprise, while isolating a hospital patient monitor or a manufacturing controller could impact safety. For this reason, most SOCs implement approval workflowsTier 2 or Tier 3 review, IR Lead authorization, or automatic validation checks to determine whether isolation is safe, permissible, and aligned with business continuity requirements.

Once a host is isolated, the SOC gains a rare advantage: time. With the host contained, analysts can perform memory captures, registry acquisition, malware extraction, and deep forensic analysis without the risk of the attacker actively interacting with the system. Isolation also prevents newly spawned processes from reaching external infrastructure and stops internal reconnaissance that would otherwise accelerate the compromise. During this period, the SOC collaborates closely with IT teams to determine remediation sequencing, ensuring that once the host is cleaned or reimaged, it re-enters the network in a known-good state.

Isolation also provides clarity during chaotic incidents. Systems still communicating on the network may continue generating noise via authentication attempts, suspicious DNS traffic, repeated malware drops which can obscure the true scope of the attack. By isolating compromised endpoints, analysts reduce environmental noise and improve their ability to track lateral movement, correlate alerts, and reconstruct attacker behavior. This makes host isolation not just a containment mechanism but also a powerful analytical tool.

Isolation must be logged and documented with the same rigor as any IR action. SOCs record who authorized the isolation, the exact time it occurred, the triggering indicators, and any impact on business operations. During post-incident reviews, these actions inform detection tuning, automated playbook design, and improvements to host-criticality mappings. Some organizations eventually implement automated isolation logicisolating hosts when ransomware behavior, mass file encryption, or credential theft patterns are detected. Even in these cases, automated isolation is usually restricted to non-critical systems, while high-impact hosts follow manual approval workflows. Isolation is not a cure-all, but when executed strategically, it becomes one of the SOC's most impactful tools, often the difference between a contained incident and a full-scale breach. It represents the moment defenders seize control, protect the environment, and carve out the space necessary for deliberate, thorough investigation and remediation. A mature SOC treats host isolation not as a panic button but as a precision instrument used to stabilize the incident, safeguard operations, and guide the organization toward recovery.

Writing IR Reports

Incident Response (IR) reports serve as the authoritative record of a security incident, documenting exactly what occurred, how it was detected, how the investigation unfolded, and what actions were taken to contain and eradicate the threat. A well-written IR report is not simply a narrative, it is an evidentiary document that must withstand scrutiny from executives, auditors, regulators, legal counsel, and, in some cases, law enforcement. Because of this, IR reports must be structured, methodical, and defensible. They should present facts with precision and avoid assumptions that are not supported by evidence.

Strong IR reports recount the entire lifecycle of the incident. They begin with the initial detection identifying the specific alert, telemetry source, or behavioral indicator that signaled suspicious activity. The report then walks through the triage and investigation phases, explaining what the analysts observed, what hypotheses guided their decisions, and what data sources were consulted. It should detail the scope of the incident by identifying all affected systems, accounts, and data assets, along with a clear timeline built from accurate and unaltered timestamps. This timeline is critical; it reconstructs attacker behavior and clarifies when each event occurred relative to detection and response.

The report must provide a clear explanation of the root cause, describing exactly how the attacker gained access or achieved execution, and should map observed behaviors to relevant MITRE ATT&CK techniques. This linkage not only provides a standardized language for describing attacker actions but also helps organizations evaluate detection coverage, identify gaps, and improve defenses. Containment and eradication actions must be described factually and sequentially, noting who approved each action, what tools were used, and whether any obstacles or delays arose. Recovery steps including reimaging, credential resets, patching, or configuration hardening should be documented with equal clarity. Because IR reports serve multiple audiences, they must balance technical accuracy with clarity. Executives rely on them to understand impact and risk; auditors use them to assess compliance; and technical teams use them to refine detection logic and hardening measures. As such, conclusions must remain evidence-based and free of speculation. Any uncertainties or limitations (e.g., missing logs, wiped systems, unavailable backups) should be openly acknowledged. A polished IR report reflects the SOC's professionalism and strengthens organizational resilience by preserving institutional knowledge for future reference.

Short-Form Incident Response Report Template

Below is a concise, professional template that fits into an MSSP or enterprise SOC workflow. It can be expanded into a full report or used as-is for rapid executive communication.

Incident Response Report (Short Form)

```
Organization:
Report Date:
Incident ID:
Prepared By:
Reviewed By (IR Lead / SOC Manager):
```

1. Executive Summary

Provide a brief, non-technical overview of what happened, how it was detected, whether the threat was contained, and current risk status.

Example:
On February 14, 2025, the SOC detected suspicious PowerShell activity on host WIN-0043. Investigation confirmed malicious script execution consistent with credential harvesting behavior. The system was isolated, malware was removed, and no lateral movement was identified. The incident has been fully contained.

2. Incident Details

`Detection Source:` (EDR, SIEM, SOAR, user report, etc.)
`Initial Alert Name:`
`Severity Level:`
`First Observed:`
`Last Observed:`

Provide a factual description of the initial detection and context.

3. Timeline of Events

List precise timestamps for all major observations and actions.

Timestamp (UTC)	Event Description
2025-02-14 10:21	EDR detected suspicious PowerShell execution
2025-02-14 10:23	Tier 1 triage escalated to Tier 2
2025-02-14 10:29	Analyst confirmed malicious behavior
2025-02-14 10:32	Host isolated via EDR
2025-02-14 10:50	Memory and log acquisition completed
2025-02-14 12:30	Containment validated; no lateral movement

4. Impact Assessment

Affected Systems:
Affected User Accounts:
Data Accessed or Modified: (If known)
Business Impact:

If impact is unknown, state limitations (e.g., missing logs, overwritten evidence).

5. Root Cause Analysis

Explain how the attacker gained access or executed code.
Map all observed behavior to MITRE ATT&CK.

Example:
The attacker used a phishing email to deliver a malicious macro. Upon execution, the macro spawned PowerShell consistent with ATT&CK techniques:

- T1059.001 – PowerShell
- T1082 – System Information Discovery
- T1056 – Credential Harvesting

6. Containment Actions

Describe when and how containment occurred, including approvals and tools used.

Example:

- EDR isolation was initiated at 10:32 UTC.
- Malicious processes were terminated.
- Firewall blocks were applied to known C2 IP addresses.

7. Eradication & Recovery

Explain how the threat was removed and how systems were restored.

Example:

- Malware artifacts removed from `%AppData%`
- Registry persistence cleaned
- Host reimaged and returned to service
- Password resets completed for impacted accounts

8. Residual Risk & Current Status

State whether any attacker activity remains or further monitoring is required.

9. Recommendations

Provide actionable improvements aligned with risk, such as:

- Enhanced logging
- New detection rules
- MFA enforcement
- Patch deployment
- User training

10. Supporting Evidence

List and attach:

- Extracted logs
- Screenshots
- Memory dumps
- File hashes
- Analytical notes

Hashes, filenames, and collection timestamps should be included for forensic integrity. Incident Response is where the SOC proves its value. Through disciplined triage, structured investigations, proper escalation, strategic containment, rigorous evidence collection, responsible host isolation, and professional reporting, SOC analysts transform alerts into decisive action. Mastery of IR is not optional; it is the skill that ultimately determines whether an organization withstands attacks or falls victim to them. This chapter equips analysts with the tactical and strategic foundation needed to perform IR with confidence and precision.

Chapter 11

Threat Hunting (Proactive Security)

Threat hunting is the discipline of proactively searching for adversaries who have bypassed existing detections. Unlike reactive alert triage, threat hunting begins without a confirmed incident. It is the deliberate process of questioning assumptions, analyzing environmental behavior, and exposing stealthy malicious activity. Modern attackers often operate quietly using legitimate tools, stolen credentials, and low-noise techniques that evade traditional detection. Threat hunting fills the gaps left by automated tooling by applying human intuition, investigative creativity, and structured methodology.

A mature SOC treats threat hunting as a continuous function, not an occasional initiative. Each hunt contributes to detection engineering, improves visibility, and enhances understanding of normal behavior. This chapter provides a full blueprint for executing professional threat hunts from hypothesis creation to reporting and detection refinement.

Hypothesis-Driven Threat Hunting

Hypothesis-driven threat hunting is the most disciplined and repeatable form of proactive security investigation. Unlike reactive analysis which begins with an alert-hunting begins with a theory about how adversaries behave and then works backward to uncover traces of those behaviors in the environment. This structured, deliberate approach is what separates true threat hunting from random log searching or intuition-based exploration. A strong hypothesis anchors the hunt and creates both focus and measurable outcomes.

A hypothesis is a predictive statement about adversary behavior, formed by combining threat intelligence, environmental knowledge, MITRE ATT&CK techniques, attack surface awareness, and recent anomalies. For example, a hunter might propose:

"If a threat actor has compromised a domain user, they may attempt privilege escalation via Kerberoasting."

This single sentence drives the entire hunt; which logs to query, what baselines to compare against, which telemetry sources to inspect, and what outcomes would either confirm or refute the prediction. A high-quality hypothesis is not broad ("Look for unusual authentication events"), nor too narrow ("Search for this exact hash"). It is testable, realistic, and tied to attacker behavior that could credibly occur in the current environment.

Professionals build hypotheses through a combination of intelligence sources. MITRE ATT&CK heat maps reveal gaps in defensive visibility. News of recent industry breaches highlights trending adversary techniques. Threat intel feeds such as Recorded Future, Microsoft TI, and CISA advisories identify current campaigns and tradecraft. Analysts also draw from internal insights, perhaps repeated failed logins against a critical server, or recurring anomalous PowerShell commands. The most experienced hunters also draw from intuition honed over years of observing how attackers pivot, disguise their movements, and blend into normal operational activity.

Designing the Hypothesis

A threat hunt begins with a hypothesis, and this hypothesis becomes the intellectual foundation upon which the entire hunt is built. It is not a guess or a vague suspicion, but a structured and testable statement about how an adversary might operate within the environment. The hypothesis defines the investigative direction, determines the analytical scope, and sets the expectations for what evidence should or should not exist. Once the hunter commits to the hypothesis, every decision in the hunt follows from it. It transforms the search from a random exploration of logs into a disciplined inquiry that resembles scientific investigation.

The process begins by defining what behaviors should be observable if the hypothesis is true. If the hunter proposes that an attacker has compromised a domain account and is attempting Kerberoasting, then certain behavioral signatures must logically follow. The environment would show signs of service principal name enumeration, unusual ticket granting service requests, and commands that query Active Directory for service accounts. If the hunter believes that persistence mechanisms have been established on a host, then they expect to find unusual scheduled tasks, unauthorized autorun entries, cloud startup policies, or modified Linux service configurations. The hypothesis allows the hunter to think in terms of cause and effect rather than isolated artifacts, making the search far more targeted.

Once expected behaviors are defined, the hunter identifies which data sources would contain the necessary evidence. Every environment produces logs that illuminate different layers of behavior. Windows Security logs reveal authentication patterns and ticketing activity. Sysmon exposes process lineage and command level details. EDR platforms reveal parent child execution relationships, memory events, and suspicious binaries. Network flow logs expose outbound reconnaissance or command and control activity. Cloud audit logs reveal configuration drift, role assumptions, or unexpected API calls. A well designed hypothesis maps directly to the correct data sources, ensuring the hunt remains efficient and technically grounded. The hunter then identifies which indicators, signals, or anomalies would confirm or contradict the hypothesis. The goal is not to prove the hypothesis correct but to create clear criteria for evaluation. A Kerberoasting hypothesis may be supported by a sudden increase in ticket granting service requests for high privilege accounts or by execution of tools that enumerate service principal names. It may be weakened or disproven if such events are absent or if correlated telemetry shows entirely benign administrative behavior. A persistence hypothesis might be reinforced by discovering new registry entries, unauthorized startup files, or unfamiliar cloud configuration changes. These signals do not exist in isolation; they function as evidence that either strengthens or challenges the investigative theory.

Equally important is the hunter's knowledge of normal baselines. Hypothesis driven hunting requires an appreciation of what is typical for each system and user. Without this baseline, the hunter cannot determine whether deviations are meaningful. For instance, if a developer frequently uses PowerShell for legitimate reasons, then PowerShell log entries alone have limited investigative value. If a domain controller regularly sends large volumes of replication traffic, then that pattern is not suspicious by itself. A thoughtful hypothesis accounts for expected behavior before drawing conclusions about anomalies. The hunter refines expectations by comparing current observations with established norms, letting deviation from normal act as a signpost toward compromise.

The hypothesis therefore serves as both anchor and compass. It anchors the hunter in a defined investigative strategy, preventing wasted effort or tangential analysis. At the same time, it guides discovery by encouraging systematic exploration of patterns, correlations, and behaviors that would logically arise from the proposed threat. A strong hypothesis is specific enough to focus the hunt, flexible enough to accommodate unexpected findings, and measurable enough to evaluate through observable telemetry. It is the intellectual engine of the hunt, transforming raw data into structured inquiry and structured inquiry into actionable security insight.

Tools and Telemetry for Hypothesis Testing

Hypothesis-driven hunts rely on a wide range of tools and data sources. The sophistication of the hunt is determined not by the number of tools but by the hunter's mastery of how and when to use them.

Endpoint Telemetry

Hunters rely heavily on EDR platforms such as:

- SentinelOne Deep Visibility
- CrowdStrike Falcon Event Search
- Microsoft Defender Advanced Hunting

- Elastic EDR Telemetry
- Velociraptor for endpoint artifact collection

These tools provide process ancestry, command-line parameters, thread injections, DLL loads, and parent-child execution chains.

SIEM Queries

SIEM platformsSplunk, Sentinel, LogRhythm, Elasticallow hunters to correlate authentication events, DNS queries, VPN tunnels, script block execution, data access patterns, and cloud API calls.

Network Telemetry

Zeek logs, NetFlow, firewall logs, IDS/IPS alerts, and PCAPs reveal lateral movement, beaconing, exfiltration patterns, and enclave boundary crossing.

Cloud Telemetry

When hunting in hybrid environments, analysts query:

- Azure AD Sign-in Logs

- AWS CloudTrail
- GCP Audit Logs
- Okta System Logs
- Microsoft Graph API

Many modern attacks occur entirely within the identity & SaaS layer making cloud telemetry indispensable.

Threat Intelligence Tools

Hunters enrich findings using:

- VirusTotal (hash correlation)
- AbuseIPDB (malicious IP reputation)
- GreyNoise (noise vs targeted activity)
- Shodan (external exposure)
- Recorded Future or Anomali (campaign indicators)

These tools transform raw signals into contextual understanding.

Executing the Hunt: Scientific Method Meets Adversary Mindset

Threat hunting sits at the crossroads of analytical discipline and adversarial imagination. A skilled hunter must think like an attacker while investigating with the precision of a scientist. Attackers are adaptive, creative, and opportunistic, often relying on subtle deviations rather than loud malicious signatures. For this reason, threat hunting cannot be a rigid procedural task. Instead, it becomes a dynamic process where creative hypotheses are tested through evidence-based inquiry. The adversarial mindset inspires the line of questioning, while the scientific method provides the structure that keeps the investigation focused and defensible.

Executing a hunt begins with translating the hypothesis into a series of targeted tests. Each test is designed to reveal whether the environment displays behaviors predicted by the hypothesis. These tests often take the form of analytical queries, correlation searches, process tree examinations, identity behavior reviews, or network flow pattern analysis. The hunter is not looking for a single data point but for behavioral patterns across multiple layers of telemetry. A hypothesis about lateral movement, for example, leads to tests involving remote service creation logs, unusual Kerberos ticket activity, suspicious authentication attempts, and cross-system process correlations. A hypothesis about cloud credential abuse may involve API auditing, unusual token creation, region anomalies, or abnormal privilege assignments. Every test is designed with intention, not guesswork, and aims to discover whether the environment is functioning within known baselines or deviating in suspicious ways.

As tests are executed, hunters maintain the objectivity characteristic of scientific inquiry. The goal is not to force the hypothesis to be correct but to determine whether the environment contradicts expectations of normal behavior. When a test reveals normal results, it reduces the likelihood that the hypothesized threat is present. When a test reveals anomalies, the hunter probes deeper, expanding pivots, correlating signals, and refining the investigative focus. This iterative process mirrors the scientific cycle of hypothesis, experiment, observation, and conclusion. Each round of analysis strengthens or weakens the initial idea. The hunter may confirm suspicious activity, uncover benign administrative operations that resemble malicious patterns, or discover environmental quirks that require no further action but inform future hunts.

Importantly, disproving a hypothesis never means the hunt has failed. Threat hunting brings value even when no adversary is present. A disproven hypothesis often exposes operational weaknesses such as misconfigured log sources, incomplete endpoint coverage, inconsistent security controls, policy violations, or gaps in visibility. These findings, while not indicators of active compromise, still contribute directly to strengthening the organization's defensive posture. Many organizations discover that hunting reveals unknown weaknesses far more frequently than it reveals attackers, yet those discoveries materially reduce risk. A hunt that uncovers minimal logging on domain controllers, recurring authentication failures tied to incorrect service configurations, or unmonitored cloud activity is considered successful because it improves resilience.

Threat hunting is therefore a continuous refinement cycle. As hunters execute tests, they adjust their investigative path based on what the data reveals. If anomalies arise, the hunter revisits the hypothesis to determine whether it should be expanded, narrowed, or replaced entirely. If the environment appears normal, the hunter evaluates whether the hypothesis was too broad, too narrow, or aimed at the wrong layer of telemetry. This ongoing refinement allows each hunt to be more precise than the last. Over time, hunters develop a mental model of adversary behaviors and environmental baselines that dramatically accelerates investigative speed and accuracy.

The marriage of scientific rigor and adversarial thinking is what elevates threat hunting from simple log review to strategic security analysis. Attackers innovate, adapt, and change techniques frequently. Scientific method provides hunters with a disciplined way to validate or disprove assumptions, while adversarial thinking ensures those assumptions remain relevant to real world threats. When executed correctly, hunting reveals not only whether attackers are present but also whether the environment is prepared to resist them. This dual insight is the hallmark of a mature and effective threat hunting program.

Expected Outcomes and Hunt Closure

A well-executed hypothesis-driven hunt always results in meaningful outcomes, even when no adversary is found. The value of threat hunting is not solely in detecting intrusions; it is in validating defenses, improving visibility, and strengthening the organization's understanding of normal behavior. Every hunt, regardless of its result, contributes to the SOC's maturity. To ensure this, the hunt must end with a structured and deliberately documented closure process.

The first possible outcome is a confirmed hypothesis. This occurs when the hunt uncovers behaviors consistent with adversary activity—whether suspicious anomalies, validated malicious actions, or clear indications of compromise. A confirmed hypothesis immediately escalates into the incident response lifecycle. The hunter transitions from exploratory analysis into incident investigation, containment recommendations, and coordination with IR leadership. In these cases, the hypothesis acts as the doorway to uncovering deeper attacker presence, root cause, lateral movement, persistence mechanisms, or external communication patterns. The hunt becomes the catalyst for rapid IR action.

The second outcome arises when the hypothesis is not confirmed, but the hunt exposes environmental weaknesses. This is far more common than actual compromise. During the process of gathering telemetry and correlating data, hunters often uncover issues such as missing logs, broken parsing rules, out-of-date endpoint agents, gaps in cloud visibility, overly permissive IAM roles, misconfigured firewall rules, stale administrative accounts, or systems operating outside intended baselines. These discoveries are extremely valuable because they highlight risk before an attacker can exploit it. A hunt that identifies configuration drift or architectural blind spots is considered highly successful, even in the absence of malicious activity. These findings become actionable improvements for engineering, governance, or IT operations. The third outcome is a disproven hypothesis with no identified gaps. In this case, the hunt confirms that the environment is behaving as expected. Although this may appear uneventful, it provides critical baseline reinforcement. Understanding what "healthy" looks like is essential for future hunts and for refining detection logic. Each disproven hypothesis adds to institutional knowledge by documenting normal behaviors, expected system patterns, and legitimate operational workflows that might otherwise be misinterpreted in future alerts or hunts. Over time, these insights form a robust reference framework for assessing deviations more quickly and accurately.

Regardless of outcome, every hunt must conclude with structured documentation. This documentation transforms the hunt from a one-time activity into a reusable source of organizational learning. At minimum, the hunter should record the hypothesis tested, the specific MITRE ATT&CK techniques associated with the behaviors under investigation, and the data sources queried during the process. Precise documentation of logs, queries, and investigative pivots ensures that future hunts can reference or reproduce the analysis. Findings—whether malicious, transitional, or benign—must be recorded with evidence and interpretation. If misconfigurations or visibility gaps were uncovered, they should be clearly identified and assigned to ownership groups for remediation. Recommendations for closing gaps, improving detections, tuning SIEM rules, or strengthening hardening policies must be included as part of the closure.

This disciplined closure process elevates threat hunting from an informal exercise into a structured, repeatable, measurable program. Over time, a repository of completed hunts provides the SOC with trend intelligence, visibility analytics, and insight into how attacker techniques map to the organization's telemetry landscape. Hunts inform detection engineering pipelines, enrich IR playbooks, improve baselines, and drive continuous security enhancement. When executed with rigor, every hunt, regardless of whether it uncovers an adversary, moves the SOC forward.

Why Hypothesis-Driven Hunting Works

Hypothesis-driven hunting is superior to other methods because it provides focus, repeatability, and strategic progression. Random searches create noise and fatigue, while reactive hunting is constrained to known alerts. A hypothesis-driven approach ensures hunters stay aligned with adversary TTPs and continually improve organizational visibility. It also standardizes how hunts are planned, executed, documented, and measured allowing leadership to evaluate the maturity and effectiveness of the threat hunting program.

Hypothesis-driven hunting maximizes the value of human intuition while grounding investigations in empirical evidence. It enables SOCs to find stealthy threats, validate security assumptions, and detect adversaries long before they trigger an alert. More importantly, it creates a feedback loop where each hunt strengthens the nextnot just improving visibility but engineering a smarter, more resilient defense over time.

Indicators, Behaviors, and Anomalies

Threat hunting is built upon three foundational pillars of investigative reasoning: indicators, behaviors, and anomalies. Each represents a different lens through which hunters examine the environment, and each offers unique advantages and limitations. Understanding how these three elements interact and how to prioritize them is essential for uncovering both known and unknown threats.

Indicators of Compromise (IOCs) represent the most atomic form of threat intelligence. These include malicious IP addresses, file hashes, domains, registry keys, mutexes, or email senders tied explicitly to adversary activity. Although IOCs are extremely useful for detecting known campaigns, they are inherently reactive; by the time an IOC is public, threat actors may already have modified their infrastructure or generated new payload variants. This makes IOC-driven hunting a necessary but limited part of the overall strategy. Hunters use IOCs primarily for scoping known activity, validating compromises, and correlating events, but they do not rely on indicators alone to find sophisticated adversaries.

Behavioral analysis offers a much deeper and more resilient framework. Attackers, despite changing tools or infrastructure, tend to reuse the same *techniques*. They must escalate privileges, move laterally, discover internal hosts, persist through reboots, and establish command-and-control channels. These behaviors manifest in characteristic patterns such as unexpected parent-child process relationships, unauthorized PowerShell invocation, remote service creation, WMI-based execution, LSASS memory access, and anomalous Kerberos ticket activity. Because techniques persist longer than indicators, behavioral hunting exposes threats even when the attacker uses novel malware, rotates domains, or employs fileless execution. Behavioral patterns, especially when mapped to MITRE ATT&CK, give hunters a durable blueprint for identifying attacker tradecraft.

Anomalies represent the third and often most subtle hunting pillar deviations from what the environment normally looks like. Unlike indicators or clearly malicious behaviors, anomalies are not inherently threatening. They merely signal something unusual. A non-interactive service account suddenly producing interactive logons, a user machine making outbound connections to a foreign ASN at 3:00 a.m., or a developer workstation generating Kerberos ticket requests it never issued before may all indicate benign misconfigurations or the earliest detectable signs of compromise. Anomaly detection requires well-established baselines and deep contextual understanding of the environment, as hunters must differentiate expected irregularities from meaningful deviations.

Anomalies are often where advanced threat actors reveal themselves first, especially in environments where they attempt to blend in.

Hunters rarely rely on a single pillar. Instead, effective investigations weave them together. Indicators provide starting points for known threats. Behaviors expose the attacker's tactics independently of tools or infrastructure. Anomalies reveal subtle deviations that indicate stealthy or emerging compromises. When combined, these pillars allow hunters to pursue leads that are grounded in both intelligence and environmental context, increasing the likelihood of discovering hidden adversaries.

This triad also dictates prioritization. IOC-only hunts produce high false positives and low discovery rates. Behavioral hunts uncover sophisticated activity but require rich telemetry. Anomaly-driven hunts are powerful but depend heavily on mature baselines and analyst intuition. A professional hunter continuously balances all three, using indicators for breadth, behaviors for depth, and anomalies for early warning signals. Together, they form a complete and modern threat-hunting strategy capable of detecting both commodity malware and advanced persistent threats.

Baseline Analysis

Effective threat hunting is impossible without a clear understanding of what "normal" looks like across an environment. Baseline analysis is the process of establishing that normality mapping out the expected patterns of system activity, user behavior, network communication, authentication flows, administrative actions, and cloud resource utilization. Without baselines, hunters are forced to treat every irregularity as a potential threat, which leads to noise, burnout, and wasted cycles. With baselines, anomalies become obvious, investigations become faster, and detections become more accurate.

A baseline is not a single artifact but a multi-dimensional profile of the environment. Analysts study which processes typically run on workstations, which service accounts authenticate against domain controllers, what types of scripts are executed by automation platforms, how much network traffic flows between internal segments, and which cloud APIs are accessed by legitimate business workflows. These recurring patterns create a behavioral fingerprint for the organization. For instance, a baseline may reveal that a specific server always executes scheduled PowerShell jobs at 2:00 a.m., or that a development team routinely interacts with an external Git repository. When such patterns are understood, analysts can immediately distinguish benign periodic actions from suspicious deviations. Baselines are not static because environments evolve constantly. New applications are deployed, cloud resources expand, employees change roles, remote work policies shift, endpoint tools update, and infrastructure undergoes modernization. These changes alter the behavioral landscape. A baseline captured a year ago, or even a month ago in fast-moving cloud environments, may no longer reflect reality. For this reason, hunters treat baseline analysis as an ongoing discipline rather than a one-time project. SIEM dashboards provide trend graphs for authentication frequency, DNS queries, VPN usage, and network flows. EDR platforms store historical process execution chains, allowing analysts to understand long-term patterns. Identity analytics platforms reveal how privilege usage changes over time, while network modeling tools such as Zeek or NetFlow analyzers help identify stable communication pathways versus sudden deviations.

A strong baseline serves two essential purposes. First, it dramatically reduces noise. When analysts can quickly classify routine system behaviors as expected, they avoid wasting time on benign events. Second, it highlights deviations with remarkable clarity. A single abnormal login, an unexpected parent-child process, or a rare outbound connection stands out instantly when a hunter has internalized what should normally occur. In mature environments, seasoned hunters develop an almost instinctive understanding of baseline activity, enabling them to spot subtle anomalies that automated tools might overlook.

The true power of baseline analysis becomes evident when confronting advanced adversaries. Sophisticated actors do not rely on signature-based malware or blatant exploitation techniques; they attempt to mimic legitimate behavior. In such cases, only a hunter who understands the environment's baseline can identify the moment something feels "off"a logon pattern that does not match historical data, a script executed by an account that never uses scripts, an API call from a host that should not be interacting with cloud services. Baselines make stealthy attackers visible.

Using SIEM Data Models

A SIEM is the central investigative engine for threat hunters, but its effectiveness depends on far more than simply ingesting logs. Raw data, in its native format, is often fragmented, inconsistent, and difficult to correlate across platforms. True investigative power emerges only when logs are normalized into data models/standardized schemas that unify fields across diverse log sources. Whether using Elastic

Common Schema (ECS), Splunk's Common Information Model (CIM), Microsoft's unified Log Analytics schema, or the Open Cybersecurity Schema Framework (OCSF), hunters rely on these models to create coherent and repeatable investigations.

Data models transform disparate logs into a predictable structure. For instance, a SIEM may ingest Windows Event Logs, Linux audit logs, Azure AD sign-in events, Okta system logs, VPN authentication logs, and firewall traffic each with different field names, formats, and event codes. Without normalization, a hunter would need a different query for each data source, significantly slowing investigation and increasing the risk of oversight. But with a unified schema, fields such as *user.name*, *source.ip*, *process.command_line*, *event.outcome*, or *host.hostname* become consistent across all logs. This allows a single query to simultaneously search multiple platforms, correlate authentication across identity providers, and trace lateral movement across endpoint, network, and cloud systems. For example, a hunter investigating suspicious logons can query *user.name* across Windows RDP attempts, Linux SSH sessions, VPN authentication logs, and Azure AD cloud identity events using the same search expression. This transforms the SIEM into a multidimensional investigative tool rather than a collection of isolated log silos. Data models also enable accelerated or indexed searches, allowing SIEM engines to retrieve results at scale without manually parsing each event type. This capability becomes critical during high-severity investigations, where time is limited and log volumes can reach millions of events per hour.

Threat hunters also leverage SIEM dashboards to visualize deviations and behavioral trends over time. Time-series analysis helps reveal patterns such as beaconing intervals, repeated authentication failures during off-hours, unexpected spikes in PowerShell executions, or unusual outbound connections from servers that typically generate little network activity. Data models enhance this visualization because dashboards remain consistent even as new log sources are added; every incoming log stream is automatically mapped to the same schema, preserving query integrity.

Advanced SIEM features further augment hunting. Lookup tables allow analysts to compare logs against enriched datasets, threat intel feeds, asset inventories, privileged user lists, or business-critical application mappings. Machine learning modules detect statistical deviations such as rare process executions or anomalous login locations. Behavioral analytics engines analyze baselines to determine when identity, endpoint, or network activity diverges from historical norms. These systems only function correctly when the SIEM's underlying data is normalized and model-driven.

Expert hunters develop mastery over the SIEM's query language, enabling them to combine fields, perform multi-source joins, pivot between identities and hosts, or trace attack paths across hundreds of correlated events. They understand how to enrich raw logs, apply schema transformations, and write dynamic queries that adapt to the SIEM's data model. They also know how to pivot across data types, querying identity logs to identify suspicious accounts, jumping into EDR telemetry for process analysis, then checking network logs for lateral movement indicators all while relying on consistent schema fields. The hunter's skill lies not only in knowing which logs to query but in knowing how the SIEM itself understands the data. Mastery of schemas, normalization, and data modeling is what transforms the SIEM from a passive log repository into an active investigative engine capable of uncovering advanced threats across the entire enterprise.

Memory Forensics Basics

Memory forensics is one of the most powerful yet chronically underutilized techniques in threat hunting. Modern attackers increasingly rely on *fileless* execution, in-memory implants, reflective DLL injection, and ephemeral payloads that never touch the disk. These techniques enable adversaries to bypass signature-based tools and leave minimal evidence within traditional logs. Because of this, a hunter's ability to analyze system memory becomes a decisive advantage. Memory captures contain the volatile truth of an attack, running processes, active threads, injected modules, open network connections, cryptographic keys, credentials in memory, and fragments of attacker tooling that would otherwise disappear.

Effective memory forensics begins with proper acquisition. Analysts typically collect memory snapshots through EDR platformsSentinelOne, CrowdStrike, Defender for Endpoint, or Velociraptor which provide controlled, low-impact acquisition capabilities. In environments lacking EDR support, specialized tools such as FTK Imager, WinPMEM, or DumpIt can be used to capture RAM images directly. The acquisition phase is critical: an improper capture can corrupt volatile data, destroy forensic integrity, or alter system state. Therefore, analysts must follow strict procedures and ensure that each memory image is hashed and logged in the chain of custody.

Once acquired, memory analysis frameworks such as Volatility, Volatility 3, or Rekall allow hunters to reconstruct the internal state of the system at the moment of capture. These tools extract detailed information about processes, threads, DLLs, handles, registry hives stored in memory, kernel structures, and even artifacts from previously terminated processes. Hunters examine process hierarchies to identify suspicious parent-child relationships, for example, Word spawning PowerShell, or LSASS spawning unknown children. They look for processes without corresponding executables on disk, often a hallmark of reflective loading or in-memory shells. Injected threads, anonymous memory regions, unsigned DLLs, and processes listening on unexpected ports all signal potential compromise.

Memory forensics is especially effective for detecting fileless malware, credential dumping techniques such as Mimikatz or direct system calls, in-memory backdoors, Cobalt Strike beacons, and lateral movement tools that rely purely on RAM. Even without deep reverse engineering expertise, hunters who understand basic memory structures can spot anomalies such as mismatched process names and PIDs, malformed PE headers, or LSASS access patterns that deviate from expected behavior. Memory also exposes operational details that SIEM and endpoint logs cannot reveal for instance, deobfuscated scripts, encryption keys used by malicious payloads, or remnants of attacker tooling long after execution has ceased.

Because memory captures reflect a system's volatile state, timing matters. A capture taken too early may miss the attacker's activity; one taken too late may miss the payload entirely. Skilled hunters often capture memory both before and after containment actions to preserve the most complete forensic picture. Once memory is fully analyzed, findings feed directly into detection engineering, threat intelligence enrichment, and the broader incident response lifecycle.

Memory forensics elevates threat hunting beyond log review. Where SIEMs provide partial visibility and behavioral indicators suggest activity, memory captures reveal the uncompromising truth of what was running. Even basic familiarity with memory structures allows hunters to flag subtle traces/threads injected into an otherwise legitimate process, unsigned DLLs hidden in expected directories, or command strings embedded within memory regions that automated alerts might overlook. For advanced threats and stealthy adversaries, memory analysis is often the only way to expose what truly occurred.

Threat Hunting Templates

Threat hunting becomes significantly more effective and repeatable when guided by structured templates. A well-designed hunting template transforms an ad-hoc, intuition-driven activity into a disciplined investigative process with consistent documentation, measurable outcomes, and reproducible steps. Templates act as the framework that ensures every hunt regardless of the analyst conducting it follows the same professional standard. They also create organizational memory, allowing the SOC to build upon prior work rather than reinventing the wheel with each new investigation.

A threat hunting template typically begins with the hypothesis, which defines the objective and sets the direction of the investigation. Supporting this hypothesis is a list of required data sources/endpoint telemetry, authentication logs, network flows, DNS data, cloud logs, or any specialized sources relevant to the expected attacker technique. By explicitly naming these data sources, templates ensure hunters do not overlook critical telemetry or rely on incomplete evidence. The template also provides space for documenting the SIEM queries, EDR searches, or forensic commands required to execute the hunt. These queries become part of the SOC's reusable library, allowing future hunts to leverage refined and proven logic.

Templates also include sections for expected behaviors and definitions of anomalies. Expected behaviors outline what legitimate activity looks like for a given technique or data source. For example, when hunting for suspicious PowerShell usage, expected behavior might include automated scripts, software deployment tasks, or configuration management functions. By documenting these expected patterns, the template helps hunters differentiate between benign automation and malicious scripting. Anomaly definitions describe what abnormal behavior looks like processes executing with unusual parameters, unexpected parent-child relationships, rare service account usage, or atypical authentication flows. These definitions guide the analysis and help prevent bias or overreaction to benign deviations.

Another critical part of the template is the investigative results section. This is where analysts capture what they found, how they validated their findings, and whether the hypothesis was confirmed, disproven, or yielded unexpected insights. Even if no malicious activity is discovered, documenting the hunt provides value by validating assumptions about the environment, exposing logging gaps, or revealing configuration drift. The results section also prompts analysts to assess the quality of data sources, identify gaps, and recommend improvements. Over time, these documented observations contribute to stronger detection engineering and more accurate baselines.

A mature threat hunting template concludes with recommendations and follow-up actions. These may include new detection rules, SIEM correlation logic, EDR alerts, or adjustments to existing thresholds and suppression logic. Recommendations may also involve operational changes such as implementing better logging, deploying additional sensors, or adjusting identity governance policies. By capturing actionable next steps, the SOC ensures that each hunt produces measurable value rather than ending as an academic exercise.

As the library of threat hunting templates grows, it becomes one of the SOC's most powerful assets. Hunts from previous months or years can be revisited to analyze trends, compare evolving attacker behavior, or validate whether improvements reduced risk over time. Templates also support collaboration: multiple analysts can work on the same hunt while maintaining consistency in notation, methodology, and results. They even enable knowledge transfernew analysts inherit a structured record of past investigations, drastically reducing onboarding time and skill gaps.

Ultimately, templates elevate threat hunting from isolated investigative episodes into an organized, continuously improving program. Each hunt strengthens the next, building a cumulative foundation of expertise, detection coverage, and environmental understanding. In a mature SOC, templates are not optional; they are the backbone of sustainable, scalable, and measurable threat hunting operations.

Threat hunting transforms the SOC from a reactive defense unit into a proactive adversary-focused force. Through hypothesis-driven methodology, behavioral analysis, baseline development, memory forensics, SIEM data modeling, and standardized templates, analysts uncover threats that evade traditional detection. A strong hunting program not only finds hidden attackers but also strengthens detections, improves telemetry quality, and sharpens analyst intuition. This chapter serves as a practical roadmap for building a mature, intelligence-driven threat hunting practice within any SOC.

Chapter 12

Malware Analysis for SOC Analysts

Malware analysis is a critical capability within any mature SOC. While not every analyst will reverse engineer binaries at an advanced level, every SOC analyst must understand how to safely analyze suspicious files, interpret malware behavior, extract indicators, and translate technical findings into actionable intelligence. Modern malware is designed to evade traditional defenses by disguising itself as legitimate software, operating filelessly, leveraging trusted system binaries, and adapting dynamically based on its execution environment. This chapter provides a practical, SOC-focused blueprint for conducting malware analysis safely, efficiently, and effectively.

Static vs. Dynamic Analysis

Malware analysis begins with a critical methodological choice: whether to study a sample statically, dynamically, or through a combined hybrid approach. Static analysis involves examining the malware without executing it, while dynamic analysis captures its behavior during runtime. Each method offers unique advantages and limitations, and a disciplined SOC analyst understands how to leverage both. In practice, static analysis often serves as the first step because it is inherently safer, quicker to perform, and does not require the overhead of executing potentially dangerous code in a sandbox environment.

Static analysis focuses on the structure, metadata, and embedded characteristics of a file. Analysts begin by identifying the file's true type using tools like file, peid, Detect It Easy, or ExifTool, since attackers often disguise malware as documents, images, or PDFs to deceive users. Metadata such as compilation timestamps, PE headers, import tables, and section information frequently reveal inconsistencies such as timestamps far in the future or past, missing signatures, or anomalous compiler information. Analysts also inspect strings extracted from the binary; even heavily obfuscated malware may leak URLs, registry paths, PowerShell commands, encryption keys, or debug messages. Entropy measurements provide insight into whether a file is packed or encrypted; high-entropy sections often indicate obfuscation or runtime-unpacking behavior designed to frustrate reverse engineering efforts. Taken together, static indicators help analysts assess risk quickly while uncovering clues that guide deeper investigation.

Dynamic analysis, by contrast, examines malware behavior during execution. This approach requires running the sample inside a controlled sandbox or virtual machine instrumented for deep observation. Dynamic environments such as Cuckoo Sandbox, Any.Run, Joe Sandbox, or an analyst-controlled VMrecord system calls, spawned processes, registry modifications, file writes, network beacons, and persistence mechanisms. Malware may attempt to alter firewall rules, inject into legitimate processes, or establish reverse shells. Dynamic analysis captures all of this in real time. It is particularly valuable when malware uses layered encryption, packing routines, reflective DLL loading, or environment checks that prevent static disassembly from yielding meaningful insight. Many modern malware families exhibit polymorphic behavior or runtime deobfuscation behaviors visible only during execution.

A mature SOC workflow blends static and dynamic approaches. Static analysis quickly identifies red flags and helps determine whether full dynamic execution is warranted. Dynamic analysis then validates the actual behavior of the malware, revealing actions that static techniques cannot uncover. For example, static inspection may show obfuscated PowerShell within a dropper script, but dynamic execution reveals the actual C2 domain, persistence mechanism, and encryption routine. Likewise, static analysis may reveal low-level indicators like hardcoded strings, while dynamic analysis shows environmental awareness such as delays, anti-VM checks, or sandbox evasion tactics.

Together, static and dynamic analysis provide a complete understanding of how malware operates, how it propagates, and how it can be eradicated. Static analysis offers speed and safety. Dynamic analysis offers depth and truth. Those who master both gain the ability to rapidly identify threats, attribute behaviors to known families, and design effective detections that prevent recurrence.

Hashing, Signatures, and YARA

Hashing forms the foundational layer of modern malware identification and forensic integrity. When analysts compute cryptographic hashes, typically MD5, SHA-1, or, most reliably, SHA-256they create a unique fingerprint for a file or artifact. This fingerprint allows the SOC to rapidly determine whether a file has been previously observed, cataloged, or associated with malicious activity. Hashes can be cross-referenced against databases from VirusTotal, MalwareBazaar, NSRL, internal threat intelligence repositories, or SIEM lookup tables to provide immediate classification. If a hash matches a known malicious sample, analysts can escalate, isolate the host, and apply remediations without performing deeper analysis. Conversely, previously unseen hashes indicate the need for further triage, static analysis, or sandbox execution. Importantly, hashing also plays a crucial role in chain-of-custody procedures; files must be hashed before storage, transfer, or evidence submission to prove they have not been altered.

Digital signatures offer an additional layer of validation and context. Modern operating systems, particularly Windows, use Authenticode to verify the publisher of a binary and ensure it has not been tampered with. While a valid digital signature does not guarantee safety attackers have stolen certificates, abused trusted publishers, and exploited signing infrastructure, unsigned executables or binaries signed with untrusted, expired, or revoked certificates warrant heightened scrutiny. SOC analysts should not only check whether a file is signed but also inspect the certificate chain, publisher reputation, and timestamping information. Enterprise environments often contain internally developed or unsigned administrative tools, so analysts must learn to distinguish between expected benign unsigned binaries and anomalous ones introduced by an attacker. Signature validation becomes especially important during supply-chain incidents, where attackers compromise legitimate software updates.

YARA adds a powerful and flexible analytical layer that extends far beyond simple hash matching. While hashes break easily when malware is recompiled, packed, or slightly modified, YARA rules detect structural and behavioral characteristics that remain consistent across variants. YARA allows analysts to define patterns, strings, binary sequences, PE header attributes, imported functions, or unique assembly instructions that identify malware families or specific threat actor tradecraft. For example, a rule may look for references to ransom note filenames, Cobalt Strike configuration strings, cryptographic routines, or suspicious API import combinations such as VirtualAlloc, WriteProcessMemory, and CreateRemoteThread. YARA effectively becomes a custom signature engine, enabling SOCs to detect obfuscated payloads, uncover malware within memory dumps, and classify samples that evade traditional antivirus.

` In advanced environments, analysts deploy YARA rules operationally across endpoints, EDR platforms, file storage systems, and network shares. They can also scan sandbox detonation artifacts, memory images, or incident data to uncover embedded malicious components. Because threat actors frequently alter malware to bypass signature-based engines, YARA's pattern-based matching provides stability in a constantly evolving threat landscape. Even when attackers rotate infrastructure, modify hashes, or introduce polymorphism, the deeper behaviors and internal structures of their malware often remain detectable. This persistence makes YARA an essential tool for long-term detection engineering, intelligence correlation, and hunt operations.

Together, hashing, signature validation, and YARA form a layered approach to malware identification and threat classification. Hashes offer rapid triage. Signatures provide trust context. YARA delivers resilience against obfuscation and variation. When used in combination, these techniques give SOC analysts a precise and reliable toolkit for cataloging threats, preserving forensic integrity, and uncovering malware that blends into the environment.

Sandbox Detonation

Sandbox detonation allows analysts to observe malware behavior safely. Sandboxed environments isolate suspicious samples and log every action the malware attempts, including file creation, registry modifications, process injections, memory allocations, network communications, and persistence mechanisms.

SOC analysts typically rely on trusted platforms such as Cuckoo, Any.Run, Joe Sandbox, VirusTotal dynamic analysis, or internal EDR sandbox capabilities. Before detonation, analysts verify that the sandbox mimics realistic environments, up-to-date operating systems, common applications installed, and internet connectivity configured. Sophisticated malware often detects sandbox conditions and suppresses execution if it believes it is being analyzed.

During detonation, analysts monitor process trees to identify parent-child relationships, observe dropped files, inspect command-line arguments, and capture outbound network traffic. DNS queries, HTTP requests, user-agent strings, and C2 patterns are especially valuable for detection engineering and blocking strategies.

Sandbox outputs must always be reviewed critically. Analysts should validate findings using multiple sources rather than relying solely on sandbox verdicts, as automated scores sometimes misclassify behavior.

Indicators to Extract

One of the most operationally valuable outcomes of malware analysis is the extraction of indicators of compromise (IOCs). Indicators represent the observable traces that malware leaves behindfile hashes, suspicious filenames, dropped payloads, network destinations, registry modifications, mutex names, scheduled tasks, user-agent strings, persistence artifacts, command-line parameters, and execution paths. Extracting these indicators with precision allows the SOC to translate raw analysis into actionable intelligence. However, not all indicators carry the same reliability or long-term value; part of the analyst's role is to assess which indicators will remain stable across variants and which represent fleeting attributes that adversaries can easily modify.

Hashes, for example, provide a definitive fingerprint for a specific malware sample, but they are fragile: a single byte change or recompilation produces a new hash, rendering hash-based detection ineffective. Similarly, IP addresses and domains used for command-and-control often rotate daily, sometimes hourly, through automation or use of bulletproof hosting. These indicators are valuable for short-lived blocking or scoping during an active investigation, but they cannot anchor long-term detection strategies. More enduring indicators stem from behavioral traits, techniques and structures attackers reuse despite changing external infrastructure. Items such as registry run keys for persistence, named pipes or mutexes used for coordination, specific PowerShell execution chains, import function patterns, or characteristic installation paths often persist across malware families and variants. These "behavioral indicators" provide higher confidence and remain relevant far longer.

When extracting indicators, analysts must balance completeness with operational usefulness. Every IOC should be evaluated for confidence, stability, and applicability across detection layers. High-confidence indicators can be deployed immediately into SIEM correlation rules, EDR custom detections, firewall blocklists, DNS response policies, or SOAR enrichment workflows. Meanwhile, medium-confidence or ephemeral indicators should be used for threat hunting, contextual enrichment, or short-term monitoring rather than deployed as rigid detection rules. Each indicator must also be documented thoroughly including source, context, associated malware family, extraction method, and timestamp so downstream teams can validate accuracy and maintain chain-of-custody requirements if the analysis becomes part of a formal investigation.

This extracted intelligence feeds directly into detection engineering pipelines. Engineers transform indicators into correlation rules, endpoint detection logic, or network signatures. Threat hunters leverage them to formulate hypotheses, validate environmental exposure, or identify lateral movement patterns. Analysts may also provide extracted indicators to customers or stakeholders in the form of advisories, ensuring rapid situational awareness. When indicators are integrated properly, malware analysis becomes a force multiplier enhancing proactive defense, hardening SOC detection capabilities, and accelerating response to future incursions.

Reporting Findings for Clients

The final stage of malware analysis and often the most overlooked is the translation of technical findings into structured, comprehensible reports. A malware analyst's work is only as valuable as the client's ability to understand and take action on it. Reports form the bridge between highly complex technical observations and the decision-making processes of executives, IT teams, regulators, and non-technical leadership. In many cases, these reports become official records for compliance audits, cyber insurance claims, incident summaries, and strategic security planning.

A strong malware analysis report does more than list indicators or describe malicious behavior. It *tells a story*. It explains how the malware entered the environment, what actions it attempted, whether those actions succeeded, how the SOC detected it, and what steps were taken to contain, eradicate, and recover from the threat. A well-written narrative gives clients confidence that the SOC fully understands the incident and has taken appropriate action. It also provides leadership with insight into attacker motives, sophistication, and potential long-term risks. Clarity and structured storytelling allow even non-technical stakeholders to follow the chain of events and understand their implications.

Effective reporting begins with an executive summary written in accessible language. This summary captures the essence of the incident, its impact, severity, and current status without overwhelming the reader with technical details. Beneath the summary, the report expands into a behavioral overview, documenting what the malware was designed to do and how it operated during execution or analysis. This section may include references to process injection, persistence mechanisms, command-and-control activity, credential access attempts, or system modification behaviors. Mapping these actions to frameworks such as MITRE ATT&CK enhances the report's value by aligning findings with industry-recognized adversary techniques.

A timeline of execution is essential for clarity and forensic accuracy. Using precise timestamps, analysts reconstruct the sequence of events from initial infection through detection and remediation. Timelines also reveal dwell time, lateral movement attempts, and whether the malware's operation overlapped with user activity. This helps IT teams correlate the attack with potential root causes, such as phishing emails, drive-by downloads, or compromised credentials. The report must also provide a validated indicator list, including file hashes, filenames, mutexes, registry paths, domains, IP addresses, dropped artifacts, and execution chains. These indicators allow clients to perform broader internal checks or enforce blocks across their environment. It is important that analysts differentiate which indicators are high-confidence and which should be considered contextual or low-confidence, especially when adversaries use rapidly changing infrastructure.

Beyond documenting the malware's behavior, analysts must provide clear and actionable remediation recommendations.

These recommendations should describe exactly what the client must do to harden the environment, prevent recurrence, and improve detection coverage. Examples include patching vulnerable applications, restricting PowerShell usage, implementing EDR policies, tightening identity governance, or enhancing logging across targeted systems. Recommendations must be prioritized according to risk and feasibility. A good report not only describes what happened but ensures the client knows how to prevent it from happening again.

Tools can significantly improve the reporting process. SOC analysts commonly use Markdown editors, Notion, Obsidian, Confluence, or Google Docs for collaborative writing; Jupyter Notebooks for embedding analysis outputs; and SOAR-driven report generators for standardized formatting. For formatting professional PDFs, tools such as LaTeX, Word Templates, or PDF export engines built into SOAR and ticketing platforms are widely used. For evidence visualization, analysts may rely on process tree graphs from EDR tools, network diagrams from sandbox analysis, and structured data exports from Volatility, Any.Run, Cuckoo Sandbox, or similar platforms.

Client-facing reports must include a reassurance component. If containment and eradication succeeded, the report should state this explicitly, explaining how the SOC validated success. If the incident exposed risks or systemic weaknesses, the report should contextualize them while providing a path to improvement rather than triggering alarm. Internally, the same report becomes part of the organization's knowledge base, informing detection engineering, SOC training, tabletop exercises, and future threat hunts. Over time, repeated use of standardized reporting structures leads to institutional intelligence enabling the SOC to track adversary patterns, toolchains, and environmental weaknesses across incidents.

Ultimately, malware analysis reporting is both a technical discipline and a communication craft. The goal is not merely to describe malware but to empower clients with understanding, confidence, and actionable next steps. A polished, well-structured report reinforces the SOC's credibility, strengthens client relationships, and contributes to the organization's long-term resilience.

Malware Analysis Report Template

(Professional Short Form)

Malware Analysis Report

```
Client Name:
Report Date:
Analyst:
Case / Ticket Number:
Sample Filename:
SHA256 Hash:
```

```
Executive Summary
```

Provide a concise, non-technical overview of the malware sample, its impact, and current status.

Example: `A malicious executable was identified on WORKSTATION-02. The sample attempted to modify registry run keys for persistence and establish encrypted outbound communication. It was detected and contained before completing execution.`

2. Scope of Analysis

Describe what was analyzed and why.

Example:

```
This report covers static and dynamic
analysis of a suspicious binary
discovered during an EDR alert
investigation.
```

3. Static Analysis Findings

Summarize key observations without executing the sample:

- File type, size, compilation timestamp
- Embedded strings of interest
- Packing or obfuscation indicators
- Import table analysis
- Signature verification results

Example:

```
The binary was unsigned and packed
with UPX. Strings indicated references
to PowerShell command generation and
credential theft modules.
```

4. Dynamic Analysis Findings

Document observed behavior from sandbox detonation or controlled execution:

- Process tree
- Registry or file modifications
- Network activity
- Persistence mechanisms
- Attempts at privilege escalation

Example:
`Upon execution, the sample spawned powershell.exe, wrote a DLL to %AppData%, and attempted to contact an external IP over port 443.`

5. MITRE ATT&CK Mapping

List techniques observed:

- T1059 Command Execution
- T1547 Persistence via Registry Run Keys
- T1105 Ingress Tool Transfer
- T1003 Credential Access

6. Indicators of Compromise (IOCs)

Provide a structured IOC table for operational use.

Indicator Type	Value
SHA256	<hash>
Domain	malicious-updates.net
Registry Path	HKCU\Software\Microsoft\Windows\CurrentVersion\Run\Updater

7. Impact Assessment

Describe whether the malware succeeded in executing, whether data was accessed, and whether additional spread occurred.

8. Containment & Eradication Actions

Document the actions taken by the SOC or IR team:

- Host isolation
- Removal of persistence keys
- File deletion
- Credential resets
- EDR scans or host reimaging

9. Recommendations

Provide actionable next steps:

- Deploy YARA rules for detection
- Block identified domains/IPs
- Patch vulnerable applications
- Enforce PowerShell Constrained Mode
- Enable additional logging

10. Appendices

Include evidence, screenshots, Volatility output, process trees, or additional technical notes as needed.

Malware analysis empowers SOC analysts to understand adversaries rather than merely react to alerts. By combining static analysis, dynamic execution, cryptographic identification, sandboxing, indicator extraction, and professional reporting, SOC teams gain the insight needed to disrupt attacks and strengthen defensive posture. This chapter equips analysts with the practical knowledge required to analyze malware safely, accurately, and in a way that directly supports SOC operations and client trust.

Chapter 13

SOC Tuning & Continuous Improvement

A SOC is never finished. The threat landscape evolves, business environments change, users adopt new tools, and attackers continually refine their techniques. A SOC that does not adapt will slowly become ineffective/overwhelmed by alerts, blind to new attack paths, and disconnected from the business it is meant to protect. Continuous improvement is not an optional enhancement; it is a core operational requirement. SOC tuning is the mechanism through which detections improve, analyst efficiency increases, alert fatigue decreases, and overall security posture strengthens over time.

This chapter provides a concrete blueprint for building sustainable feedback loops, reducing alert fatigue, measuring detection quality, capturing lessons learned, and deliberately maturing the SOC through structured "hardening" cycles.

Feedback Loops: The Engine of SOC Improvement

Feedback loops are the engine that turns a SOC from a reactive alert desk into a learning, evolving system. Without them, every investigation is an isolated event and every alert is handled as if it were the first time anyone has seen something similar. With them, each alert, incident, and false positive becomes raw material for making the SOC smarter, faster, and more efficient. The central idea is simple: the outcome of today's work must influence tomorrow's detections, processes, and priorities in a systematic way, not just informally through hallway conversations or chat messages.

Effective feedback starts at the analyst level. Tier 1 analysts are the first to see alert patterns and quickly recognize when certain rules generate repetitive, low-value noise. Tier 2 and Tier 3 analysts see a different side of the picture: they encounter complex investigations where alerts fired too late, fired without enough context, or didn't fire at all. Threat hunters, in turn, discover blind spots and missing telemetry as they execute hypothesis-driven hunts. Each of these perspectives is valuable, but only if it is captured in a structured form. A mature SOC doesn't rely on memory or tribal knowledge; it bakes feedback into the tooling and workflows. Analysts tag tickets as "false positive," "low value," "late detection," "missed detection," or "tuning required." They add short, standardized investigation notes that explain *why* an alert was benign, why it was hard to investigate, or what would have made it easier or faster to resolve.

Ticketing systems such as Jira, ServiceNow, Zendesk, Azure DevOps, or even GitHub Issues can all serve as the backbone of this feedback capture. The key is consistency. Each closed alert or case should include fields for final disposition (true positive, false positive, benign-but-interesting, test, etc.), contributing factors (weak rule logic, missing context, noisy data source), and recommended actions (tune rule, add enrichment, add new detection, adjust

SLA, refine SOP). SOAR platforms can help as well by automatically tagging cases based on closure reasons or analyst input. Over time, the SOC accumulates a rich dataset of labeled outcomes tied directly to specific rules, data sources, clients, and environments.

Detection engineers and SOC managers then treat this feedback not as anecdotal commentary but as a backlog of work that must be triaged and prioritized like any other engineering effort. This is where project management tools become essential. Jira boards, ServiceNow change queues, Azure DevOps backlogs, Trello boards, or Asana projects can all be used to manage "SOC improvement tasks." False-positive clusters are turned into tuning stories. Missed detections become detection-engineering tasks. Telemetry gaps become logging or configuration change requests directed at IT or cloud teams. Each task is given an owner, a priority, and a due date. Some SOCs even adopt light-weight Agile practices running weekly or biweekly sprints focused purely on tuning, detection engineering, and automation enhancements.

Regular cadences give structure to the feedback loop. Many SOCs hold a weekly tuning and improvement meeting where the SOC manager, detection engineers, IR lead, and one or two senior analysts review the prior week's data. Instead of arguing from memory, they look at ticket tags and metrics: which rules generated the most false positives, which alerts took the longest to triage, which incidents revealed gaps, which data sources caused confusion or delays. A single false positive is just noise; ten identical false positives from the same rule across multiple clients is clearly a problem. Similarly, multiple escalations involving the same missed behavior, lateral movement that never triggered a meaningful alert indicate a detection gap that needs immediate attention. These themes are converted into actionable items in the project management tool and tracked to completion.

Key performance indicators (KPIs) and metrics both feed and validate the feedback loop. A mature SOC tracks, at minimum, metrics like mean time to triage (MTTT), mean time to detect (MTTD), mean time to respond (MTTR), alert volume per analyst per shift, false-positive rate per rule, ratio of automated vs. manual tasks, incident count by root cause, and the percentage of alerts coming from high-value detections versus generic baseline rules. These KPIs can be visualized in dashboards using tools such as Power BI, Grafana, Kibana, Splunk dashboards, Microsoft Sentinel workbooks, or ServiceNow performance analytics. Over time, the SOC should see measurable improvements in these metrics if feedback loops are working: fewer low-value alerts, faster triage times, higher automation coverage, and fewer surprises during major incidents.

Project and KPI visibility also create accountability and alignment. When tuning and detection engineering tasks live in a backlog with clear priorities, analysts see that their feedback leads to changes, and leadership can see the improvement work being done, not just incident firefighting. SOC managers can justify staffing and tooling changes by pointing to trends: for example, a sustained reduction in false positives after a set of tuning sprints, or a decrease in MTTR following the implementation of new SOAR playbooks. Feedback loops also feed capacity planning: if KPIs show that certain clients or environments generate disproportionate noise, the SOC can target those for focused improvement.

At a higher level, the SOC can integrate feedback loops with broader organizational project management frameworks. Tuning initiatives, new detection development, and SOAR automation projects can be rolled into quarterly objectives (OKRs) or roadmap items. This ensures continuous improvement is not something done "when there is time," but a core part of the SOC's mandate with explicit goals and measurable outcomes. For instance, a quarterly objective might be "reduce false-positive rate from 40% to 25% on top 20 rules" or "increase automated triage coverage to 60% of recurring alert types." These objectives are then tracked through the same project management tools used for operational tasks, closing the loop between strategic intent and day-to-day work.

Ultimately, a mature SOC treats feedback as data. Every closed alert is a labeled training sample. Every investigation outcome is a signal about rule quality, data quality, or process quality. The SOC's job is to capture those signals, organize them, prioritize them, and act on them with project management tools coordinating the work and KPI dashboards measuring the impact. When this discipline is in place, the SOC stops repeating the same mistakes and starts compounding its own learning. Over time, the environment becomes quieter, detections become sharper, analysts become more effective, and the organization becomes significantly harder to breach not because the threats went away, but because the feedback loops never stop running.

Reducing Alert Fatigue

Alert fatigue is one of the most pervasive and dangerous threats to SOC effectiveness. It occurs when analysts are overwhelmed by excessive volumes of low-value, repetitive, or poorly contextualized alerts. Over time, this constant stream of noise desensitizes them, slows their response time, degrades their judgment, and increases the likelihood that a real threat will go unnoticed. Alert fatigue is not a human failure it is an engineering failure. A SOC that depends on analyst endurance rather than signal quality is structurally flawed and guaranteed to underperform.

Reducing alert fatigue requires a systematic, engineering-driven approach, not arbitrary suppression or "working harder." The first step is to identify which alerts provide limited or no investigative value. These are typically alerts that always resolve as benign, alerts generated by normal administrative or automated activity, or alerts that consistently lack the context analysts need to reach a meaningful conclusion. Analysts must be empowered to label these alerts accurately within the ticketing or SIEM system, using standardized dispositions such as *Benign*, *Expected Behavior*, *False Positive*, or *Insufficient Context*. When this labeling is consistent, SOC managers can measure noise objectively rather than relying on anecdotal complaints from the queue.

SOC leadership must treat this feedback like operational telemetry. Repeated false positives from the same detection rule indicate broken logic, insufficient enrichment, or poorly defined thresholds. For example, a rule that triggers every time a service account authenticates across systems when cross-system authentication is expected should not remain active without modification. Rather than blaming analysts for being overwhelmed, managers must interpret recurring noise as a sign that tuning or detection engineering is overdue. Regular review cycles weekly or biweekly ensure that the SOC continuously identifies and corrects its noisiest rules.

Enrichment-driven suppression is a second major lever for fatigue reduction. A large percentage of alerts become trivial once additional context is applied. SOAR platforms can enrich alerts automatically with identity history, MFA results, device posture information, known "safe" IP ranges, or prior event frequency. For instance, an "Impossible Travel" alert may become benign instantly if enrichment confirms the user is connected via a company VPN endpoint. Similarly, a PowerShell event becomes low-risk if enrichment shows it originated from an authorized deployment tool. By attaching context early in the workflow, the SOC prevents analysts from burning time on alerts that can be safely auto-closed or deprioritized. Enrichment transforms raw signalsoften ambiguous and noisyinto informed evaluations that dramatically reduce alert load.

Correlation further multiplies these gains. Instead of generating multiple standalone alerts for each event in a wider sequence, the SOC should group related activities into a single investigative case. A brute-force attempt followed by a successful login should not produce two unrelated alerts; it should trigger a single correlated detection that tells the story. Similarly, a chain of suspicious processes on an endpoint should consolidate into one case that reflects the full activity graph. Correlation reduces cognitive fragmentation, enabling analysts to see the bigger picture and investigate with clarity instead of piecing together scattered signals.

In mature SOCs, engineers also implement event de-duplication, dynamic thresholds, behavioral scoring, and probabilistic detection frameworks. These methods ensure that alerts fire only when meaningful deviations occur, not simply when a static rule fails to account for regular environmental noise. Identity analytics, UEBA systems, and ML-based detectors help refine baselines automatically, enabling detections that adapt to normal user and system behavior instead of rigidly matching signatures.

Reducing alert fatigue is fundamentally a quality-of-signal problem, not a human-capacity problem. The goal is not to have analysts “handle more alerts”the goal is to generate fewer but better alerts. When detection logic is tuned, enrichment is automated, correlation is applied, and noise is treated as a metric, analysts regain the mental bandwidth needed to detect real attacker behavior. In this model, alert fatigue does not get solved by individual tolerance, it gets solved through intentional engineering.

Detection Quality Metrics

You cannot improve what you do not measure. Detection quality metrics provide objective insights into how well the SOC is performing and where improvement is needed. These metrics shift the SOC from reactive firefighting to data-driven management.

High-quality SOCs track metrics such as mean time to triage, mean time to detect, mean time to contain, false-positive rate, alert closure accuracy, and alerts per analyst per shift. Detection-specific metrics include rule firing frequency, percentage of alerts escalated per rule, investigation outcome distribution, and coverage across MITRE ATT&CK tactics.

These metrics should be reviewed visually through dashboards on a regular cadence. Trends matter more than absolute values. A rising false-positive rate signals environmental or behavior changes that require tuning. A decreasing time-to-triage often reflects improved automation or analyst familiarity. Detection coverage metrics reveal where the SOC is blind or overly dependent on a small subset of detections.

Metrics must be used constructively. They are tools for improvement, not punishment. When analysts trust that metrics exist to improve workflows rather than evaluate individuals unfairly, the feedback loop remains healthy.

Lessons-Learned Cycles

Every security incident, whether a catastrophic breach, a contained intrusion, a malware detonation, or even a close call contains valuable lessons for the SOC. These lessons are often hidden within the noise of investigation timelines, alert sequences, communication patterns, and detection gaps. Lessons-learned cycles (often called "post-incident reviews" or PIRs) formalize the process of extracting these insights and converting them into measurable operational improvements. In high-performing SOCs, lessons-learned cycles are not optional rituals performed only after major breaches; they are continuous improvement engines that fuel detection enhancements, workflow optimization, tool tuning, and organizational growth.

A lessons-learned cycle typically begins after the SOC resolves an incident or identifies a significant investigative event even if no compromise occurred. "Near misses" are just as important as confirmed incidents because they often reveal structural weaknesses that attackers could exploit if they tried again. The timing of the review is also strategic: too early, and root causes may still be unclear; too late, and human memory fades, losing nuance that could improve future performance. Most SOCs conduct the review within 24–72 hours after the incident's containment, when details remain fresh but emotions have cooled.

A proper lessons-learned session asks a consistent, structured set of diagnostic questions. These questions are not designed to identify *who* is at fault but rather *where* the system, process, or tooling can be improved. For example:
How was the activity initially detected? If detection occurred through an EDR alert, phishing report, or user complaint, analysts examine whether this was the earliest possible signal or merely the first one the SOC noticed.

Was detection early enough? Many incidents reveal dwell time, attackers lingering in the environment longer than expected. If detection occurred late, the SOC must determine whether earlier signals were overlooked, suppressed, or nonexistent.

What signals were missed initially? Analysts review logs, SIEM dashboards, and EDR telemetry to determine whether detection logic failed or if insufficient data was collected.

What slowed down the investigation? Common issues include missing context, low-value alerts, unhelpful enrichment, noisy rules, documentation gaps, unclear procedures, or reliance on subject matter experts who were unavailable.

Were escalation paths followed and understood? Confusion about escalation criteria, handoff timing, or communication responsibility often extends the duration of incidents.

Were containment actions timely and effective? If host isolation, credential resets, or network blocks were delayed or misapplied, containment procedures must be revisited.

What would we change next time? This question is the heart of the review, it extracts improvements and converts them into real operational change.

The answers to these questions must result in tangible action items, not abstract observations. Lessons learned without follow-through simply become "postmortem folklore." Real improvement involves writing or tuning detection rules, adding missing SIEM fields, revising SOAR playbooks, enhancing logging on under-monitored systems, refining SOPs, improving ticketing workflows, adjusting SLAs, or updating escalation matrices. Some lessons may require engineering-level projects, such as deploying Sysmon across workstations, enabling Azure AD risk-based policies, onboarding additional cloud logs, or remediating identity governance weaknesses.

Tools play a critical role in managing lessons-learned cycles. A SOC may track improvement actions through Jira, ServiceNow Change Requests, Azure DevOps boards, Trello workflows, or GitHub Issues. These tools ensure accountability by assigning owners, due dates, workflows, and priority levels. KPIs and dashboards built in Power BI, Grafana, Splunk, or Sentinel Workbooks help visualize recurring root causes, incident types, detection failures, and investigation bottlenecks. Mature SOCs even integrate post-incident data into knowledge bases stored in Confluence, Notion, WikiJS, or internal SharePoint libraries, ensuring that the lessons become part of the institutional memory accessible to future analysts.

A key principle of effective lessons-learned cycles is blamelessness. These reviews must be collaborative, transparent, and psychologically safe. Blame-driven reviews discourage truthful reflection and create defensive behaviors that obscure systemic weaknesses. A blameless review focuses on workflows, tools, telemetry, SOPs, and structural factors, not individuals. This cultural foundation allows analysts to share what they struggled with, where they hesitated, and what information they lacked. These insights are critical: analysts often know exactly what the SOC needs, but they lack a structured forum to express it.

Over time, lessons-learned cycles accumulate into what can best be described as a SOC maturity compounding effect. Each review adds new detection logic, improves automation, clarifies communication, and expands coverage. The SOC becomes faster, quieter, more accurate, and more confident. False positives decrease, SLA performance improves, and incidents shrink in duration and impact. Newly onboarded analysts learn faster because they inherit a repository of previous mistakes and improvements instead of repeating them. Ultimately, the SOC becomes significantly harder to breach not because its analysts work harder, but because its systems improve continuously and systematically.

Lessons-learned cycles are not the conclusion of an incident; they are the beginning of better future outcomes. The SOCs that master them become learning organizations constantly evolving, constantly improving, and constantly increasing the cost of attack for adversaries.

"SOC Hardening" and Maturity Growth

SOC hardening is the disciplined, ongoing process of strengthening every aspect of Security Operations, not just detection rules or alert logic, but the entire ecosystem of people, processes, tooling, architecture, communication, and governance. It is the operational equivalent of hardening a server or network, but applied to the SOC as a living, evolving organism. Whereas tuning focuses on improving individual detections, SOC hardening improves the *system as a whole*, ensuring that every component from data ingestion pipelines to IR workflows to analyst training operates with precision, efficiency, and resilience.

Hardening begins with procedural refinement. Standard Operating Procedures (SOPs) must be reviewed, rewritten, tested, and validated regularly. Ambiguous instructions create inconsistent investigations, wasted effort, and unnecessary escalations. SOC hardening ensures that SOPs clearly define triage expectations, escalation paths, evidence handling procedures, client communication standards, and IR activation thresholds. As lessons accumulate from investigations and incidents, SOPs become sharper, more prescriptive, and more aligned with real-world workflows. This reduces friction and speeds analyst decision-making, which directly strengthens the SOC's response capability.

Access control is another foundational pillar of SOC hardening. SOC tooling often contains highly sensitive information, endpoint telemetry, identity logs, network traffic data, threat intelligence, and sometimes even decrypted payloads. Proper hardening enforces least privilege across all SOC platforms. Analysts should have access only to the tools and permissions necessary for their duties. Administrative privileges must be limited, audited, and regularly reviewed. This includes MFA enforcement, session logging, change auditing, and role-based access control (RBAC). SOCs that neglect access control risk insider threats, accidental misuse, and unnecessary exposure of sensitive data.

Tooling resilience is equally important. A SOC's architectural backbone is SIEM, SOAR, log ingestion pipelines, EDR deployment, threat intelligence feeds, and case management systems must be hardened against operational disruptions. This may involve implementing redundancy and failover paths so ingestion does not halt during outages; improving SOAR error handling so automations do not break silently; adding monitoring to ensure enrichment sources remain healthy and responsive; and deploying fallback pipelines that preserve visibility even during partial system failures. As SOCs evolve, their tooling becomes more interconnected, making resilience essential to preventing cascading failures during high-severity incidents.

Another dimension of SOC hardening is *coverage expansion*. As the SOC learns from past incidents and hunts, it identifies gaps in telemetry missing logs, blind spots in cloud platforms, insufficient endpoint visibility, inconsistent Sysmon coverage, overlooked service accounts, or under-monitored SaaS applications. Hardening involves closing these gaps by onboarding new log sources, enabling advanced audit logs, deploying agent updates, capturing identity risk signals, and adding specialized sensors to detect lateral movement or command-and-control activity. This continuous closing of visibility gaps is one of the clearest indicators of operational maturity.

Hardening also applies to the SOC's intellectual infrastructure: detection engineering, threat hunting, and adversary alignment practices. As the SOC matures, detection engineering shifts from generic, signature-based detections toward behavior-driven logic and adversary TTP recognition. Engineers begin to map existing detections to MITRE ATT&CK, identifying which techniques are well-covered and which require new content. Threat hunters evolve beyond reactive queries and begin utilizing hypothesis-driven hunts, adversary emulation, memory forensics, and analytics-based anomaly detection. SOCs incorporate purple teaming and intelligence-led exercises to simulate real adversary behavior, using the results to refine detections and strengthen response procedures.

SOC hardening extends deeply into operational governance. Evidence-handling procedures become stricter and more forensic in nature. Ticketing workflows become standardized and enforced. Documentation quality improves not just SOPs, but internal runbooks, enrichment explanations, data dictionaries, and architectural diagrams. Internal communication mechanisms mature, forming predictable channels for escalations, IR coordination, and executive briefings. Senior leadership gains visibility into SOC performance through dashboards that track KPIs such as

MTTD (Mean Time to Detect), MTTR (Mean Time to Respond), alert closure rates, false positive ratios, and automation coverage. Hardening transforms the SOC from a reactive, alert-driven function into a structured operational program with measurable outputs and predictable results.

As a SOC hardens, its maturity grows but maturity is not linear. Early in the SOC's development, improvements generate dramatic gains. Tuning a handful of noisy rules can reduce alert volume by 30–50%. Adding simple enrichment layers can cut triage times in half. Clarifying escalation paths can eliminate hours of confusion during major incidents. Deploying Sysmon or upgrading EDR coverage can uncover previously invisible attacker activity. These early-stage improvements often feel transformative because they directly address chronic pain points.

As the SOC advances, maturity becomes more nuanced. Improvements no longer come from basic rule tuning but from sophisticated engineering work: identifying long-tail anomalies, aligning detections with adversary tradecraft, conducting intelligence-led hunts, strengthening cloud identity governance, and refining automation pipelines. The SOC begins measuring detection effectiveness with ATT&CK heatmaps, using frameworks such as the

SOC-CMM (SOC Capability Maturity Model), NIST CSF maturity tiers, or service excellence assessments. These benchmarks provide helpful structure, but true operational maturity is demonstrated by outcomes rather than labels.

Ultimately, SOC maturity is measured by results: fewer missed incidents, faster response times, more confident analysts, smoother escalations, stronger collaboration with IT and leadership, and a consistent ability to prevent small incidents from escalating into business-impacting crises. Mature SOCs are trusted by their stakeholders because they operate predictably, communicate clearly, and improve continuously. They generate signals not noise. They contain threats quickly, detect subtle patterns early, and align operations with business risk. SOC hardening never ends. Each tuning improvement, each procedural refinement, each new detection rule, each closed telemetry gap, and each lessons-learned cycle adds to the resilience of the system. Over time, these incremental improvements transform the SOC from a reactive firefighting team into a strategic security asset one that learns from every incident and emerges stronger after each challenge.

SOC tuning and continuous improvement are what separate stagnant security teams from resilient, high-performing operations. Through structured feedback loops, alert fatigue reduction, rigorous detection metrics, disciplined lessons-learned cycles, and intentional SOC hardening, organizations ensure their SOC evolves alongside the threat landscape. This chapter provides the blueprint to transform daily operational experience into long-term defensive strength keeping the SOC effective, adaptive, and trusted.

SECTION V SOC MANAGEMENT & CLIENT COMMUNICATIONS

Chapter 14

Managing Client Relationships & Bridge Calls

No matter how technically mature a SOC becomes, its success is ultimately measured by trust. Clients and executives rarely judge security teams by the sophistication of detections or dashboards; they judge them by how clearly, calmly, and competently they handle incidents especially when pressure is highest. Bridge calls are the moment when SOC operations become visible to the business. Poorly handled bridge calls erode confidence instantly, while well-managed ones strengthen long-term relationships even in the face of bad news. This chapter provides a practical blueprint for leading bridge calls, de-escalating tense situations, communicating with confidence, translating technical findings into business language, managing expectations, and delivering difficult information professionally.

What a Bridge Call Is and How to Lead One

A bridge call is a live, multi-party communication session established during a security incident to coordinate response efforts, share accurate status updates, and align technical actions with business priorities. It is not an investigation forumthe SOC continues technical analysis in the background. The bridge exists to provide structure, control, and clarity when the situation feels chaotic. Participants may include SOC analysts, IR leads, IT operations personnel, legal and compliance representatives, security leadership, executive stakeholders, and occasionally outside vendors or cyber insurance partners. The effectiveness of the bridge call relies heavily on leadership; it must have a designated lead, typically the SOC Manager or IR Lead who guides the discussion, maintains order, and ensures timely, fact-based communication. The bridge lead begins by immediately asserting control of the call, setting expectations, and providing a calm, structured overview of what is known, what is still being investigated, what actions are underway, and when the next update will be provided. This reduces uncertainty, which is the primary driver of client anxiety during an incident.

Tone and language are critical. The bridge lead must avoid emotionally charged phrases like "we have a breach," which triggers panic. Instead, they should use measured language that reflects both realism and containment, such as "we've identified suspicious activity and have isolated the affected systems while we verify scope." Problems must never be presented without solutions or paths forward. Stating, "We've lost multiple systems," leaves clients feeling helpless; reframing as, "We're seeing impact to several systems, and we're already implementing containment and recovery measures," communicates control. Accurate but steady communication prevents escalation of fear among stakeholders. The bridge lead also makes clear distinctions between confirmed facts and hypotheses under investigation, avoiding speculation that could mislead legal decisions or executive perceptions.

The structure of the call should be predictable and disciplined. After opening the call and establishing roles, the bridge lead presents a concise snapshot of the situation: what is impacted, what is not impacted, what has been contained, and what the team is actively investigating. This snapshot must be factual and tightly focused. The call then moves into coordinated updates from each workstream such as forensics, containment, IT operations, business impact assessment, and legal review with each update limited to what has been done, what has been found, and what the next steps are. If participants begin veering into speculation or excessive technical depth, the bridge lead gently redirects them to maintain a clear, high-level operational picture. Bridge calls also serve as decision forums. When containment actions, system shutdowns, firewall changes, or regulatory notifications require approval, the bridge lead frames the decision, explains the rationale, outlines business impact, and requests authorization in a controlled manner.

Throughout the call, reassurance is woven into the communication not through false optimism but through clarity, structure, and reference to established processes. Statements like, “This is the type of incident we train for,” or, “These containment steps align with standard response procedures,” remind stakeholders that the team is not improvising under pressure. Effective bridge leadership also prevents surprises by signaling potential downstream considerations early, such as regulatory notification requirements or temporary system outages, ensuring executives are not blindsided later. Clients remain calm when they understand the plan, feel heard, see action underway, and know when they will receive the next update.

The bridge call concludes with a structured summary that includes the current status, actions completed during the call, next steps with assigned owners, risks still being assessed, and the timing for the next update. This final recap reinforces control and alignment. After the call, the bridge lead or designated scribe documents decisions, timelines, commitments, and open questions to ensure consistency across subsequent bridge calls and to support post-incident reporting. Ultimately, a well-run bridge call becomes a stabilizing force during a stressful event. When executed with clarity, discipline, and controlled language, it assures clients that even in the midst of an attack the response is coordinated, professional, and firmly under control.

De-Escalation Techniques

Security incidents create emotional responses: fear, frustration, blame, and urgency. De-escalation is therefore a critical SOC skill. Effective de-escalation begins with tone. A calm, steady voice reassures stakeholders that the situation is under control even when it is complex. Analysts and leaders should speak slowly, avoid filler language, and never raise their voice or display defensiveness.

De-escalation also requires acknowledgment. When stakeholders express concern or anger, the SOC lead should acknowledge those concerns directly without assigning blame. Phrases such as *"That concern is understood"* or *"Here's how we are addressing that risk right now"* redirect emotion toward action.

Another key technique is separating urgency from panic. Not every action must happen immediately, but every action must be intentional. Communicating *why* certain steps are being taken and *why others are not yet appropriate prevents* rushed decisions that could cause additional harm, such as unnecessarily isolating critical systems.

Finally, de-escalation improves when updates are predictable. Establishing a fixed update cadence during an incident reduces interruptions and prevents stakeholders from repeatedly re-asking the same questions.

Speaking Confidently Under Pressure

Confidence during incidents is not about bravado; it is about clarity and discipline. SOC personnel must communicate only what they know, avoid speculation, and resist the temptation to over-explain. Confidence is conveyed by structure: presenting facts in sequence, stating what actions are in progress, and explaining decision rationale without technical sprawl.

One of the most common mistakes analysts make under pressure is filling silence with assumptions. Silence is acceptable. If information is not yet available, it is better to say *"We are validating that now and will update in 15 minutes"* than to guess incorrectly. Guessing erodes trust faster than admitting uncertainty. Preparation builds confidence. SOCs should train analysts using mock bridge calls and incident simulations so they become accustomed to speaking under observation. Knowing how to articulate findings succinctly is as important as discovering them. Over time, confident communication becomes a learned operational skill rather than an innate personality trait.

Translating Technical Findings to Non-Technical Audiences

One of the SOC's most critical and often overlooked responsibilities is translating the ability to convert highly technical, forensic-level findings into clear, business-relevant language that executives, clients, and non-technical stakeholders can understand and act upon. Most leaders do not need to hear about registry hive modifications, encoded PowerShell parameters, LSASS memory access attempts, or SMB enumeration sequences. They need to understand risk, impact, exposure, likelihood, business interruption, and mitigation. The SOC's job is to bridge that gap without diluting truth or amplifying fear.

Translation begins by reframing technical observations into *outcomes*. For example, saying "PowerShell executed with encoded arguments" may be accurate, but it creates unnecessary confusion, raises anxiety, or leads executives to misinterpret severity. A more effective translation would be: *"An attacker attempted to run unauthorized commands on a workstation, and the action was blocked before it caused impact."* This version maintains accuracy while shifting the focus from the mechanism (PowerShell parameters) to what matters: defensive success and business safety.

Similarly, "Credential dumping was attempted" may sound dramatic or ambiguous to a non-technical audience. Translating it into, *"We detected and stopped an attempt to access password information, and no accounts were compromised,"* clearly communicates both the threat and the outcome. This framing gives clients confidence while ensuring they understand the significance. The goal is not to soften reality, it's to express reality in a way that is useful.

Good translation requires intentional balance. Oversimplifying to the point of distortion is dangerous because executives may believe a threat was smaller than it was, delaying needed investments or corrective actions. Overly technical explanations are equally damaging because they overwhelm listeners, erode confidence, and cause decision paralysis. Effective SOC communicators understand their audience: they speak differently to IT engineers than they do to a CEO, CFO, or board member. The content remains accurate, but the framing shifts from *how* something occurred to *what it means* and *what needs to happen next.*

For example:

- Technical version: "We observed Mimikatz LSASS memory scraping attempts across three hosts."
- Executive version: "There was an attempt to steal user passwords from several systems, but no password data was accessed. We've isolated the affected systems and enforced resets as a precaution."

The executive version conveys:

- What happened
- What was prevented
- What actions were taken
- What risk remains

This is everything a leader needs to make informed decisions without drowning in jargon.

Analogies can be powerful tools for translation when used appropriately. They should simplify concepts while keeping severity clear. For instance:

- Malware persistence can be described as "an attacker hiding a spare key so they can sneak back in later."

- Lateral movement becomes "an intruder walking through the building checking which doors are unlocked."

- Privilege escalation is "an attacker finding a way to get master keys instead of guest badges."

- Data exfiltration attempt is "someone trying to quietly copy documents out of the building."

These analogies help non-technical stakeholders visualize events quickly and accurately without requiring them to understand system internals. They convert abstract cyber actions into intuitive physical scenarios that immediately convey seriousness.

However, analogies must be chosen carefully. They should illuminate, not exaggerate. A poor analogy can trivialize a serious event or unintentionally amplify fear. The SOC lead must also be cautious not to rely on analogies alone; after using one, they must tie it back to real conditions: *"In practical terms, here is what that means for your environment..."*

Another key element of translation is prioritization. Executives do not need fifteen technical bullet points. They need a structured communication model:

1. What happened (high-level description)
2. How it affects us (impact, risk, exposure)
3. What has been done (containment, protections, verifications)
4. What we are doing next (investigation, monitoring, recovery)
5. What we need from leadership (approvals, resources, coordination)

This structure prevents information overload and ensures leaders can make timely decisions.

Finally, effective translation builds trust not by sugarcoating, but by clearly explaining:

- What is known
- What is not yet known
- What is being done to close those gaps
- How soon updates will follow

Uncertainty is inevitable during incidents, but uncertainty delivered with confidence and clarity is manageable. Uncertainty delivered through technical chaos is not.

In this sense, translation becomes one of the SOC's most strategic capabilities. It aligns technical truth with business context, enabling executives to understand threats, approve actions, allocate resources, and maintain calm even in high-pressure scenarios. A SOC that communicates well is not just a technical defender it is a stabilizing force for the entire organization.

Managing Expectations

Many client frustrations arise not from incidents themselves, but from mismatched expectations. Managing expectations is therefore a proactive activity that begins *before* an incident occurs. SOCs must clearly define what they monitor, how quickly they respond, what actions they can take autonomously, and what requires client approval.

During incidents, expectation management involves setting realistic timelines. SOC leads should avoid promising immediate answers when investigations take time. It is better to say *"We expect clarity within one hour"* than *"We're almost done"* without certainty.

Expectation management also includes clearly differentiating between containment, eradication, and recovery. Clients often assume an issue is "fixed" once a system is isolated, when in reality recovery may take days. Clarifying where the SOC is in the IR lifecycle prevents confusion and disappointment.

Consistency builds trust. When update timelines are met consistently, confidence grows even during prolonged incidents.

Delivering Bad News Professionally

Delivering bad news is one of the most difficult but essential responsibilities of a SOC, and the way it is communicated often has more impact on client trust than the incident itself. Whether the news involves confirmed data exposure, ransomware encryption, unauthorized access, regulatory implications, or operational shutdowns, the SOC must approach the disclosure with professionalism, clarity, and emotional intelligence. Bad news should be communicated early and factually rather than delayed in hopes of gathering "complete information." Waiting too long creates the impression of concealment or mismanagement, and stakeholders may learn partial details from other teams, log anomalies, or user reports. When the SOC takes ownership of the narrative upfront, it reinforces reliability and leadership.

The delivery should begin with what is definitively known, phrased in calm, precise language that avoids dramatization. Overly emotional or alarmist phrasing intensifies fear, while excessive technical depth confuses stakeholders and undermines decision-making. Instead of presenting a mountain of log data or technical jargon, the SOC lead summarizes the confirmed event succinctly, then distinguishes clearly between established facts and areas still under investigation. This helps stakeholders understand that the situation is being handled methodically rather than reactively. It also reduces the risk of misinterpretation, which can cause unnecessary escalation to legal, HR, or external partners.

Blame must never be included in the initial disclosure. Even if a misconfiguration, outdated system, or human error contributed to the incident, the SOC's job during active response is not to assign fault. Pointing fingersdirectly or indirectlycreates defensiveness and shifts focus away from containment and recovery. Instead, the SOC frames the situation using neutral language centered on the event itself: what happened, how it was discovered, when it occurred, and what the impact appears to be. By focusing on the situation rather than people, the SOC maintains a constructive and solution-oriented environment that keeps teams aligned rather than divided.

Tone plays a significant role. During high-pressure moments, leadership and clients look to the SOC for emotional cues. A steady, composed tone communicates that the situation is serious but manageable. Dramatic phrasing such as "catastrophic breach" or "everything is compromised" does nothing to improve response and may cause executives to make rushed or fear-driven decisions. Similarly, overly technical descriptions can overwhelm non-technical stakeholders and obscure the real implications. Effective communicators translate the technical reality into business-relevant terms, discussing operational impact, risk exposure, regulatory considerations, and immediate actions in language that leadership understands.

Bad news must also be paired with actionable next steps. Even when the full scope is not yet known, the SOC should outline what is happening now, what will happen next, and what decisions leadership may need to make. This could include system isolation, password resets, communication plans, or legal notification workflows. Providing clear recommendations helps stakeholders regain a sense of control, shifting focus from fear toward coordinated action. When people know what comes next, uncertainty decreases and collaboration improves.

The communication should conclude with a forward-looking plan. This reassures stakeholders that the incident is being managed in a structured way and that recovery is possible even in severe cases. A strong closing statement might summarize containment progress, describe the ongoing investigation, and provide a timetable for future updates. This maintains confidence by showing that the SOC is not only responding to the immediate event but also planning ahead to minimize further risk.

Ultimately, delivering bad news professionally is not simply about informing stakeholders, it is about protecting trust, guiding decision-making, and maintaining stability during a crisis. A SOC that communicates difficult truths with calm authority, factual clarity, and actionable recommendations becomes a dependable partner in the eyes of clients and executives. Even in the worst incidents, a well-managed disclosure can strengthen relationships rather than damage them. Managing client relationships and bridge calls is a core SOC competency not a soft skill to be learned incidentally. Through disciplined leadership, emotional intelligence, structured communication, and professional transparency, SOC teams transform high-stress incidents into opportunities to reinforce trust. This chapter provides the operational blueprint for ensuring that when pressure is highest, the SOC remains calm, credible, and in control.

Chapter 15

Reporting & Executive Communications

A SOC that cannot communicate its value will eventually be perceived as a cost center rather than a strategic asset. Reporting is the bridge between technical security operations and business leadership. While alerts, investigations, and response actions occur continuously behind the scenes, executives and clients experience the SOC primarily through reports, dashboards, and briefings.
Well-designed reporting demonstrates effectiveness, maturity, and return on investment. Poor reporting obscures success, increases scrutiny, and weakens trust.

This chapter provides a complete blueprint for building reporting structures, KPI dashboards, executive summaries, and MSSP-style deliverables that clearly communicate impact, risk reduction, and business value.

Daily, Weekly, and Monthly Reporting

Effective SOC reporting follows a cadence. Each reporting interval serves a different purpose and audience, and reports must be tailored accordingly. Daily reports are operational in nature. Their goal is situational awareness and continuity, not long-term analysis. A daily SOC report typically summarizes alert volume, notable incidents, active investigations, SLA status, and any high-risk trends observed during the last operational period. These reports are brief, standardized, and designed for SOC leadership, IR leads, and operational stakeholders. They enable smooth shift handovers and rapid escalation when needed.

Weekly reports shift the focus from immediate operations to pattern recognition. They identify trends in alert categories, recurring false positives, emerging threat patterns, and performance metrics such as time-to-triage and time-to-contain. Weekly reports are where stakeholders begin to see *direction*: whether security posture is improving, stagnating, or degrading. These reports often include summaries of completed incidents and highlight upcoming risks or required changes.

Monthly reports are strategic. They summarize SOC performance over time, correlate security activity with business impact, and communicate progress toward maturity and risk reduction goals. Monthly reports are designed for executives, board members, and external clients. They should emphasize outcomes, not volumewhat threats were stopped, what risks were reduced, and how the SOC contributed to business resilience.

KPI Dashboards

KPI dashboards serve as the operational heartbeat of a SOC. They are not passive visual displays; they are decision-making instruments that guide resourcing, tuning, engineering priorities, and executive strategy. While static reports provide a snapshot in time, dashboards deliver continuous, near–real-time visibility into SOC health, performance, and detection efficacy. When properly designed, dashboards help identify bottlenecks before they become outages, expose detection weaknesses before they become breaches, and provide leadership with clarity rather than noise. When poorly designed, dashboards become screensaver pretty but meaningless.

The most important principle in dashboard development is intentionality. A dashboard should never exist simply because the capability to create it exists. Every metric should answer a real operational question, support a staffing decision, guide an engineering effort, or inform a leadership conversation. When dashboards become cluttered with vanity metrics/alert counts, event volumes, or meaningless charts, they lose function and become distractions. The goal is clarity, relevance, and actionability.

Operational Dashboards: Monitoring the SOC's Daily Pulse

Operational dashboards support frontline SOC leaders and managers by illustrating how effectively the team is handling the live workload. These dashboards reveal triage velocity, alert queue depth, SLA progression, resource distribution, and overall SOC throughput. When designed well, they allow managers to quickly rebalance analyst loads, identify bottlenecks, detect backlogs forming, and intervene before SLA breaches occur.

Key components of an operational dashboard typically include:

- Alert queue health, showing the volume of unassigned, in-progress, and overdue alerts.
- Alert aging, which visualizes how long alerts remain in each status category.
- SLA countdown indicators, highlighting alerts nearing breach in "red zone" time windows.
- Analyst distribution, showing how many alerts each analyst is handling to ensure workload fairness.
- Case progression timelines, demonstrating how quickly alerts progress from triage to closure.

Operational dashboards must update frequently/ideally every few minutes because their purpose is to influence real-time decision-making. A SOC manager might use such dashboards during daily standups or shift handoffs, or keep them displayed on wall monitors as a running operational heartbeat.

Detection Quality Dashboards: Measuring the Strength of the Signal

If operational dashboards represent the SOC's pulse, then detection quality dashboards represent its immune system. They reveal how well the SOC is detecting real threats, how often rules produce noise, and where detection gaps exist. This allows detection engineers, SOC leads, and threat hunters to make informed decisions about where to tune, where to add new logic, and where telemetry gaps are weakening the defense.

Detection quality dashboards commonly include:

- False-positive ratios per detection rule, a critical metric for determining rule health and tuning priority.
- Alert-to-incident conversion ratios, showing how often a detection identifies a legitimate threat.
- Detection firing frequency trends, highlighting when rules fire too often

(noise) or not at all (broken logic).

- MITRE ATT&CK coverage heatmaps, mapping detection rules across attack techniques to visualize gaps.
- Telemetry coverage indicators, showing what percentage of endpoints, servers, cloud assets, or identities are providing usable logs.

A well-constructed detection quality dashboard transforms tuning from anecdotal complaint-driven effort into data-driven engineering. Instead of relying on analysts saying "This rule fires too much," engineers rely on objective measurements. Over time, these dashboards reduce alert fatigue, increase visibility, and strengthen the SOC's defensive posture.

Executive Dashboards: Communicating Security Outcomes, Not Alerts

Executive dashboards serve an entirely different purpose than operational or engineering dashboards. While the SOC floor requires granular detail to manage daily investigations, executives require a narrative of security posture framed within business outcomes, not technical artifacts. The distinction is crucial. Executives must be able to look at a dashboard and immediately understand whether the organization's risk is increasing or decreasing, whether response processes are improving, and whether strategic investments are producing measurable results. In other words, executive dashboards answer the question: *Are we safer than we were before?*

Unlike analyst-facing interfaces that highlight alert queues or ingestion statuses, executive dashboards deliberately abstract away the noise. They are not the place for correlation charts, SIEM schema details, or raw alert counts—these metrics lack business meaning and often create unnecessary confusion. Instead, executive dashboards translate SOC performance into risk signals that leaders can use to make informed decisions. This translation is what makes the SOC visible and valuable at the highest levels of the organization.

A well-designed executive dashboard provides clarity at a glance. It highlights whether incident severity is trending downward, whether detection and response times are improving, and whether preventive controls are reducing exposure. Monthly incident trends listed by category such as credential misuse, endpoint malware attempts, cloud misconfigurations, or insider behaviors help executives see patterns across business units or technology platforms. These trends become the basis for informed budget decisions, resource planning, and executive prioritization. Two of the most important metrics for executives are Mean Time to Detect (MTTD) and Mean Time to Respond (MTTR). These metrics are universally understood across industries because they communicate operational effectiveness in terms of speed and efficiency. A dashboard that shows a reduction in MTTD clearly demonstrates that the SOC is beginning to catch attacks earlier in the kill chain. A reduction in MTTR shows that analysts are responding faster and containing threats before they escalate. Together, these metrics form the backbone of executive confidence.

Executive dashboards also highlight prevention success—not just detection. Many high-risk attacks are thwarted by automated containment, policy enforcement, identity controls, or EDR intervention long before an analyst becomes involved. Showing how many ransomware precursors, credential theft attempts, suspicious authentications, or device exploit attempts were successfully blocked reinforces the SOC's strategic value. Prevention metrics shift the executive conversation from

"How many alerts fired?" to "How many attacks never became incidents?"

Compliance alignment is another essential component. Most organizations operate within one or more governance frameworks; NIST, ISO, HIPAA, PCI, CJIS, SOX, FedRAMP and executive leadership is ultimately accountable for meeting these requirements. Dashboards should visually present compliance posture across key domains such as logging coverage, detection maturity, evidence-handling readiness, retention compliance, and incident documentation quality. This gives executives a clear understanding of regulatory exposure and remediation priorities.

Risk trend indicators deepen the strategic insight. Instead of showing isolated findings, executive dashboards should highlight whether identity compromise risk is rising, whether endpoint coverage is slipping, whether privileged access is increasing, or whether cloud misconfigurations are accumulating. These risk curves create a forward-looking perspective that drives investment decisions. If cloud misconfigurations are increasing quarter over quarter, leadership may choose to invest in cloud security posture management. If endpoint coverage drops below acceptable thresholds, executives can prioritize funding for agent deployment or remediation staffing.

A defining characteristic of an effective executive dashboard is its simplicity. Visuals are prioritized over text, and the number of panels is intentionally limited. Executives should be able to interpret the dashboard in under sixty seconds. Trend lines, color-coded risk gauges, pie charts, and minimalist bar graphs provide clarity without overwhelming the viewer. The dashboard should convey business risk in intuitive language: *low, moderate, high*, rather than technical jargon. Its purpose is not to educate executives on detection engineering, it is to empower them to steer the security strategy of the organization.

Design Principles for High-Value SOC Dashboards

Dashboards must be treated as evolving products rather than static artifacts. What matters today may become obsolete tomorrow. A SOC should review dashboards at least quarterly to ensure they remain relevant to operational and strategic decision-making.

Effective dashboards share several principles:

1. Every metric must have a purpose
   If a metric does not drive a decision, clarify risk, or reveal an actionable

insight, it should not exist.

2. Dashboards must be role-specific
   Analysts, managers, engineers, and executives all require different perspectives. One-size-fits-all dashboards fail everyone.

3. Simplicity wins
   Cluttered dashboards mislead more often than they inform. A few high-quality visualizations outperform a wall of mediocre charts.

4. Dashboards must prompt action
   If a dashboard cannot trigger or justify a change in behavior, staffing, or tooling, it is decorative not operational.

5. Metrics must be accurate and consistently sourced
   Inconsistent data undermines trust. All dashboards should pull from authoritative data sources with transparent definitions.

6. Dashboards should highlight exceptions, not just data
   Heatmaps, thresholds, red/yellow/green indicators, and trend deviations help prioritize attention rapidly.

Retiring Metrics: Knowing When a Dashboard Has Outlived Its Usefulness

One of the biggest pitfalls in dashboard development is accumulating too many metrics that once mattered but no longer influence decision-making. A mature SOC routinely retires or replaces dashboards that do not serve a current operational purpose. This keeps the environment lean and responsive.

A metric should be retired when:

- It no longer correlates with risk reduction
- It is no longer used in managerial decision-making
- It becomes automated elsewhere
- It reflects activity rather than outcome
- It encourages vanity behavior (e.g., closing alerts quickly instead of correctly)

Dashboards are tools, not trophies. Their job is to improve situational awareness and guide action not to serve as digital wallpaper. A SOC that masters KPI dashboarding gains powerful visibility into itself. Operational dashboards ensure day-to-day efficiency, detection quality dashboards strengthen the defensive foundation, and executive dashboards translate security into business value. Together, they create a feedback loop of continuous improvement, ensuring the SOC evolves, matures, and adapts to changing threats. Properly designed dashboards are not just visual aids, they are strategic assets that transform raw data into insight, insight into action, and action into security resilience.

Executive Summaries

Executive summaries are the most important section of any SOC report. Many executives read nothing else. A strong executive summary condenses complex technical activity into a clear, accurate narrative.

An effective executive summary answers five essential questions:
What happened?
How was it detected?
What was the impact or potential impact?
What actions were taken?
What should leadership know or decide next?

Language must be concise, factual, and free of unnecessary technical detail. Instead of listing alert types or tools, summaries should describe risk and outcome. For example, rather than stating *"Multiple EDR alerts occurred,"* the summary should state *"Unauthorized access attempts were identified and blocked before systems were impacted."*

An executive summary should also reinforce confidence. Even when incidents occur, demonstrating that controls worked, response was fast, and lessons were incorporated strengthens executive trust.

Communicating Impact and Value

Communicating the value of a SOC is one of the most strategically important responsibilities of security leadership, yet it is often done poorly. Many SOCs focus on technical outputs, alert counts, log volumes, triage hours, or tickets closed because those are easy to measure. But these metrics rarely resonate with executives. Business leaders do not care how many alerts were processed; they care how risks were reduced, how disruptions were prevented, and how the SOC protected revenue, reputation, and operational continuity. In other words, true SOC value is measured not by what happened, but by what did not happen.

To communicate impact effectively, SOC reporting must shift from technical activity to business-aligned outcomes. Blocking a credential theft attempt should not be described as "stopped LSASS scraping on three hosts." Instead, it should be framed as preventing unauthorized access to financial systems, safeguarding sensitive internal data, and reducing the probability of a costly breach. When the SOC stops a malware execution chain, the message is not "malware quarantine successful"it is "this prevented operational downtime and avoided potential data exposure." When a phishing attack is neutralized, the SOC should emphasize how this protected customer trust and avoided brand damage. Executives understand risk, cost avoidance, and business continuity far more intuitively than they understand telemetry or detection rules.

Mapping SOC activity to business risks is one of the strongest techniques for demonstrating value. Each major detection category can be tied directly to high-impact business concerns:

– *Stopping credential theft protects financial systems and access to sensitive records.*

– *Detecting ransomware precursors prevents revenue-stopping outages and regulatory fallout.*

– *Identifying lateral movement attempts protects internal segmentation and prevents multi-system compromise.*

– Surfacing cloud misconfigurations avoids compliance violations and unintended data exposure.

This approach transforms technical events into strategic risk reductions, which is the language boards and executives speak fluently.

Another powerful method is trend analysis. Executives respond to directionality progress over time. Showing that Mean Time to Respond (MTTR) has improved over several quarters, or that false-positive volume has been cut in half, or that detection coverage has expanded across key MITRE ATT&CK techniques instantly communicates maturity. Trend lines demonstrate trajectory: the SOC is not merely operating but getting better. By highlighting measurable improvement, leadership gains confidence that the SOC is evolving and that their investment in cybersecurity is producing tangible returns.

Communicating value also requires connecting actions directly to outcomes. Rather than simply reporting that analysts tuned a detection rule, SOC leaders should explain that the tuning reduced noise, improved analyst focus, and enabled earlier detection of high-risk anomalies. Instead of reporting that additional logs were onboarded, explain that this new telemetry fills a prior blind spot, reducing the likelihood of hidden lateral movement. Each technical action should be framed in terms of the risk reduction it creates and the business exposure it prevents. The SOC must position itself not as a technical cost center but as a business enabler. By articulating how operational security protects revenue, minimizes downtime, ensures compliance, reduces legal exposure, and supports customer trust, the SOC becomes a strategic asset. When executives understand the value in their language, they champion security investments, support staffing strategies, and trust the SOC during crises. In this way, effective communication is not an optional soft skillit is a fundamental operational capability that elevates the SOC from reactive responders to proactive partners in the organization's success.

MSSP-Style Client Deliverables

For Managed Security Service Providers, reporting is not simply documentation, it is a core product that directly shapes client trust, satisfaction, and perception of value. Unlike internal SOC reporting, MSSP deliverables function as both a service update and a strategic communication tool. They must demonstrate proficiency, stability, vigilance, and partnership. The client should walk away from every report feeling *protected*, *informed*, and *supported, never* confused, alarmed, or overwhelmed. MSSP reporting must balance three competing objectives: transparency, professionalism, and reassurance. Transparency ensures clients understand what was observed in their environment, what actions were taken on their behalf, and what risks remain. Professionalism ensures the language, structure, and visual formatting reflect a high level of expertise and operational maturity. Reassurance ensures that information is framed appropriately; clients must see that risks are being managed, not spiraling out of control.

Because many MSSP stakeholders are mixed audiences (CEOs, IT managers, compliance officers, board members), the report must be both technical enough to satisfy security teams and digestible enough for non-technical leaders. This duality requires disciplined writing, structured storytelling, and refined visual design.

Structure and Content of MSSP Deliverables

A standard MSSP monthly (or quarterly) report should follow a consistent, predictable structure. Clients appreciate familiarity; they want to know where to find information, how to interpret it, and how metrics have changed since the previous report. Consistency also allows clients to compare progress over time without re-learning the format.

A well-structured deliverable typically begins with a Service Overview, summarizing the MSSP's scope of work, available services, and monthly activities performed. This reminds clients what the MSSP is responsible for and what protections are in place. It also subtly reinforces the breadth of service, helping clients recognize the value they are receiving.

Next, the report provides an Incident Summary, outlining any significant detections, investigations, escalations, or confirmed incidents that occurred during the reporting period. The narrative should focus on outcomes rather than technical minutiae. For example, instead of stating that abnormal Kerberos requests were detected, the summary should explain that an attempted unauthorized privilege escalation was blocked early, preventing potential lateral movement. Clients respond best to descriptions of what was prevented, not just what was observed. A key part of MSSP value communication is demonstrating operational reliability. For this reason, SLA Performance is typically included. This section shows how the MSSP met or exceeded triage time requirements, notification guidelines, response commitments, and escalation timelines. SLA transparency builds credibility even if an SLA was breached, acknowledging it and explaining the corrective plan increases trust more than hiding it.

Following SLA performance, Notable Detections and Trends provide insight into the client's unique threat landscape. This includes recurrent phishing attempts, anomalous authentication patterns, malware detections, cloud misconfigurations, or exposure trends. These insights should not simply list events, they should connect activity patterns to evolving risks. If the SOC sees an increase in password-spray attempts, the deliverable should explain what this likely signifies and how the MSSP is mitigating it.

Many MSSPs also include Exposure Insights or Vulnerability Observations, even if they do not provide vulnerability management as a formal service. These might include outdated endpoints, risky configurations, unmonitored assets, or missing patches that the MSSP observed during investigations. The tone must remain supportive rather than accusatory exposures are opportunities for improvement, not failures

Writing for Mixed Technical and Non-Technical Audiences

One of the biggest challenges in MSSP deliverables is tailoring content for a mixed readership. The report must satisfy IT and security personnel without alienating executives. Achieving this balance requires careful layering of information. High-level summaries should lead each section, followed by optional technical appendices or detail tables for those who wish to dive deeper.

Clear headings, short paragraphs, and clean visuals improve readability. Jargon should be minimized or accompanied by plain-language explanations. For example, instead of saying "the endpoint initiated SMB enumeration," it is more effective to note "a device attempted to scan nearby systems to see what was accessible, this behavior is commonly associated with early-stage attacker movement."

One highly effective technique is to add a brief section titled "What This Means for You." This distills technical findings into direct business context. If MFA bypass attempts increased, the section might explain how this relates to identity protection. If endpoint detections decreased, the summary might reinforce that the client's posture improved due to recent configuration changes. This short narrative prevents misinterpretation and enhances decision-making.

Recommendations: Actionable and Prioritized

Clients value reports that give them direction, not just data. Recommendations must be specific, actionable, and prioritized according to risk. Vague statements such as "improve endpoint security" or "increase monitoring" add no real value. Instead, recommendations should be concrete: enable MFA for administrative accounts, deploy EDR to the remaining 12% of endpoints, close unused RDP ports, upgrade unsupported operating systems, or apply conditional access policies in the cloud environment.

Prioritization is essential. A client who receives ten recommendations with equal weight will often act on none of them. A client who receives three high-priority items framed in business risk terms is far more likely to act. The MSSP should also indicate which recommendations can be implemented by the client and which can be implemented by the MSSP itself, further reinforcing partnership.

Visual Refinement and Presentation Quality

MSSP deliverables must look professional. Layout, typography, color consistency, and graphical clarity all contribute to the client's perception of competence. Even the most insightful security analysis will lose credibility if presented in a cluttered or amateur-looking format. Many MSSPs adopt branded templates with standardized sections, headers, icons, and charts to provide a polished, uniform experience.

Charts, risk meters, heatmaps, and trend lines help communicate patterns quickly. However, visuals must serve clarity, not decoration. A simple, well-labeled line graph showing declining MTTR over four months carries far more meaning than a complex, multi-variable chart that requires interpretation. The rule of thumb is: if a visual element does not directly strengthen understanding, it does not belong in the deliverable.

Why Consistency Matters

Clients should quickly recognize the format of each month's report. Familiarity builds trust and reduces cognitive load. A consistent structure helps clients compare progress, trends, risks, and improvements over time. For example, if the report always begins with a high-level executive overview followed by operations, detections, SLA metrics, and recommendations, clients will intuitively know where to find what matters most.

Consistency also reinforces operational maturity. A SOC that produces reports in varying formats appears improvisational. A SOC that maintains a stable, professional reporting structure demonstrates control, predictability, and methodological discipline.

Deliverables as Relationship Builders

Above all, MSSP deliverables must demonstrate *partnership*, not mere monitoring. A client should finish reading the report feeling that:

- The MSSP is watching over their environment closely
- The SOC understands their unique risks
- The findings were explained clearly
- The recommended actions are realistic and valuable
- The service justifies its cost

- The client is not alone in mitigating threats

When done well, these deliverables become one of the strongest retention tools in an MSSP's entire business model. They show competence, reliability, and long-term strategic value qualities that keep clients loyal even through difficult incidents or market changes.

Reporting and executive communication are where SOC credibility is established and maintained. Through disciplined reporting cadences, thoughtfully designed dashboards, concise executive summaries, and business-aligned messaging, SOCs demonstrate tangible value and strategic relevance. For MSSPs, reporting is not just communication, it is a deliverable that defines the client experience. This chapter provides the blueprint to ensure every report reinforces confidence, clarity, and trust.

Chapter 16

SOC Budgeting, Scaling & Roadmapping

A SOC that cannot scale responsibly will eventually fail, either by becoming financially unsustainable, operationally overwhelmed, or strategically misaligned with the business it protects. Budgeting, scaling, and roadmapping are not administrative afterthoughts; they are core SOC competencies. Mature SOC leaders understand that every detection, analyst shift, data source, and automation decision carries both technical and financial consequences.

This chapter provides a practical blueprint for forecasting SOC costs, designing scalable staffing models, maintaining documentation integrity, auditing operational health, and building a realistic one-year SOC roadmap that aligns security operations with business growth.

Tool Cost Forecasting

Tool cost forecasting is an essential discipline for every modern SOCinternal or MSSP. Without structured forecasting, tooling expenses grow quietly and exponentially until leadership is blindsided by a massive invoice that forces reactive cuts. A mature SOC treats tooling costs with the same rigor used for performance metrics, risk analysis, and capacity planning. Cost forecasting is not merely financial management, it is a security control that ensures the SOC remains sustainable, predictable, and strategically aligned with business needs.

Understanding Pricing Models Across Security Tools

Each category of SOC tooling has unique pricing mechanics, and forecasting depends on understanding exactly how consumption maps to spend. SIEMs typically charge based on data ingestion volume, either through daily GB ingested or events-per-second (EPS). Even modest increases such as enabling verbose audit logs or onboarding a new cloud service can double or triple ingestion costs overnight.

SOAR platforms often use action-based billing, charging for the number of automated playbook steps executed each month. EDR products license per endpoint, meaning workforce growth, new servers, VDI deployments, and cloud workloads directly impact annual subscription costs. Cloud security tools (AWS, Azure, GCP) fluctuate based on log volume, retention length, and analytic query frequency, making them volatile if not actively monitored. To forecast accurately, SOC leaders must understand these pricing levers and recognize how operational decisions, adding new log sources, increasing retention, and expanding automation directly alter monthly billing.

Establishing Baselines: The Foundation for Cost Modeling

Forecasting begins with detailed measurement. A SOC cannot model future costs without knowing current consumption. At minimum, baselines must include:

- Daily ingestion volume per log source
- Average alert creation rates
- Daily storage consumption and retention impact
- Number of SOAR actions executed
- Total endpoints under EDR coverage
- Cloud logging volume (CloudTrail, Defender for Cloud, Azure Monitor, etc.)

With these baselines, the SOC models "growth curves" using conservative assumptions. Typical modeling scenarios include:

- 15–25% annual increase in endpoints due to hiring or device expansion
- Cloud adoption growth, including new SaaS logs and container workloads
- Retention expansion, often driven by compliance (PCI, HIPAA, FedRAMP)
- Increased log verbosity due to tuning, Sysmon deployment, or audit requirements

Forecasting isn't just multiplying today's spend, it is projecting what tomorrow's security maturity will cost.

Modeling Cost Growth Over Time

Accurate cost modeling is one of the most important and least understood responsibilities in SOC leadership. Security operations rarely remain static; they evolve as the organization grows, regulatory pressures increase, and infrastructure becomes more complex. Because of this, SOC costs are not linear. They expand in waves, influenced by hiring cycles, technology adoption, seasonal workloads, cloud usage surges, and retention mandates. To plan effectively, SOC leaders must build multi-year financial forecasts that anticipate these dynamics rather than react to them.

Effective cost modeling begins with a clear understanding that today's SOC architecture will not look the same in a year or two. Cloud transformation, new applications, M&A activity, endpoint expansion, remote work adoption, and compliance audits can dramatically alter ingestion volumes and tool workloads within months. For this reason, the strongest forecasts are built using quarterly modeling rather than annual snapshots. Quarterly intervals reveal cost inflection points, such as renewal cycles, infrastructure refreshes, or expected periods of increased activity (for example, year-end reporting, tax seasons, or product launches). This format also aligns with executive budgeting calendars, giving leadership a predictable cadence for evaluating SOC financial performance.

A robust cost model does not assume a single future. Instead, SOC leaders build multiple scenarios, each representing different levels of organizational growth and threat pressure. The baseline scenario assumes conservative growth, stable tooling, and minimal architectural changes. This model represents steady-state operations and forms the financial floor. The moderate scenario anticipates increased cloud workloads, adoption of automation workflows, and predictable expansion of monitored assets. This is the most realistic trajectory for most maturing organizations. The high-growth scenario reflects aggressive digital transformation: multi-cloud adoption, expanded compliance retention requirements, additional telemetry sources, and new business units onboarding into SOC visibility. This scenario is critical because it exposes the upper limit of operational cost under stress, enabling executives to prepare for worst-case operational spending.

Each scenario produces a different cost trajectory, and these trajectories become the foundation for strategic budgeting discussions with the CFO, CIO, and executive leadership. When presented clearly, these models allow leaders to compare financial impact across different operational futures, enabling more intelligent resource allocation and long-term planning.

Within these models, several key components shape the cost curve over time. Projected SIEM ingestion costs are often the largest variable. Leaders must model ingestion growth across a 12–36 month window, factoring in log verbosity changes, new applications, increased audit requirements, and cloud-native telemetry sources. SIEM retention strategy also affects cost significantly. Short-term hot storage grows quickly, while archival tiers offer savings but require careful access planning. Forecasting must visualize these cost curves so executives understand the trade-offs between detection performance, compliance obligations, and budget allocation.

Endpoint Detection and Response licensing follows headcount and asset expansion. Cost models should map hiring forecasts, device onboarding rates, and remote workforce expansion to EDR licensing trajectories. Similarly, SOAR workloads must be modeled not just by platform licensing but by action volume. As automation expands, so do per-action costs for cloud-based SOAR platforms. High-automation SOCs may see SOAR become a major budget line item within two years if growth is not modeled accurately.

Threat intelligence subscriptions often renew annually with cost escalators tied to usage or organizational size. Cost models should account for increases in API usage, collection frequency, or access tier. Additionally, cloud logging expenses merit separate forecasting due to their dependence on retention mandates, audit requirements, and the unpredictable nature of cloud service adoption. When organizations expand into new cloud platforms or adopt new managed services, logging automatically expands, sometimes exponentially.

A mature cost forecasting dashboard brings all these components together into a single visual model. It shows SIEM ingestion projections, retention cost curves, EDR licensing growth, SOAR action costs, cloud logging trajectories, and renewal cycles across three distinct scenarios. This allows leadership to simulate decisions; *what happens if the organization shifts to multi-cloud, accelerates automation, or expands to new regulatory frameworks? How do these changes impact SOC spend over the next three years?*

Accounting for Hidden and Indirect Tooling Costs

One of the most common reasons SOC budgets spiral out of control is the failure to account for hidden and indirect tooling costs. Many organizations budget only for the flagship systems such as the SIEM, the EDR platform, and the SOAR engine. These tools may represent the core of SOC capability, but they are only the visible portion of a much larger financial ecosystem. The supporting technologies that surround them often create more cumulative cost than the core platforms themselves. SOC leaders must therefore understand and plan for the full financial landscape, not just the headline purchases.

A realistic SOC budget must include a wide array of supporting technologies. Threat intelligence services often represent the first major layer of additional expense. These include paid intelligence feeds, enrichment platforms, reputation databases, adversary tracking services, dark web monitoring, and geopolitical intelligence modules. Many organizations add these slowly over time, often during incidents or audits, which leads to budget drift. Malware sandboxing and cloud detonation services are similarly underestimated. Dynamic analysis platforms often charge by submission volume, which increases rapidly during active investigations or widespread phishing campaigns. Forensic tooling is another major category of indirect cost. Disk imaging tools, memory capture frameworks, registry differential analyzers, timeline creation tools, and portable IR field kits are often purchased on demand during major investigations. Because these tools are reactive acquisitions, they frequently escape the formal forecasting process. Vulnerability management platforms also impose recurring costs due to licensing models based on asset count, scan frequency, cloud agent usage, and compliance reporting modules. Log archival storage is another silent budget driver. While short term SIEM retention is usually included in initial planning, cold storage, object storage, and retrieval fees grow steadily as retention requirements expand to meet regulatory obligations.

Cloud based SOCs must also consider API gateway charges and ingestion taxes created by large scale automation or cross platform enrichment. Every SOAR action, automated API query, or bulk lookup may incur fractional charges that accumulate significantly over time. Network based tooling introduces additional indirect costs. Packet capture appliances, traffic analyzers, east west visibility solutions, and network threat analytics tools may require hardware refresh cycles, high speed storage, and maintenance contracts. Endpoint platforms often expand through add ons that organizations do not initially plan for. These include modules for device control, identity behavior analytics, data loss prevention, and cloud workload protection. Each of these add ons can double or triple endpoint licensing costs across a large enterprise.

These indirect costs often represent the difference between a stable budget and an unexpected overrun. A mature SOC therefore evaluates every tool through the lens of measurable operational value. Tools must be mapped to specific outcomes such as reduced mean time to respond, reduced false positive rates, expanded ATTACK framework coverage, increased automation reliability, improved detection fidelity, or reduced analyst workload. This mapping transforms tooling decisions from preference based choices into measurable performance investments.

When a tool cannot demonstrate clear value relative to its cost, it becomes a candidate for consolidation or retirement. Many organizations run overlapping tools simply because they accumulated them over time. Others maintain legacy platforms because they fear the migration process. A disciplined SOC continually evaluates whether each tool still contributes to operational effectiveness. Anything that does not support the mission is removed, and anything that duplicates functionality is merged or replaced.

Quarterly Cost Reviews and Tool Rationalization

SOC tooling cannot operate on a "set it and forget it" mindset. Even the most carefully planned security architecture will evolve as environments change, logging expands, workloads multiply, and automation matures. For this reason, a disciplined SOC conducts quarterly cost reviews that compare actual spend to projected forecasts. These financial audits are just as important as operational reviews because they reveal where the SOC is drifting from its expected consumption model and why.

A quarterly review typically begins by examining changes in ingestion volume. SIEM costs increase in direct proportion to log volume, and even small spikes can have significant financial impact. These spikes are often caused by well intentioned engineering teams enabling verbose logging on cloud services or identity platforms without notifying the SOC. In other cases, a new application may begin producing ten times the expected telemetry, or a development environment may suddenly generate production level audit logs. Without continuous monitoring of ingestion trends, these increases can remain unnoticed until the monthly bill arrives.

SOAR action consumption is another area that must be monitored carefully. Automation platforms often charge based on the number of executions or API actions performed. When a playbook contains inefficient loops, redundant enrichment calls, or poorly designed branching logic, the SOC may incur silent but significant cost growth. Quarterly reviews help identify where automations need optimization, consolidation, or rate limiting. This is especially important as analysts increasingly rely on automated enrichment, containment, and validation tasks. As automation usage grows, so does the financial footprint behind it.

Unused licensing represents another recurring source of waste. Over time, organizations decommission systems, retire endpoints, or restructure departments. When these assets are not removed from EDR or SIEM licensing pools, the SOC continues paying for seats that deliver no value. Quarterly license reconciliation ensures that licensing accurately reflects the active environment rather than historical asset inventories. Similarly, cloud workloads can multiply rapidly, especially in development or staging environments. Each new workload introduces additional telemetry, authentication logs, and cloud audit activity, which in turn drives cost. Quarterly reviews provide the opportunity to examine these expansions and determine whether they align with business needs.

A particularly important component of quarterly financial review is the identification of overlapping or redundant tools. Many SOCs accumulate tools gradually over the years, adding a new threat intelligence service here, a new enrichment platform there, or a niche analytics tool during an incident. These tools frequently offer overlapping features. When multiple platforms provide the same value, analysts become fragmented across several consoles, training overhead increases, and operational workflows lose efficiency. Reducing redundancy strengthens the SOC by simplifying its toolchain and sharpening focus. Another hidden generator of cost is under integrated technology. Organizations sometimes purchase a tool for a specific purpose, deploy it partially, and never finish the integration. The platform remains licensed, supported, and maintained, but contributes very little operational value. Quarterly reviews force the SOC to confront these partially implemented systems and make a decision: complete the integration to unlock value or retire the tool to reduce cost and complexity. Cost overruns often have external drivers as well. Regulatory requirements change, especially in industries that follow payment card standards, healthcare mandates, defense compliance frameworks, or financial reporting requirements. A compliance shift from ninety days to one hundred eighty days of retention can instantly double storage cost. A new audit mandate may require ingesting entire classes of logs the SOC never previously collected. Quarterly reviews ensure that these expanding obligations are incorporated into the financial model before they create unexpected deficits.

Rationalization is the natural outcome of these quarterly assessments. Tool rationalization is not simply cost cutting; it is the strategic removal, consolidation, or restructuring of technology to eliminate waste, reduce operational friction, and strengthen the overall architecture. Every tool retired is one less platform to maintain, less training required, fewer integration points to secure, and fewer consoles competing for analyst attention. Rationalization shrinks the attack surface and improves SOC unity by ensuring every tool in the ecosystem serves a defined purpose within a coherent operational model.

A mature SOC views quarterly cost reviews as both a financial safeguard and a security control. Tools that drain the budget without delivering measurable outcomes are liabilities, not assets. Tools that duplicate functionality confuse analysts and slow investigations. Tools that remain unintegrated silently siphon resources. Through disciplined quarterly reviews, the SOC identifies these inefficiencies early and adapts before financial or operational degradation occurs. This disciplined approach allows the SOC to scale sustainably, maintain financial predictability, and concentrate resources on technology that truly improves detection, response, and resilience.

Using Industry Frameworks for Cost Governance

Cost governance in a SOC cannot rely on intuition or ad hoc decision making. As environments expand, cloud workloads scale, and regulatory requirements become more demanding, SOC leaders require structured frameworks to ensure that financial decisions align with operational needs and compliance expectations. Several industry frameworks serve as anchors for disciplined cost management, each reinforcing the principle that financial stewardship is an essential security control rather than a budgeting afterthought.

The NIST Cybersecurity Framework is the most widely adopted standard for operational alignment and resource planning. In the Identify and Protect functions, NIST explicitly emphasizes the need for capacity planning, asset inventory accuracy, and controlled development of security capabilities. For a SOC, this means that cost forecasting is directly linked to the requirement to understand what is being monitored, how much telemetry is being ingested, and what resources are needed to sustain long term visibility. The NIST framework reinforces the idea that financial forecasting is part of risk management. Without adequate funding to ingest cloud logs, maintain endpoint coverage, or operate automation platforms, the organization will not meet the baseline protective controls described in the framework.

The Security Operations Capability Maturity Model, or SOC CMM, provides a more granular view of operational maturity specific to SOC functions. One of its core domains addresses budget and resource optimization, recognizing that a SOC cannot progress through maturity stages without predictable and strategically allocated funding. SOC CMM encourages leaders to evaluate not only the presence of tools but the efficiency with which those tools are used. A SOC may have a world class SIEM, SOAR, and EDR stack but still operate at a low maturity level if cost governance is absent and financial unpredictability undermines sustained operations. By mapping SOC processes to specific SOC CMM maturity levels, leaders can justify budgets, demonstrate cost effectiveness to executives, and identify where financial shortfalls will hinder progress.

ISO 27001 also reinforces cost governance, even though its primary intent is to establish an information security management system. The standard requires controlled procurement, asset management discipline, and formal management of support services. In practice, this means that a SOC cannot simply acquire new tools whenever a problem arises. Every purchase must align with documented needs, approved processes, and monitoring expectations. ISO expects organizations to monitor the effectiveness of financial and operational controls, which naturally extends to reviewing ingestion spend, storage requirements, licensing coverage, and renewal cycles. When a SOC aligns cost governance with ISO 27001, budget planning becomes traceable, auditable, and deeply integrated into the wider security governance framework.

FinOps, the modern discipline for cloud financial management, is increasingly relevant to SOCs that rely on cloud based SIEMs, cloud telemetry pipelines, and elastic storage systems. The FinOps model encourages cross functional ownership of cloud cost decisions, continuous visibility into spend, and shared accountability for consumption. For a SOC, this means analysts, engineers, and leadership work together to understand how query frequency, ingestion volume, retention duration, and automation activity translate into cost. FinOps introduces techniques such as cost allocation tagging, real time spend dashboards, and usage optimization reviews. When applied to a SIEM or cloud based logging system, FinOps transforms cost forecasting from a static budget estimate into a dynamic operational practice that can be adjusted as conditions change. This is essential for organizations where cloud workloads and telemetry volume grow at unpredictable rates.

Integrating these frameworks does more than promote operational rigor. It ensures that the SOC's forecasting and cost governance practices align with recognized audit and compliance expectations. Regulators, auditors, and third party assessors routinely evaluate whether an organization has exercised due diligence in planning and sustaining its security operations. A SOC that uses NIST, SOC CMM, ISO, and FinOps principles can demonstrate not only technical readiness but financial stability. This makes budget discussions easier, strengthens trust with executives, and reduces the likelihood of sudden cost overruns that threaten operational continuity. In short, cost governance grounded in industry frameworks is a hallmark of a mature and strategically aligned SOC.

When tool cost forecasting is treated as a continuous program rather than a once-a-year budgeting exercise, the SOC becomes predictable, financially stable, and operationally mature. Cost discipline ensures:

- The SOC scales sustainably
- Tools support measurable outcomes
- Redundancy and waste are eliminated
- Security investments align with risk reduction
- Leadership receives clear, data-backed financial planning

A SOC that understands and governs its tooling costs protects more than the network; it protects the organization's financial resilience and long-term strategic viability.

Staffing Models

Staffing represents the single largest recurring cost in any SOC budget and the most challenging element to scale intelligently. Unlike tooling, which can be expanded through licensing tiers or automation, human staffing requires navigating expertise gaps, burnout risks, training cycles, retention challenges, and organizational maturity constraints. An effective SOC staffing model is not simply a matter of "how many analysts are needed," but rather how work flows, how automation absorbs repetitive tasks, and how the SOC grows in capability rather than size.

Traditional SOC structures follow the Tier 1 → Tier 2 → Tier 3 escalation model, supported by incident response leads, detection engineers, threat hunters, platform engineers, and SOC managers. While this tiered model remains effective, it cannot scale purely through hiring additions. As environments expand and threats evolve, SOC leaders must adopt a staffing philosophy built on *efficiency and leverage*, not headcount alone. The most scalable SOCs achieve efficiency by shifting repetitive or low-value work away from human analysts and into automation, better detections, and well-defined workflows.

Aligning Staffing Models With SOC Requirements

A SOC cannot function effectively unless its staffing model is designed around the operational realities of the environment it protects. Staffing must be directly aligned with the organization's risk profile, expected alert volume, and the service level obligations defined in its operational agreements. This alignment ensures that the SOC has the capacity to meet detection and response requirements without overwhelming analysts or jeopardizing response quality. A SOC that provides continuous twenty four hour monitoring for hospitals, financial institutions, government agencies, or critical infrastructure faces a fundamentally different operational landscape from a business hours SOC serving lower risk commercial clients. Environments with high consequence failure require immediate response at all times, which means the SOC must maintain full alert handling capability across nights, weekends, and holidays. This requires more than simply rotating analysts through shifts. It demands overlapping shift structures, formal on call escalation procedures, and built in redundancy to handle unexpected absences or turnover. In these environments, a single missed alert can result in regulatory violations, major outages, or patient safety concerns. As a result, staffing must be proactive rather than reactive.

By contrast, business hours SOCs can often operate with a smaller footprint, especially when supported by strong automation, mature tuning practices, and clearly defined after hours escalation procedures. These SOCs focus their daytime staffing on expected operational peaks, then rely on a small on-call team to handle only high severity alerts during off hours. This approach is cost effective for organizations whose risk tolerance allows delayed response for lower severity events. The success of a business hours model, however, depends heavily on accurate severity classification and a reliable automation layer that prevents low value alerts from waking on call personnel unnecessarily. The true differentiator between staffing models is not simply the number of analysts employed but the architecture of how work is performed. SOC leaders must understand how many alerts are generated on an average day, what percentage requires human decision making, how long each type of investigation typically takes, and what service levels must be met. These variables form the backbone of staffing decisions. Without quantification, staffing becomes guesswork, and leadership may over hire, under hire, or allocate personnel inefficiently.

One of the most important metrics is the alert per analyst ratio. This metric captures the realistic number of alerts a trained analyst can handle in a single shift without compromising investigation quality. For example, if analysts can consistently triage and investigate twenty to thirty alerts per shift, and the SOC receives two hundred alerts per day, the staffing model must reflect this demand to maintain acceptable response times. If SLAs require triage within a specific time frame, such as fifteen minutes for high severity alerts or sixty minutes for lower severity ones, staffing must be calculated backward from these obligations. This ensures that analysts are not forced into rushed triage, which increases the likelihood of missed detection or incorrect classification.

Beyond raw alert volume, staffing models must account for the complexity of investigations. A SOC handling primarily authentication anomalies and low level malware detections may require fewer senior analysts than one regularly responding to lateral movement, cloud privilege escalation, or ransomware precursor activity. Investigation depth, average investigation duration, and expected containment activity all influence how staffing must be structured. SOC leaders must also incorporate operational realities into staffing forecasts. Analysts require breaks, training time, knowledge sharing sessions, meetings, and vacation time. Shifts must overlap to ensure continuity. Workloads fluctuate throughout the day and across seasons. New technologies, new log sources, and increased cloud adoption will drive alert volume upward over time. If staffing models do not account for these dynamics, SOC performance will degrade while leadership remains unaware of the root cause.

The most successful SOC staffing models blend quantitative workload analysis with qualitative understanding of team capability, environmental complexity, business risk, and cultural expectations. Staffing becomes not an exercise in headcount allocation but a strategic function that directly influences detection quality, response speed, analyst retention, and overall SOC maturity.

Preventing Burnout Through Sustainable Workload Distribution

Analyst burnout is a silent threat to SOC performance. High alert volume, repetitive triage tasks, and constant exposure to serious security incidents can degrade morale and lead to turnover one of the most expensive SOC costs. A sustainable staffing model includes mechanisms to distribute workload evenly, rotate analysts into higher-skill investigative work, and reduce low-value tasks through automation and tuning.

Instead of expecting Tier 1 analysts to shoulder the full weight of initial triage, SOCs can use SOAR workflows to automate enrichment, benign resolution checks, risk scoring, and context gathering. This not only reduces workload but also improves analyst engagement, as they focus more on meaningful investigative tasks rather than clicking through benign alerts. Over time, reducing the monotony of Tier 1 triage slows attrition, increases skill retention, and preserves institutional knowledge.

SOCs should monitor specific metrics to identify burnout conditions early, including:

- Average alerts handled per analyst
- SLA pressures on each shift
- Backlog accumulation trends
- Mean investigation time per alert type
- Analyst overtime hours

By reviewing these indicators at least semi-annually, SOC leaders can proactively adjust staffing levels, rotate responsibilities, add automation, or modify SLAs before burnout becomes a retention crisis.

Leveraging Automation to Shift Work Left

A scalable SOC does not simply hire more Tier 1 analysts as demand increases, it reduces the amount of Tier 1 work that requires humans. This concept, often called "shifting left," relies on SOAR playbooks, real-time enrichment, correlation logic, and detection engineering improvements. Automation can resolve benign alerts, enrich suspicious alerts with context, run containment actions, or apply business logic before humans ever touch the ticket.

When properly deployed, automation allows a SOC to:

- Reduce the number of alerts needing manual triage
- Lower the cognitive load on analysts
- Increase investigation depth and quality
- Maintain SLA performance with fewer staff
- Scale support for additional clients (in an MSSP model)

By integrating automation early and aggressively, SOCs can maintain efficiency even as endpoint counts, cloud workloads, and telemetry volume increase. Without automation, hiring becomes the only solutionan expensive and unsustainable path.

Building a Skills Pipeline Through Career Progression

Staffing models must also include career progression paths to retain talent and improve capability. Without a growth trajectory, analysts become stagnant and leave for better roles, forcing the SOC into costly and disruptive hiring cycles. A mature SOC maps clear skill transitions:

Tier 1 → Tier 2 → Tier 3 → IR Lead / Threat Hunter / Detection Engineer / SOC Manager

Analysts at each stage should receive structured training, certification pathways, shadowing opportunities, and exposure to increasingly advanced investigative work. Supporting analyst growth not only reduces attrition but also enhances the SOC's long-term effectiveness, as experienced analysts develop intuition, pattern recognition, and cross-domain expertise.

An internal mentorship model pairing junior analysts with senior ones greatly accelerates skill development and provides continuity during incidents.

Reviewing Staffing Models Semi-Annually

A SOC is a living, adaptive system. Its workload, complexity, and operational maturity change continuously as new technologies are introduced, cloud environments expand, threat landscapes evolve, and automation capabilities strengthen. For this reason staffing cannot be treated as a fixed decision. A staffing model that worked twelve months ago may be completely inadequate today. To maintain operational excellence, SOC leaders must conduct formal staffing reviews at least twice per year, aligning personnel levels and skill distribution with real workload metrics and service level expectations.
A semi annual staffing review begins by evaluating the number of alerts handled per analyst per shift. This single metric provides immediate insight into whether analysts are operating within a sustainable workload. When analysts routinely exceed reasonable capacity, the consequences can be severe. Alert quality decreases, true positives are missed, documentation suffers, investigations become rushed, and morale declines. Conversely, if analysts are consistently underutilized, the SOC may be overspending on personnel or failing to leverage analysts for proactive tasks such as hunting or detection engineering.

Understanding this balance is essential for strategic workforce planning.

SLA adherence is another critical measure. When staffing levels fail to match workload, SLA breaches become more frequent, especially during high volume periods or major incidents. A semi annual review examines which SLAs were met consistently, which were missed, and why. If investigations routinely exceed expected timelines, or if triage delays become common, staffing adjustments or process refinements are required. In many cases these issues point to a staffing bottleneck rather than an analyst skill issue. SOC leaders must distinguish between performance problems and capacity problems to prescribe the correct remediation. Backlog length offers an additional indicator of staffing health. A growing backlog is an early warning sign that analysts are struggling to keep pace with incoming events. Backlog growth often correlates with increased false negatives, lower investigation quality, and delayed containment actions. A semi annual review quantifies backlog trends and helps determine whether the SOC needs more analysts, stronger automation, improved tuning, or a broader redistribution of responsibilities across tiers.

Escalation patterns also inform staffing decisions. If Tier 2 or Tier 3 analysts receive more escalations than they can reasonably support, investigations slow, containment decisions are delayed, and high severity incidents risk losing momentum. A semi annual review examines how many escalations occurred, what types of alerts drove them, and whether Tier 1 analysts require additional training to handle early stage investigation work more effectively. In many cases, an increase in escalations indicates either rising threat sophistication or insufficient Tier 1 readiness. Both scenarios require staffing or training adjustments.

Automation metrics provide another perspective. Specifically, SOC leaders must examine the percentage of alerts resolved by automation. A declining automation resolution rate may signal broken playbooks, misconfigured integrations, or an increase in alert types not supported by current automations. In these cases hiring more analysts will not solve the underlying issue. Instead the SOC must invest in refining automation logic and expanding playbook coverage. In contrast, if automation handles the majority of low level triage and enrichment tasks, staffing can shift from high volume triage roles to more advanced positions focused on threat hunting, detection engineering, or proactive security measures. Analyst turnover rates must be evaluated. High turnover is often the result of burnout, unclear progression paths, insufficient training, or overwhelming alert volume. Each resignation carries both financial cost and operational risk. If turnover accelerates, SOC leadership must evaluate whether staffing levels are contributing to analyst fatigue. Semi annual staffing reviews provide a structured opportunity to assess employee experience, team morale, and workload sustainability.

The purpose of the semi annual staffing review is not merely to count personnel but to understand how staffing intersects with performance, workload, risk, and strategic growth. When performed consistently and guided by measurable evidence, these reviews allow the SOC to evolve deliberately rather than reactively. They ensure that analysts remain supported, SLAs remain intact, automation remains optimized, and the organization is continuously prepared to meet rising security challenges.

Successful SOC staffing models are not defined by how many analysts sit in seats, but by how efficiently work flows through the system. Automation absorbs repetitive tasks. Detection engineering reduces noise. Threat hunting identifies gaps early. Career progression retains talent. Operational reviews catch inefficiencies before they become failures. When staffing aligns with workload, risk tolerance, and maturity level, the SOC becomes scalable, stable, and resilient, capable of growing in capability without equal growth in cost.

SOC Scalability Framework

Scalability is often misunderstood as the ability to "grow bigger," but true scalability has nothing to do with size. It is about adapting to increased complexity, increased volume, and increased threat velocity without requiring proportional increases in human effort or financial cost. A scalable SOC absorbs growthmore alerts, more assets, more logs, more clients, more cloud resources, more adversary activity while maintaining consistent performance, predictable spending, and operational calm. This is not achieved through hiring sprees or oversized tooling budgets, but through architectural design, procedural discipline, and cultural maturity.

Architectural Scalability: Building a System That Expands Without Breaking

A SOC's architecture must evolve at the pace of the organization it protects. As businesses move workloads to the cloud, expand globally, adopt new applications, and increase digital transformation, the volume and diversity of telemetry rise dramatically. A SOC built on rigid or monolithic foundations will eventually buckle under this pressure. True scalability is not simply the ability to ingest more logs. It is the capacity to expand without creating bottlenecks, without requiring disruptive redesign, and without sacrificing detection quality or operational stability. Scalable architectures protect the SOC from both technical failure and financial inefficiency by ensuring that growth does not translate into chaos.

Modern SOCs therefore rely on cloud native SIEM platforms and modular ingestion pipelines that scale horizontally. Instead of fixed storage appliances or vertically scaled compute clusters, cloud based SIEMs allow elastic expansion. When telemetry rises, compute and storage expand automatically, allowing the SOC to adjust to new log types, increased event frequency, or large incident spikes. This prevents the operational panic that often accompanies traditional SIEM deployments where increasing ingestion requires expensive hardware refreshes or complex reconfiguration. Cloud platforms also separate storage from processing, which means more logs can be retained without slowing queries or overloading ingestion engines.

A core architectural pillar is queue based ingestion. Rather than pushing logs directly into the SIEM, modern SOCs rely on message brokers such as Kafka, Event Hubs, or cloud based queue services. These systems accept incoming logs and hold them until downstream processors are ready, smoothing out ingestion spikes. This design prevents data loss during periods of high activity such as ransomware outbreaks, mass authentication failures, or cloud misconfigurations that generate rapid bursts of audit events. The queue becomes a shock absorber, ensuring telemetry flow remains consistent and manageable. Without this buffering layer, SIEM ingestion can fall behind, leading to delayed alerts or even data gaps.

Scalable architectures also rely on multi-tiered storage strategies. Hot storage retains recent data for immediate search, warm storage keeps slightly older data at reduced cost, cold storage maintains long term retention for compliance, and archive tiers hold rarely accessed logs at the lowest possible cost. This tiering allows a SOC to meet regulatory retention requirements without overwhelming the budget. It also ensures that heavy investigative activity focuses on performant data while less frequently used logs remain available but inexpensive. This separation dramatically improves query speed and overall SOC efficiency.

Modularity is another fundamental design requirement. Every component of the ingestion pipeline should be replaceable, upgradable, or augmented without rearchitecting the entire system. Parsing engines, enrichment modules, filtering rules, routing logic, and storage destinations must be loosely coupled, allowing changes to occur independently. This prevents cascading failures and shortens development cycles. When a new data source needs onboarding, the SOC should not require custom scripts or bespoke connectors. Instead, standard templates, schema based validation, and dynamic routing rules should permit plug and play onboarding. If adding new logs requires multiple engineering teams to coordinate complex adjustments, the architecture is brittle rather than scalable.

Equally important is the separation of duties within the pipeline. Ingesters collect logs, parsers normalize fields, enrichers add context, routing engines distribute data to appropriate destinations, and analytics platforms apply detection logic. Each component should independently scale based on load. For instance, during a surge in Windows Event logs, only the parsing layer needs to scale, not the enrichment or analytics layers. This prevents wasteful overprovisioning and reinforces architectural resilience.

A scalable SOC architecture must also support evolving detection strategies. As the SOC matures, it will shift from rules based alerts to entity behavior analytics, machine learning models, correlation engines, and cloud identity risk scoring. These advanced analytics require more data, more compute, and greater flexibility in how data is queried and linked. A rigid architecture built around static indices and fixed schemas will falter under these demands. Scalable systems support schema evolution, dynamic fields, and real time data transformation, enabling future ready threat detection without costly overhauls.

Scalability also extends beyond technology. Documentation, onboarding procedures, access models, and governance must scale as well. As the SOC grows to support more business units, more cloud tenants, or more customers (in the case of MSSPs), the architecture must enforce strict tenant isolation, role based access models, and easily repeatable onboarding workflows. Human scalability is just as important as technical scalability. A SOC that expands its ingestion capacity without expanding its operational support processes will quickly become overwhelmed.

Finally, architectural scalability must be tested deliberately. Synthetic log generation, load testing, failover simulations, and ingestion stress tests reveal weaknesses before they cause incidents. Continuous monitoring of ingestion rates, queue depth, storage consumption, and processing latency is essential. Scalable architectures do not remain scalable by accident; they remain scalable through active maintenance, careful design, and ongoing validation.

In summary, a scalable SOC architecture is modular, resilient, elastic, and future ready. It separates ingestion from processing, decouples storage from analytics, supports dynamic growth, and ensures that increases in telemetry do not degrade operational effectiveness. When scalability is treated as a design principle rather than an afterthought, the SOC becomes capable of expanding seamlessly alongside the organization it protects.

Procedural Scalability: Processes That Work at 10 Alerts or 10,000

Technical scalability is only half of the equation. Even the most advanced SIEM, SOAR, or log pipeline will fail under pressure if the operational processes around it cannot scale. True SOC scalability is achieved when procedures remain stable regardless of whether the SOC is handling a quiet day with ten alerts or a crisis day with ten thousand. This requires building processes that are predictable, repeatable, and resilient. A scalable SOC is one where every analyst can rely on the same workflows, every investigation follows the same structure, and every containment action is executed with the same level of rigor. This standardization transforms the SOC from a collection of individual analysts into a unified operational system.

The foundation of procedural scalability is the creation of clear and enforceable standard operating procedures. SOPs define how analysts triage alerts, where they document their work, what evidence they must gather, what queries they must run, and when they must escalate. Without SOPs, analysts behave inconsistently, which results in uneven quality, duplicate work, and wasted time. SOPs reduce cognitive load by giving analysts decision support. Instead of improvising steps for each case, analysts follow a tested and validated sequence that ensures no part of the investigative process is overlooked. When procedures are repeatable, training becomes significantly easier. New analysts can be ramped up faster, and senior analysts spend less time correcting errors or filling procedural gaps.

Reusable playbooks extend this concept into day to day operations. Playbooks guide analysts through common scenarios such as phishing investigations, credential abuse, lateral movement detection, endpoint malware events, or cloud misconfigurations. These playbooks are not limited to automated SOAR versions. They should also exist as documented workflows for human analysts to follow during investigations. A SOC that has established playbooks can scale because each analyst, regardless of experience level, approaches a problem using the same structure. Playbooks reduce variability, increase accuracy, and prevent the SOC from having to reinvent investigative logic every time a familiar alert appears. With this consistency, the SOC can add new staff, expand coverage, or onboard new clients without collapsing under procedural inconsistency.

Equally important is the creation and enforcement of consistent data schemas. Logs are the raw material of SOC operations. If they arrive in inconsistent formats, investigations become slow and unreliable. Data normalization frameworks such as the Elastic Common Schema, the Common Information Model, or the Open Cybersecurity Schema Framework ensure that logs conform to predictable field names and structures. This uniformity allows correlation rules, dashboards, and detection logic to be reused across multiple technologies and business units. It also simplifies onboarding new telemetry sources, because the detection engineering team does not need to rebuild entire logic sets for each unique log format. When schemas remain consistent, the SOC scales analytically, since one rule can apply across many environments with minimal customization.

Enrichment must also be standardized if the SOC wants to grow without friction. Raw alerts are rarely actionable. Analysts need contextual information such as user identity, group membership, device importance, observed attack patterns, asset ownership, network location, and threat intelligence reputation. Procedural scalability requires that this enrichment occur automatically before analysts ever view the alert. When enrichment pipelines operate uniformly across all alert types, analysts receive complete investigative packages rather than fragments that require manual lookups. This dramatically reduces triage time and allows analysts to operate at scale because they are no longer reinventing the initial data gathering process for every alert.

The final cornerstone of procedural scalability is an automation first mindset. As alert volume increases, human analysts become the bottleneck unless repetitive tasks are automated. A scalable SOC does not depend on analysts to gather evidence manually or perform basic checks. Instead, tasks such as identity lookups, host inventory checks, file reputation queries, domain age analysis, sandbox submissions, and repeated historical searches are executed by automation before an analyst opens the case. Even benign alert resolutions can be automated when supported by strong logic. Analysts should spend their time making decisions, not clicking through screens or performing redundant queries.

Over time, automation allows the SOC to grow alert capacity without equivalent increases in staffing. For example, if a SOAR platform automatically enriches and resolves fifty percent of low risk alerts, analysts can focus on the remaining subset that truly requires human judgment. This not only improves scalability but improves morale because analysts spend less time on repetitive and low value tasks.

Procedural scalability therefore transforms the SOC from a reactive team into a disciplined operational program. With SOPs to guide consistency, playbooks to guide investigations, schemas to guide data structure, enrichment pipelines to guide context, and automation to guide efficiency, the SOC becomes capable of handling enormous increases in alert volume without sacrificing quality. It becomes predictable, measurable, and resilient. When these procedures mature, the SOC can scale indefinitely, because its effectiveness no longer depends on individual improvisation but on engineered processes that perform reliably at any volume.

Cultural Scalability: Thinking in Systems, Not Silos

A SOC can engineer the most advanced architecture, implement flawless log pipelines, create mature playbooks, and design a world class automation program. Yet none of this will scale if the culture surrounding the SOC remains fragmented or reactive. Cultural scalability is the human dimension of SOC growth. It determines whether the SOC can absorb increasing complexity, expanding telemetry, larger client portfolios, and heightened threat activity without collapsing under its own operational weight. When culture does not scale, processes break, people burn out, automation stagnates, and technical investments fail to produce meaningful results. A truly scalable SOC is built on a culture that thinks in systems, not silos.

Systems thinking means viewing the SOC as an interconnected organism rather than a collection of isolated tasks. Analysts do not treat alerts as isolated events. Engineers do not treat ingestion issues as isolated technical bugs.

Leadership does not treat performance problems as isolated human errors. Instead, every problem is viewed through the lens of the larger system. When an alert repeatedly generates false positives, analysts log the pattern, detection engineers adjust the rule logic, and automation engineers update enrichment pipelines. The SOC learns from its own feedback loops. Insights travel upward and downward, enabling continuous improvement. In this environment, every alert becomes an opportunity to strengthen the entire system rather than an isolated box to close.

Culturally scalable SOCs also embrace automation as a partner, not a threat. Analysts understand that automation removes repetition, not responsibility. They recognize that the most valuable work they perform is decision making, not manual data gathering. Instead of resisting automation out of fear of job displacement, analysts become champions of it. They identify repetitive tasks that waste time and energy. They propose ideas to detection engineers and SOAR developers. They test new playbooks, refine logic, and provide feedback that makes automation safer and more reliable. This culture creates a positive loop: automation reduces manual effort, analysts gain more time for strategic work, strategic work improves detections, and improved detections produce better automation opportunities.

Cross functional collaboration is another essential component of cultural scalability. Many SOCs struggle not because of technical limitations but because of organizational friction. When SOC, IR, engineering, cloud, network, and IT operations work in isolation, handoffs become slow, misunderstandings grow, and errors multiply. A scalable SOC creates clear communication channels and shared understanding across all supporting teams. SOC analysts understand how cloud engineers structure identity policies. IR leads understand how SOC triage works. Engineering teams understand the operational impact of parsing and ingestion changes. These relationships are built through transparency, routine communication rituals, shared dashboards, and structured escalation paths. As silos dissolve, the SOC begins to operate like a unified command center instead of a patchwork of disconnected departments. Documentation and knowledge sharing form the backbone of a scalable culture. When knowledge resides only in the minds of senior analysts, the SOC becomes fragile. Staff turnover erases institutional memory, slows onboarding, and disrupts operational stability. A scalable SOC captures knowledge in runbooks, internal wikis, process documents, decision trees, training modules, and post-incident summaries that are accessible to the entire team. Analysts write what they learn and share what they solve. Senior staff mentor new hires and teach investigative reasoning, not just tool navigation. Over time, the knowledge base becomes a living artifact that expands with every alert type, every new detection, every hunt, and every technical improvement. This documentation driven culture means each new hire strengthens the system rather than straining it.

Training and professional development are equally essential. A scalable culture invests in its people as much as its tools. Analysts receive structured training paths that evolve from triage fundamentals to advanced investigation, and eventually to detection engineering or threat hunting roles. Engineers receive training on emerging log schemas, evolving adversary tradecraft, and new automation capabilities. Leadership invests in soft skills such as communication, analytical reasoning, and decision quality. This creates a pipeline of talent where junior analysts grow into senior analysts, senior analysts grow into detection engineers or incident responders, and the organization gains internal resilience.

Perhaps the most defining feature of a culturally scalable SOC is psychological safety. Analysts must feel comfortable raising concerns, reporting mistakes, identifying fragile processes, and suggesting improvements without fear of punishment. A SOC that punishes error invites silence, and silence destroys scalability. Scalable cultures treat mistakes as data points in system improvement. Leaders encourage open discussion about detection gaps, broken workflows, and operational inefficiencies. This environment creates a virtuous cycle where issues are surfaced early, resolved quickly, and documented for future prevention. Cultural scalability is about building a team that grows with complexity rather than collapsing under it. It is about fostering an environment where analysts think holistically, engineers anticipate the needs of operations, leadership invests in people, and every individual contributes to the strength of the whole system. When culture scales, every part of the SOC benefits. The SOC becomes smarter, faster, more resilient, and more capable of defending the organization against ever evolving adversaries.

If the technical foundation is the skeleton of the SOC, cultural scalability is its nervous system. One cannot function without the other, and neither can expand alone. Only when both grow together does the SOC achieve true mastery.

Measuring Scalability Across SOC Layers

SOC leaders must evaluate scalability using measurable indicators across four domains: data ingestion capacity, detection performance under load, analyst workload tolerance, and response coordination efficiency.

Data ingestion capacity must be assessed under anticipated growth scenarios. Leaders should simulate log increases from new SaaS applications, expanded cloud environments, or new compliance logging requirements. If ingestion creates latency or performance degradation, the architecture is not yet scalable. Detection performance should be evaluated by monitoring whether rules flood the SOC during volume spikes or whether correlation logic remains stable as event count increases. Poorly designed detection rules may trigger thousands of alerts during activity spikes, overwhelming analysts and damaging incident visibility.

Analyst workload tolerance is measured by tracking alerts per analyst, SLA adherence, mean investigation time, and backlog accumulation. If workload increases linearly with asset growth, the SOC relies too heavily on human effort. If workload increases only marginally despite major telemetry expansion, the SOC is scaling correctly.

Response coordination efficiency reflects how quickly teams align during incidents. This includes bridge call coordination, on-call cross-coverage, containment execution speed, and clarity of roles during escalations. As environments grow, response coordination must remain smooth.

Designing for Scalability from the Start

The most scalable SOCs design every new use case, log source, detection rule, or tool integration with one question in mind:

"What will this look like at 2×, 5×, or 10× today's volume?"

This forward-looking mindset prevents technical debt, runaway alert volume, and cost overruns. When onboarding a new log source, scalable SOCs consider; "*How many alerts will this generate? How will enrichment handle the increased load? Does this introduce parsing complexity? Will detection logic fire too often? Does this materially improve risk visibility?*" When implementing a new detection rule, they consider; "*How this rule scales across thousands of endpoints? Whether it requires expensive queries? Whether automation can handle resolution? How many false positives it might generate?"*

A scalable SOC is not defined by the number of analysts, the size of the SIEM, or the volume of alerts it can ingest. It is defined by its ability to grow without breaking, its efficiency per unit of telemetry, its automation maturity, its cultural adaptability, and its architectural resilience.

Documentation and Versioning

Documentation serves as the institutional memory of the SOC. It is the backbone that supports day to day operations and the historical record that preserves lessons learned. Without disciplined documentation, a SOC becomes dependent on tribal knowledge that exists only in the minds of experienced analysts. When those individuals leave, or even when they simply move to another shift, much of that operational wisdom disappears. Processes become inconsistent. Alert quality drifts over time. Investigations vary widely based on who is working the case. Mistakes that were solved last month suddenly reappear because no written guidance prevented their return. In short, documentation is not paperwork. It is the glue that binds operational excellence together.

Mature SOCs treat documentation as a living system rather than an assortment of detached files. This system grows and evolves as workflows change, detections improve, and new threats emerge. Playbooks are updated when tuning occurs. SOPs evolve alongside new tools or data sources. Escalation paths are revised after major incidents reveal bottlenecks. Every meaningful operational adjustment is reflected in the written record. This mindset ensures that documentation stays current and does not decay into a graveyard of forgotten PDFs.

Modern SOCs use version controlled repositories to manage this continuous evolution. These repositories may live in GitHub, GitLab, Bitbucket, Confluence with version tracking, or internal knowledge bases with revision history. Version control is essential because it preserves the lineage of every update. Analysts can examine older versions of a rule to understand why a threshold was changed. Managers can audit which team member approved an escalation path revision. Engineers can determine whether a recent spike in false positives correlates with a tuning update from last week. This traceability transforms documentation from static text into an accountable, auditable operational asset. Versioned documentation becomes especially critical during external audits or legal reviews. Auditors routinely request evidence that procedures existed at a specific moment in time and that analysts followed approved workflows. Legal or compliance investigations often rely on historical documentation to reconstruct events accurately. Without versioning, a SOC cannot demonstrate procedural consistency or defend decisions made under pressure. With it, the SOC can show precise change records, approval paths, and operational reasoning. This assurance strengthens trust with regulators, clients, and executive leadership.

Documentation also plays a central role in onboarding new analysts. A SOC that does not invest in structured knowledge forces new hires to learn through inconsistent verbal explanations, informal shadowing, or trial and error. This creates variability in performance and extends the training timeline. High quality documentation, however, shortens the learning curve significantly. New analysts arrive with access to clear triage guides, escalation flows, detection engineering references, ticketing expectations, and communication templates. They are not left guessing how to approach each alert type. They have a playbook that reflects real experience gathered over months or years. As a result, the SOC gains consistency, reliability, and predictable performance across analysts and shifts.

Robust documentation must cover the full operational ecosystem. This includes playbooks that outline step by step triage workflows, incident response procedures that guide analysts through containment and eradication, threat hunting frameworks that define methodology, communication guidelines that govern client notifications, and tool reference material that explains how to use SIEM queries, EDR timelines, or identity investigation panels. The documentation should not only state what to do but also explain how to do it in practical terms. Screenshots, diagrams, examples, caution notes, and scenario driven explanations give analysts the confidence to execute tasks properly even under pressure.

Another major advantage of documentation and versioning is the ability to prevent regression. When a detection or workflow fails after a recent change, engineers can immediately track the exact modification that created the issue. This rapid diagnosis dramatically reduces operational downtime and prevents prolonged false positive storms. Without historical documentation, teams must rely on memory and assumptions to determine what went wrong. With documentation, they rely on data.

For documentation to function as a true operational pillar, it must be woven into the culture of the SOC. Teams must contribute to it regularly rather than treating it as a secondary chore. Every detection tuning change should include a corresponding entry in the repository. Every update to a containment workflow should be recorded before analysts rely on it. Every procedural improvement should be reviewed, approved, versioned, and published. Leadership must reinforce this discipline by validating documentation compliance during post incident reviews, shift handoffs, and team meetings.

Documentation and versioning define whether a SOC operates with maturity or improvisation. Immature SOCs rely on memory, fragmented notes, and informal knowledge sharing. Mature SOCs rely on structured information, repeatable processes, and clearly recorded reasoning. This difference determines whether the SOC can scale with growing telemetry, pass demanding audits, maintain operational continuity during turnover, and maintain investigative quality across analysts and time zones. Documentation is more than a record. It is the operational soul of the SOC. When maintained with discipline and versioned with precision, it becomes a force multiplier that enhances capability, continuity, and trust for the entire organization.

SOC Audits & Health Checks

SOC audits and health checks function as the objective mirror through which an organization examines its operational integrity, its consistency, and its readiness for real threats. Daily operations reveal only surface level patterns. Analysts see the alerts in front of them. Engineers see the rules they create. Managers see the immediate workload and performance metrics. What they do not see are the deeper systemic issues that accumulate gradually. These hidden weaknesses often form during routine work, unnoticed until an incident exposes them at the worst possible moment. Audits uncover these slow moving risks. They force the SOC to confront whether it is operating as it believes it is or whether process drift, tooling misalignment, or cultural shortcuts have altered critical workflows. A SOC that does not audit itself becomes vulnerable to silent degradation. A SOC that embraces audits grows predictably and significantly over time.

Audits appear in several different forms, each serving a unique role. Internal audits are conducted by the SOC leadership team or by internal governance groups. These reviews allow the SOC to measure adherence to standard operating procedures, evaluate the accuracy of escalation decisions, and verify whether analysts follow established workflows. Internal audits also reveal disconnects between what the SOC believes it is doing and what is actually happening on the ground. External audits, performed by third party assessors, bring an unbiased outside perspective. These auditors evaluate whether the SOC operates with maturity, consistency, and evidence based practices. Clients, regulators, and executives often place great trust in external audit results because they come without internal influence.

Compliance driven audits represent a separate category. These reviews are required under regulatory frameworks such as PCI DSS, HIPAA, SOX, FedRAMP, ISO 27001, or SOC 2. Compliance audits are not concerned solely with technical performance. They examine documentation, governance, and evidence of procedural consistency. They test whether the SOC is capable of providing accountability. These audits also influence business outcomes directly, because a failure in compliance may restrict the organization's ability to operate in regulated industries or to gain new customers. Maturity focused audits, often aligned to models such as NIST CSF, SOC CMM, or MITRE ATT and CK evaluation frameworks, measure not only whether the SOC performs required tasks but whether it performs those tasks effectively and strategically. These audits help leadership understand the SOC's developmental stage and what investments are required to advance it.

Health checks operate at a different tempo and with a different purpose. They are less formal than audits, yet they are equally important. A health check measures whether the SOC is functioning properly in its daily operations. It assesses the overall health of detections, processes, response times, and staff workload. A well designed health check examines detection coverage to determine whether important attack surfaces remain unmonitored. It reviews false positive rates to identify rule deficiencies or tuning gaps. It measures adherence to service level commitments, ensuring the SOC does not drift away from contractual or operational expectations. Health checks also evaluate alert fatigue and analyst workload to detect early signs of burnout, which can degrade performance quietly for months before becoming noticeable.

Health checks must also examine tooling configuration. SIEM parsers may silently break during system updates. Correlation rules may be disabled accidentally or misconfigured without triggering obvious errors. SOAR playbooks may fail silently when an API changes. Ticketing platforms may be misaligned with escalation workflows. These issues directly affect detection fidelity and response speed, yet they rarely reveal themselves until the environment is reviewed comprehensively. Health checks ensure that tools behave as documented and that engineers maintain disciplined configuration management. When discrepancies appear, corrective actions must be immediate to prevent long term degradation.

Timing is critical. Audits and health checks must be scheduled proactively. Waiting until a major incident or client complaint triggers an audit is already a sign of organizational failure. Quarterly internal health checks offer a natural cadence that balances depth with continuity. These reviews allow teams to catch drift early and correct it long before the issues become visible to clients or leadership. Semi annual or annual external audits provide a deeper, more formal assessment that often reveals blind spots internal teams have learned to overlook. A combination of these rhythms creates a layered governance structure that maintains both daily stability and long term strategic growth.

The tone of an audit influences its impact. When audits are framed as punitive exercises, analysts hide mistakes, engineers resist transparency, and managers avoid acknowledging problems. This creates a culture of fear that undermines the purpose of auditing. A healthy audit culture is built on improvement, not punishment. Findings are not failures. They are opportunities for growth. Each identified issue becomes a directive to refine tuning, to bolster staffing, to enhance documentation, or to redesign workflows. When the SOC treats audit results as strategic input for its roadmap, audits shift from administrative requirements to engines of operational advancement.

A mature SOC sees audits as validation of its discipline. It welcomes scrutiny because scrutiny confirms the rigor of its workflows and the reliability of its detections. Regular audits become part of the rhythm of operations, reinforcing standards, revealing dormant risk, and ensuring that the SOC remains aligned with evolving adversary tradecraft and the expectations of regulators and executive leadership. Over time, audit readiness becomes a sign of operational maturity, not merely a compliance obligation.

Building a One-Year SOC Roadmap

A one year SOC roadmap serves as the guiding instrument that transforms security operations from a state of reactive maintenance into a disciplined program of strategic advancement. Without a roadmap, the SOC drifts from crisis to crisis, chasing whatever problem appears next. With a roadmap, the SOC evolves deliberately, strengthens predictably, and aligns its operational plans with the broader mission of the enterprise. The roadmap establishes what the SOC intends to build, refine, retire, and mature over the next twelve months, anchored by business priorities and organizational risk appetite.

A strong roadmap begins by assessing the SOC's current state through audits, health checks, incident trends, and capability evaluations. Leadership must understand the SOC's strengths, operational bottlenecks, staffing gaps, tooling limitations, and environmental blind spots. This assessment becomes the foundation for the roadmap's progression. Once the baseline is established,

SOC leaders identify strategic themes that will define the upcoming year. Common pillars include expansion of telemetry, rationalization of existing tools, maturation of core detections, increase of SOAR driven automation, growth of threat hunting programs, and advancements in reporting and executive communication. These themes ensure that efforts are not scattered but organized around coherent goals.

Each theme is then broken down into specific initiatives. Initiatives should be actionable and measurable. For example, improving detection quality may include creating new use cases aligned to ATT and CK, tuning noisy rules, redesigning correlation logic, and expanding schema standardization across log sources. Expanding telemetry coverage may include onboarding cloud logs, increasing endpoint visibility, improving identity logging, or integrating new network sensors. Strengthening automation may include building enrichment micro automations, redesigning playbooks, expanding containment coverage, or eliminating redundant manual steps. The roadmap must also account for industry or regulatory expectations. Many organizations require milestones tied to compliance frameworks such as PCI DSS or ISO 27001, which influence the scope and timing of SOC initiatives.

Every initiative in the roadmap should have an assigned owner, timeline, budget estimate, and required dependencies. Ownership drives accountability. Timelines prevent drift. Budget estimates allow leadership to evaluate financial feasibility. Dependencies highlight prerequisites that must be completed before other tasks begin. Initiatives without clear ownership or dependencies often stall, creating long term operational debt. A well crafted roadmap avoids this by ensuring that each body of work has a responsible leader, a clear definition of success, and alignment with ongoing SOC operations. A one year SOC roadmap is never static. It must be reviewed quarterly to incorporate new information. Incident trends may reveal a surge in identity based attacks, prompting earlier investment in identity detections. Audit findings may show gaps in containment procedures, requiring reprioritization of runbook development. Business expansion into new cloud services may introduce new telemetry requirements. Emerging threats, especially those driven by global campaigns, may force the SOC to accelerate detections related to lateral movement, privilege abuse, or cloud control plane manipulation. A roadmap that does not evolve with environmental conditions is not a roadmap; it is a list of outdated objectives.

Although the roadmap is a technical document, it is also an essential communication tool. Executives and clients rarely understand the inner workings of SOC processes, but they understand deliberate plans and strategic direction. A clear roadmap demonstrates that the SOC is not merely reacting to events but steering toward measurable improvement. This level of transparency builds trust and encourages continued investment. It also helps manage expectations, since leadership can see what the SOC intends to achieve within the year and what requires additional resources to accomplish. A well communicated roadmap supports funding discussions. When SOC leaders present initiatives within a structured and forecasted plan, it becomes easier for executives to approve investments in automation, tooling upgrades, staffing additions, or expanded detection coverage. The roadmap links spending to outcomes, such as reduced response time, improved telemetry depth, better compliance alignment, or increased resilience against modern attack chains. This framing shifts the SOC in the eyes of leadership from a cost center to a strategic capability that protects business continuity.

The strength of a SOC roadmap lies not only in what it contains but in how consistently it guides decision making. When the roadmap is used actively, it shapes weekly priorities, monthly progress reviews, quarterly planning cycles, and long term architectural decisions. It helps leaders determine which initiatives are foundational and which are enhancements. It also ensures the SOC avoids overextension, focusing on achievable progress rather than a laundry list of idealistic goals.

A mature SOC understands that budgeting, scaling, and roadmapping form the structural core of sustainable operations. Cost forecasting prevents financial surprises. Staffing models ensure analysts are neither overwhelmed nor underutilized. Scalable architecture and disciplined processes allow the SOC to absorb growth without losing quality. Documentation and versioning preserve institutional knowledge. Regular health checks keep the SOC aligned with its standards. Finally, a strong roadmap ties all these elements together into a cohesive vision. It allows the SOC to grow stronger rather than more fragile, more intentional rather than reactive, and more aligned with both business objectives and the realities of an evolving threat landscape.

SECTION VI

TOOLS: EXPLANATIONS & HOW THEY WORK

Chapter 17

Deep Dive: SIEM Tools

A SIEM is not a single product category, it is a philosophy of security data engineering. While vendors market SIEMs as dashboards or alerting platforms, their real value lies in how they ingest, normalize, correlate, store, and analyze massive volumes of telemetry. Understanding how major SIEM platforms function internally allows SOC teams to design better pipelines, write higher quality detections, control costs, and avoid architectural mistakes. This chapter examines four leading SIEM platformsSplunk, Microsoft Sentinel, Elastic, and LogRhythmnot from a feature checklist perspective, but from the standpoint of *internal mechanics and operational behavior*.

Splunk: Index-Centric, Search-Driven Architecture

Splunk is fundamentally designed around an index centric architecture that allows it to manage extraordinary volumes of machine data while giving analysts the freedom to search and interpret that data in dynamic ways. At its core, Splunk ingests raw events from countless sources and transforms them into structured entries that live inside time organized indexes. When logs arrive, Splunk immediately enriches them with metadata such as timestamp, host, source, and sourcetype. These metadata fields become the anchors for filtering, categorization, and long term retrieval. What distinguishes Splunk from many other platforms is its decision to delay most field extractions until search time. This allows analysts to customize searches for new requirements without altering ingestion pipelines, giving Splunk unmatched adaptability. The tradeoff is simple but important. Splunk demands efficient query design and strong engineering practices to avoid overwhelming the search infrastructure.

The architecture of Splunk can be understood through three essential components: forwarders, indexers, and search heads. Universal forwarders sit closest to the data. These small and efficient agents collect logs from endpoints, servers, network devices, and applications, then send the data to indexers. Heavy forwarders add an additional layer of processing for organizations that need filtering or transformation before ingestion. Once data reaches the indexer tier, Splunk performs the bulk of its work. Indexers parse incoming events, extract preliminary fields, assign metadata, build index structures, compress data for storage efficiency, and store it in time series buckets that optimize both speed and retention. Search heads act as the analytical brain. They execute user queries, distribute work across indexers, merge results, and power dashboards, visualizations, and incident reviews. This distributed model allows Splunk to scale outward as telemetry grows, but it requires careful planning of hardware, cluster layout, and resource allocation.

Splunk Enterprise Security builds on this architectural foundation by introducing correlation searches. These scheduled searches evaluate patterns across multiple indexes and event types, identifying sequences of behavior that may indicate adversary activity. Each time a correlation search identifies concerning conditions, it generates a notable event. These notable events populate the Incident Review dashboard, where analysts triage, assign severity ratings, escalate cases, and document findings. Over time, this workflow becomes an operational heartbeat for SOC teams. The structure encourages consistency, promotes disciplined review habits, and provides a reliable timeline of analyst decisions.

One of Splunk's most advanced features is its risk based alerting model. Rather than sending alerts from single events, Splunk assigns risk scores to entities such as users, hosts, applications, or service accounts. A single suspicious action may register as low risk, but when several unrelated but unusual behaviors occur within a defined period, the cumulative risk may reach a threshold that automatically triggers an alert. This approach mirrors how real adversaries operate. They rarely reveal themselves in a single event; rather, their patterns become suspicious only when viewed collectively. Risk scoring allows Splunk to reduce false positives dramatically while improving the accuracy of true positive detection. Environments that invest in this model gain a strategic advantage because their alerts are tied to entity behavior instead of individual log lines.

However, Splunk's flexibility creates operational responsibilities that cannot be ignored. Because Splunk delays much of its parsing until search execution, poorly written queries can cause slow searches, delayed alerts, and even timeouts. These issues grow worse as ingestion increases. Splunk licensing also ties cost to daily ingest volume, so careless or redundant data onboarding can lead to unexpected expenses. To avoid these pitfalls, mature SOCs adhere to strict engineering practices. They define clear sourcetypes. They maintain logical index structures. They enforce naming conventions. They optimize search performance with base searches, summary indexes, and data model acceleration. They validate field extraction patterns to ensure consistency across log sources. They also leverage Splunk's Common Information Model to normalize data so that searches and dashboards operate uniformly across Windows, Linux, cloud telemetry, identity systems, and network appliances. A successful Splunk deployment therefore requires balance. It must balance ingestion volume with search performance. It must balance field flexibility with compute cost. It must balance detection fidelity with correlation complexity. When these elements are managed well, Splunk becomes more than a SIEM. It becomes a real time analytics engine, a forensic search platform, a pattern recognition system, and the central nervous system of the SOC. When poorly managed, Splunk can suffer from slow searches, ingest bottlenecks, and runaway cost growth.

When Splunk is engineered with discipline, governed by strong data standards, and operated by teams that understand search optimization and detection science, it becomes one of the most capable security analytics platforms in the world. It supports advanced threat detection, rapid incident investigations, unified visibility across diverse environments, and scalable operational growth. In the hands of a mature SOC, Splunk transforms from a log repository into a strategic powerhouse that elevates security operations far beyond traditional monitoring.

Microsoft Sentinel: Cloud-Native, Analytics-Driven SIEM

Microsoft Sentinel represents a complete rethinking of what a SIEM can be when it is built entirely inside a cloud ecosystem. Rather than relying on physical servers, storage arrays, clustered search heads, or manually tuned index pipelines, Sentinel uses Azure as its operational backbone. All scaling, storage expansion, compute allocation, and backend optimization occur behind the scenes. As a result, Sentinel allows SOC teams to focus almost entirely on security outcomes rather than on SIEM infrastructure management. This design is especially valuable for organizations that want global reach, rapid onboarding, and the ability to scale detection capabilities without rearchitecting their monitoring environment every few years.

In Sentinel, all telemetry begins with connectors. Microsoft provides a large catalog of prebuilt connectors for Azure AD, Entra ID, Microsoft Defender, Exchange Online, Teams, Intune, Azure Firewall, and hundreds of third party products. These connectors send logs to Azure Monitor and then into Log Analytics workspaces. A Log Analytics workspace functions as the logical core of Sentinel. It is where tables such as SecurityEvent, Syslog, DeviceEvents, AuditLogs, and SigninLogs are stored. Every table is timestamped, indexed, and optimized for analytical queries. The cloud native design means the SOC never has to worry about storage performance, ingest bottlenecks, or hardware procurement cycles. If capacity increases, Azure expands automatically.

One of the most important operational differences between Sentinel and traditional SIEM platforms is the choice to parse and normalize logs at ingestion time. Sentinel performs JSON flattening, field extraction, schema alignment, and structural enrichment before data is written to disk. This approach improves search performance dramatically because Kusto Queries read data that is already structured. It also enhances correlation because events across products share consistent field names. However, ingestion time parsing requires discipline. A misconfigured parser can generate malformed tables or inflated ingestion costs. Increasingly, Microsoft aligns Sentinel to the Open Cybersecurity Schema Framework, allowing multi vendor logs to conform to a common set of fields. This reduces confusion, simplifies use case development, and accelerates engineering work.

The core analytical engine behind Sentinel is the Kusto Query Language, which is optimized for time series investigation, massive scale filtering, security analytics, and rapid data exploration. KQL is both expressive and efficient. Analysts can perform joins across billions of rows, calculate anomaly scores, model behavioral patterns, and pivot between identity logs, endpoint activity, and cloud resource changes with remarkable speed. This responsiveness changes how analysts work. Instead of waiting for long searches to complete, they can explore hypotheses rapidly and iterate during live investigations. KQL becomes both a triage tool and a forensic platform.

Sentinel detection logic revolves around scheduled Analytics Rules that execute KQL queries at defined intervals. These rules can detect simple threshold spikes, multi step attack chains, lateral movement sequences, cloud privilege misuse, identity anomalies, or behavioral signals tied to machine learning models. When a rule fires, Sentinel automatically generates an Incident. Unlike alerts in some other SIEM platforms, Sentinel incidents consolidate related events so analysts receive a unified case rather than a scattered collection of atomic alerts. This grouping reduces noise and helps analysts see the broader pattern of the attack.

A major advantage of Sentinel is its deep and seamless integration with the Microsoft security suite. Defender XDR, Entra ID, Exchange Online, SharePoint, Teams, and Azure workloads feed rich telemetry that correlates automatically. Analysts gain immediate visibility into the relationships between identity events, endpoint behavior, email delivery and malware scanning, cloud resource modifications, and network communication patterns. This unified visibility is extraordinarily difficult to achieve with traditional SIEM deployments that require extensive parsing and normalization work.

Automation is another area where Sentinel excels. Azure Logic Apps serve as the SOAR layer, allowing playbooks to run enrichment routines, notify analysts, quarantine devices, disable accounts, block suspicious IP addresses, or trigger forensic collection workflows. These automations scale effortlessly because Logic Apps are built on the same elastic infrastructure as the SIEM. The result is an automation system that grows with the organization rather than requiring reengineering whenever load increases.

Investigations occur inside Sentinel's Incident Queue, a workspace where analysts can assign severity, track case progress, review related evidence, and examine entity timelines. Graph based mapping shows relationships between accounts, devices, IP addresses, events, and resources. For cloud environments, this visualization capability is especially useful because attacks often unfold across identity, compute, and storage layers rather than within a single server or endpoint. Despite its strengths, Sentinel introduces two operational challenges. First, cost predictability is difficult without careful ingestion management. Azure charges for ingestion volume and retention duration. Verbose logs or redundant tables can inflate monthly spend significantly. SOC leaders must review diagnostic settings, filter unnecessary categories, and tune retention tiers to control budget growth. Secondly, Sentinel requires analysts to develop competence in KQL, Azure identity architecture, cloud resource configuration, and Microsoft Defender telemetry. Without sufficient training, teams may fail to unlock Sentinel's full potential and depend too heavily on default rule templates.

Nevertheless, when deployed with discipline, Microsoft Sentinel becomes one of the most scalable SIEM platforms available. It supports rapid expansion, global operations, elastic automation, and seamless correlation across identity, cloud, endpoint, and application layers. For modern enterprises embracing cloud first strategies, Sentinel offers a security foundation that grows effortlessly while enabling sophisticated analytics and real time operational insight.

Elastic SIEM: Schema-Driven, Search-First Analytics

Elastic SIEM is built upon the broader Elastic Stack, a collection of tightly integrated technologies that include Beats, Logstash, Elasticsearch, and Kibana. Together they form a powerful and highly customizable security analytics ecosystem. What distinguishes Elastic from many traditional SIEM platforms is its schema first philosophy. Rather than waiting to interpret and normalize data at search time, Elastic emphasizes early normalization through the Elastic Common Schema. ECS provides a standardized way to represent processes, network connections, authentication events, cloud activity, file operations, and host telemetry. By enforcing consistency from the beginning, Elastic significantly reduces ambiguity, improves detection reliability, and creates a clean foundation for correlation and threat hunting. Analysts spend less time deciphering inconsistent field names and more time interpreting attacker behavior.

Ingestion begins with Beats, which are lightweight agents tailored for specific telemetry types. Filebeat handles logs from systems and applications, Winlogbeat collects Windows event logs, Auditbeat monitors audit frameworks and system integrity, Packetbeat observes network traffic, and Metricbeat provides performance statistics from hosts and workloads. This specialization means agents collect exactly what they need without the complexity often found in general purpose log forwarders. Many organizations route Beats into Logstash, which acts as an enrichment and transformation engine. Logstash pipelines can extract fields from raw logs, normalize them to ECS, enrich them with threat intelligence, perform geo location lookups, apply custom transformations, and prepare the data for indexing. This approach shifts analytical value upstream. When events reach Elasticsearch, they are already structured, enriched, and ready for rapid search.

Elasticsearch is the heart of Elastic SIEM. It is a distributed search engine designed for massive scale and lightning fast analytics. Logs are stored across indices and shards, allowing the system to distribute load horizontally across nodes. Elastic clusters grow simply by adding more nodes, without requiring monolithic upgrades or rearchitecture. Elasticsearch excels at full text search, complex aggregations, nested queries, time series analysis, and real time correlation. For SOCs that rely heavily on threat hunting, timeline reconstruction, or rapid multi source investigations, Elastic provides a level of speed and responsiveness that is difficult to match. Even when analysts query billions of events, Elasticsearch can return results in seconds, enabling rapid experimentation during investigations.

Detection logic in Elastic is implemented through rules that evaluate ECS aligned fields. Because the underlying data is normalized and consistent, the rules tend to be more stable and easier to maintain compared to SIEM platforms with unpredictable schemas. Elastic supports several types of detection logic. Threshold rules identify spikes or suspicious patterns. Indicator rules match known bad hashes, IP addresses, domains, or filenames. Event sequence rules capture multi step attacker behaviors. Behavioral rules identify anomalies or deviations from expected system or user activity. Elastic also includes a substantial library of ready to use detections aligned with the MITRE ATT and CK framework. This library accelerates early deployment and gives SOC teams a reliable baseline for common attack patterns.

Elastic Security extends the SIEM with investigation tools, case management features, entity timelines, relationship graphs, and visualizations that allow analysts to reconstruct events across multiple indices. Kibana, the visualization layer, provides dashboards, saved searches, interactive filters, and custom visual representations of data. Kibana's timeline interface allows analysts to stitch together events drawn from different log sources into a coherent narrative, revealing attacker movement across hosts, cloud platforms, or identity systems.

One of the most attractive qualities of Elastic is the control it offers. Many organizations choose to self host Elastic to avoid cost models that charge by ingestion volume. With self hosting, cost is determined primarily by hardware and storage allocation rather than daily ingest limits. This makes Elastic appealing for large enterprises and MSSPs that regularly process enormous volumes of telemetry. The tradeoff, however, is operational effort. Elastic clusters require careful tuning to avoid performance degradation. Engineers must monitor shard allocation, JVM memory usage, index lifecycle policies, disk I O performance, node health, and cluster stability. High availability configurations require architectural planning, and poorly tuned clusters can slow searches, delay alerts, or increase the risk of data loss. Elastic provides powerful capabilities, but it expects technical maturity from the teams managing it.

Detection effectiveness in Elastic depends heavily on clean, consistent, and complete ECS adoption. If logs arrive with inconsistent field names, missing timestamps, improper formatting, or incomplete enrichment, detection rules may fail silently. Threat hunts may generate misleading results. Correlation across sources may break. Analysts depend on fields such as process executable, process command line, source IP, destination port, event action, and file hash to behave predictably across all telemetry. When those assumptions hold, Elastic becomes exceptionally powerful. When they do not, detection quality deteriorates. Few SIEM platforms reward good data hygiene as clearly as Elastic.

Despite these operational challenges, Elastic SIEM is one of the most versatile, high performance, and cost efficient SIEM platforms available. It is ideal for organizations that want complete control over ingestion, search, retention, and cluster design. It supports deep, rapid threat hunting, aggressive indexing strategies, large scale detection engineering programs, and fully customizable dashboards. Elastic's architecture appeals to teams that prefer engineering discipline and flexibility rather than vendor imposed constraints. With the right expertise, Elastic becomes a formidable foundation for advanced SOC operations, enabling analysts to identify sophisticated threats with precision, speed, and analytical depth. Elastic's greatest strength is also its greatest demand: it gives the SOC complete control. For teams with the skill and maturity to manage it, Elastic becomes a powerful, adaptable, and deeply transparent security analytics engine capable of supporting world class detection and response programs.

LogRhythm: Appliance-Oriented, Correlation-Centric Design

LogRhythm represents one of the more traditional SIEM architectures still widely deployed in enterprise environments. Unlike cloud-native or open-search architectures, LogRhythm is built around dedicated appliancesphysical or virtualeach assigned a specific role within the overall SIEM ecosystem. This appliance-centric design appeals to organizations that prioritize deterministic performance, tight environmental control, and simplified compliance alignment. Many regulated industries including healthcare, financial institutions, and defense contractors continue to rely on LogRhythm because of its predictable architecture and strong case workflow capabilities.

Log ingestion in LogRhythm begins with system agents or syslog collectors that forward data to the platform's Mediator component. The Mediator acts as the central parsing and distribution hub. As logs are ingested, they are normalized against LogRhythm's proprietary schema, which standardizes fields across disparate data sources. This standardization is a core strength of LogRhythm: analysts do not need to memorize multiple field names or log formats because the SIEM enforces consistency at ingestion. Once normalized, data moves into one of LogRhythm's defining features: the AI Engine. The AI Engine is the analytical heart of the platform, applying rule-based correlation, statistical analysis, and behavioral modeling. Despite the name, the AI Engine does not operate like machine learning systems in modern behavioral analytics products. Rather, it executes highly structured correlation logic created by engineers or drawn from LogRhythm's extensive rule library. These rules can evaluate sequences of events, deviations from baselines, threat intelligence context, and multi-source correlations. For many SOCs, this deterministic, rule-driven structure provides clarity and auditabilitytwo qualities that are essential for compliance-heavy sectors.

Where LogRhythm stands apart from other SIEMs is in the tight integration between detection, investigation, and response. When the AI Engine generates an alarm, it flows directly into LogRhythm's Case Management module. This module provides guided workflows that walk analysts through triage and investigation steps. Instead of requiring analysts to construct custom searches or pivot between disparate tools, LogRhythm consolidates investigation actions into a structured sequence. This is especially appealing to SOCs that rely heavily on Tier 1 analysts or prefer standardized, repeatable IR processes. With each alarm, analysts receive context, recommended steps, and integrated tools needed to escalate or resolve the issue. Because of this integrated design, LogRhythm often excels in organizations that value workflow stability over architectural flexibility. Whereas Splunk encourages free-form searches and Elastic rewards deep engineering, LogRhythm provides an operationally disciplined environment. It allows SOC managers to implement consistent procedures across teams, reducing investigation variability and bringing less-experienced analysts quickly up to speed.

However, this design comes with limitations. LogRhythm's architecture is more closed than platforms like Splunk or Elastic. The proprietary schema, while helpful for consistency, restricts the extent to which detections can be customized. Custom parsing, correlation logic, and enrichment layers are possible but far more constrained than in open platforms. Organizations that rely on cutting-edge detection engineering, advanced threat hunting, or machine learning models may find LogRhythm's environment too rigid.

Scalability is another critical consideration. Because LogRhythm's capacity is tied to appliance specifications, scaling requires adding more appliances either through additional indexers, data processors, or mediators. This makes long-term capacity planning essential, as exponential growth in telemetry or increased data retention demands can strain the platform. For MSSPs or large enterprises with dynamic scaling needs, LogRhythm may require more forward planning than cloud-native SIEMs, where storage and compute expand elastically.

Despite these constraints, LogRhythm remains a highly capable SIEM when deployed with intention. Its strengths lie in its guided workflows, tightly integrated detection and response pipeline, stable performance, and predictable behavior. For SOCs that value structure, compliance alignment, and repeatability over open-ended customization, LogRhythm provides a reliable and cohesive operational foundation. When supported by disciplined architecture planning and well-maintained correlation rules, LogRhythm contributes meaningfully to mature, process-driven SOC environments.

Comparative Operational Considerations

Every SIEM platform expresses a particular worldview about how security operations should function. These philosophies shape not only the technology but the workflows, staffing requirements, tuning strategies, and long term financial patterns of the SOC. Understanding these divergent philosophies is essential for any leader tasked with building or maturing security operations, because the SIEM ultimately determines how analysts think, how detection engineers work, and how the organization manages risk at scale.

Splunk represents a philosophy of boundless flexibility and search driven exploration. It excels in environments where engineers need full control over data structure, parsing, correlation, and advanced analytics. Splunk allows nearly any machine data to be ingested and interpreted in whatever form the organization chooses. This creative freedom is why threat hunters, detection engineers, and seasoned analysts often praise Splunk as a platform for deep investigation and custom detection logic. Yet this freedom carries an operational price. Because Splunk extracts many fields at search time, inefficient queries can place heavy load on search heads and indexers. Engineers must constantly tune parsing, retention, index configuration, and summary searches to maintain performance. Licensing based on daily ingestion volume introduces constant budget pressure. In short, Splunk rewards strong engineering maturity and predictable financial planning, but it penalizes environments with inconsistent pipelines or unclear ingestion strategy.

Microsoft Sentinel embodies a very different principle. It is designed for organizations that prefer cloud native elasticity, seamless integration, and rapid onboarding. Sentinel thrives in ecosystems anchored in Microsoft services, where Azure AD, Defender, Office 365, and Entra telemetry already exist in standardized forms. Because Microsoft handles scaling, updates, and backend architecture, SOC teams avoid the traditional burden of maintaining infrastructure. This allows them to focus on detections, investigations, and automation. However, the convenience of cloud native ingestion introduces new challenges. Ingestion costs accumulate rapidly when verbose or unnecessary logs are enabled without careful filters. Retention costs and search charges must be continually monitored. SOCs must adopt disciplined ingestion hygiene to avoid runaway cost patterns. Sentinel excels when organizations lean into its integrated ecosystem and provide analysts with strong KQL proficiency, but it demands careful governance to maintain predictable cost models.

Elastic SIEM expresses yet another architectural vision. It is built for speed, transparency, and engineering control. Elastic's schema first approach ensures that logs are normalized early, yielding consistent field structures across all sources. This uniformity enables fast correlation, reliable detection logic, and near instant search performance. Elasticsearch provides blazing fast analytics even across enormous datasets, and the open nature of the platform appeals to organizations that want to customize every layer of ingestion, enrichment, and storage. However, Elastic is not a set and forget platform. It requires continual tuning of clusters, shards, indices, retention policies, and resource allocation. Poor ingestion design or inconsistent ECS adoption can undermine detection quality. Elastic thrives where DevOps and detection engineering teams collaborate closely and treat the pipeline as a living, evolving system that must be nurtured over time. When properly curated, Elastic becomes a powerful and cost efficient cornerstone for advanced SOC operations.

LogRhythm represents a more structured and appliance oriented interpretation of SIEM. It favors predictable workflows, guided investigations, and integrated case management. Many highly regulated industries appreciate the stability, consistency, and audit friendliness of this approach. LogRhythm provides clearly defined ingestion pipelines, correlation policies, and investigation pathways that reduce analyst friction and enforce operational discipline. The tradeoff is a reduction in customizability and a narrower engineering surface. Organizations that require highly tailored detections, experimental analytics, or large scale multi cloud ingestion may encounter limitations. Scaling often requires additional hardware or virtual appliances, which means that capacity planning must be taken seriously from the outset. LogRhythm excels in environments that value structure over creative freedom and operational predictability over experimentation.

Selecting a SIEM should never be approached as a simple feature comparison exercise. It is a strategic decision that touches every layer of the SOC. The right choice depends on internal skill sets, the maturity of engineering practices, existing technology footprints, compliance obligations, growth expectations, and financial tolerance. A company that operates primarily in Azure and relies heavily on Microsoft identity systems will derive immense operational value from Sentinel. A research driven SOC that values deep hunting, unusual telemetry sources, or custom detections may prefer Splunk or Elastic. Organizations with strong governance requirements and limited engineering bandwidth may find LogRhythm the most stable path.

Understanding how each SIEM processes data internally is essential for avoiding common architectural pitfalls. Over ingestion, inefficient correlation searches, inconsistent schemas, and unstructured pipelines can cripple any SIEM regardless of brand. A SOC that understands its chosen platform deeply can create a finely tuned ecosystem that surfaces adversary behavior clearly and reduces noise to manageable levels. A SOC that treats the SIEM as a black box will eventually drown in alert fatigue, slow investigations, and unpredictable cost patterns.

SIEM selection is not a technology choice but a people and strategy choice. The best SIEM is the one that empowers analysts to think clearly, engineers to build effectively, leaders to plan confidently, and the organization to detect threats with precision. A SIEM is not simply a repository of logs. It is a distributed data processing system designed to reveal adversarial intent across vast volumes of telemetry. When chosen wisely and engineered deliberately, it becomes a precision instrument rather than a source of confusion. Through this understanding, SOC teams gain leverage and transform SIEM platforms from expensive dashboards into tools of clarity, insight, and operational mastery.

Chapter 18

Deep Dive: SOAR Tools

SOAR platforms are the execution engines of modern SOCs. While SIEMs detect and SIEM rules generate alerts, SOAR platforms decide, act, and coordinate. A mature SOC does not automate randomly; it encodes decision logic, escalation policy, and institutional knowledge into repeatable workflows. Understanding how SOAR platforms operate internally enables teams to build reliable playbooks, avoid automation failures, scale safely, and maintain analyst trust.

This chapter provides a deep technical and operational breakdown of four major SOAR platformsPalo Alto Cortex XSOAR, Tines, IBM

Resilient, and Microsoft Sentinel Automation/Logic Apps focusing on internal design philosophy, execution models, and real-world operational tradeoffs.

Palo Alto Cortex XSOAR: Stateful, Incident-Centric Automation

Cortex XSOAR occupies a unique place in the automation landscape because it does not treat orchestration as a loose collection of independent tasks. Instead, it builds its entire framework around a persistent incident object that acts as the authoritative source of truth for every step of the workflow. This single object holds the full timeline of activity: the alerts that initiated the case, the enrichment results, analyst comments, evidence attachments, process decisions, timestamps, and SLA progression. By treating the incident as the anchor for all automation, XSOAR creates a stateful environment that resembles a living investigation rather than a disconnected chain of actions. This design gives SOC teams a forensic quality record that supports both real time response and retrospective analysis.

When a new alert enters XSOAR, whether through SIEM forwarding, EDR webhooks, cloud event ingestion, or a custom API pipeline, it is immediately transformed into an incident type. The incident type is not merely a label. It defines a structured schema that includes required fields, classification logic, severity assignment, default SLAs, layouts, and the appropriate automation logic for that particular category of case. A phishing incident receives a completely different schema and workflow than a ransomware precursor event, an insider threat case, or a cloud misconfiguration. By enforcing separation at the incident type level, XSOAR ensures that every category of response follows a consistent and well governed process that matches organizational policy.

Once the incident object is created, XSOAR binds it to a playbook. Playbooks operate like dynamic state machines that evolve as the investigation progresses. Each playbook consists of task nodes connected through conditional paths. These tasks can call Python scripts, execute integration commands, launch sub playbooks, or pause the workflow until a human approval is provided. The branching logic allows playbooks to respond intelligently to changing conditions. If a sandbox detonation reveals a high confidence malware family, for example, the playbook can escalate automatically. If a reputation lookup returns uncertainty, the playbook can request analyst review. This adaptive structure gives XSOAR unparalleled ability to orchestrate complex multi step investigations. A defining strength of XSOAR is the context data store, a persistent memory layer associated with the incident. Key value pairs recorded during any task remain accessible to every later task. This eliminates redundant API calls and allows the playbook to make decisions based on enriched intelligence collected earlier in the workflow. For example, once a file hash reputation is pulled, the score is preserved and available for containment decisions. If EDR telemetry reveals a suspicious parent process or lateral movement attempts, those facts remain in context and influence subsequent steps. Over the course of long running investigations, this stateful memory becomes essential for maintaining continuity, speed, and accuracy.

XSOAR excels in investigations that require multiple rounds of enrichment and analysis. A malware event may require a sequence of enrichment steps such as sandbox detonation, hash lookups, firewall traffic correlation, EDR process tree reconstruction, user login analysis, and indicator extraction for wider threat hunting. A traditional stateless automation engine would treat these steps as isolated commands. XSOAR, however, binds them to a cohesive investigative narrative. Each step modifies the state of the incident, and each subsequent task interprets the updated state before acting. This gives the SOC a tool that performs automation with context rather than automation in a vacuum.

Human involvement remains a core principle in XSOAR's design. While it can automate extraordinary volumes of repetitive work, it does not assume that all decisions can be made by machines. Analysts can be asked to validate ambiguous indicators, approve containment actions, classify the final disposition of an alert, or supply additional fields required by playbook logic. XSOAR pauses confidently and resumes seamlessly once the analyst responds. This controlled interaction allows XSOAR to handle sensitive or high risk operations without undermining governance or accountability.

The power of XSOAR introduces responsibilities that should not be underestimated. Without structured engineering discipline, the platform can quickly become unwieldy. Playbooks may multiply without purpose. Scripts can diverge in function and naming. Integrations may drift from their intended access control boundaries. Inconsistent incident types can confuse analysts or generate unpredictable workflows. For these reasons, XSOAR requires lifecycle management. Version control, peer review, staging environments, naming standards, integration audits, and periodic playbook evaluations are essential to keep the platform reliable and maintainable.

Permissions governance is particularly critical. XSOAR can isolate endpoints, disable accounts, update firewall rules, perform cloud policy changes, or modify configuration settings across an enterprise. If service accounts are over privileged or role based access control is misconfigured, the platform could unintentionally introduce substantial operational risk. Therefore, every integration must be scoped carefully, and every automated action must honor least privilege principles.

Organizations that invest in engineering maturity, structured governance, and continuous review discover that XSOAR becomes an enormous force multiplier. It eliminates repetitive tasks, accelerates enrichment, ensures consistent workflows, and frees analysts to focus on complex reasoning rather than clerical execution. In environments with high alert volume or strict SLA requirements, XSOAR can transform operational tempo, reduce fatigue, and significantly improve the quality and reliability of incident response.

Despite its complexity, XSOAR stands as one of the most capable automation platforms available. It is particularly valuable for SOCs that require deep case management, branching orchestration paths, broad integration support, and a structured investigative record that matures over the lifespan of an incident. With the right governance, XSOAR becomes a cornerstone of a modern, well engineered, and highly effective security operations program.

Tines: Event-Driven, Stateless Automation

Tines represents a very different vision for security automation. Where platforms like Cortex XSOAR anchor their workflows to a persistent incident object, Tines embraces an event driven and stateless model that focuses on the flow of data rather than the management of cases. The core building blocks of Tines are Stories, which function as small and powerful automation programs composed of individual actions that pass structured data from one step to the next. Each Story is a chain of logic, triggered by an inbound event such as a webhook, SIEM alert, email, or scheduled process. Once the Story is triggered, Tines begins moving the event through a series of connected actions, each performing a discrete and self contained task.

Internally, Tines treats every event as an independent unit of work. The platform does not maintain a long running state or a persistent memory object the way incident centric platforms do. Instead, each action receives data, performs its task, and emits a new event that moves on to the next action in the Story. The data that flows between these actions is expressed as JSON, which provides a flexible, consistent, and easily manipulated structure for enrichment, transformation, and decision making. Because of this stateless design, Tines can process astonishing volumes of events in parallel. There are no concerns about shared memory conflicts or complex state transitions. This architectural simplicity makes Tines exceptionally strong in scenarios that demand speed, concurrency, and large scale automation.

Scalability is perhaps the greatest operational advantage of Tines. Thousands or even millions of events can pass through the same Story without interference because Stories do not maintain a shared state. This makes Tines especially powerful in automation intensive environments such as high volume enrichment pipelines, large email security operations, fraud detection systems, identity lifecycle automation, and the demanding pipelines used by many MSSPs. The platform thrives in programs where enormous quantities of small tasks must be performed reliably and at speed.

A defining principle of Tines is the concept of human assisted automation. Rather than embedding approval gates directly inside the platform, Tines frequently offloads decisions to communication channels such as Slack, Teams, or email. The Story pauses at that point and waits for a human response. Once the analyst replies in the communication tool, Tines captures the response and resumes the automation. This approach allows organizations to include analysts in critical decisions without confining them to a single user interface. It also reinforces a more natural operational model where analysts continue to work in the communication platforms they use throughout the day, making the interaction feel seamless and intuitive.

Because Tines is intentionally lightweight and focused on orchestration, it does not attempt to provide full incident management. It has no built in incident object, no long form case timeline, and no native evidence repository. For long running investigations, this means Tines relies on external systems such as Jira, ServiceNow, XSOAR, or other case management tools to provide context and historical tracking. In practice, this is not a limitation but a design choice. Tines concentrates the bulk of its capability on rapid action, reliable orchestration, and scalable automation, while allowing more fully featured platforms to handle the investigative lifecycle. Many SOCs and MSSPs pair Tines with an external ticketing or incident management system for exactly this reason.

This stateless model has significant implications. It reduces complexity because workflows do not depend on historical context. It increases reliability because each event is self contained. It accelerates performance because parallelization is natural rather than engineered. However, it also means that SOCs must design clear boundaries around what Tines handles and what the broader tool ecosystem supports. Tines excels when it is the automation engine, not the investigation workspace.

For organizations prioritizing speed, scalability, low overhead, and clean integration patterns, Tines offers a powerful and elegant solution. It demonstrates how security automation can be simple, modular, and fast without sacrificing capability. When paired with strong governance, a well defined architecture, and appropriate external systems for case management, Tines becomes a flexible and dependable automation layer that blends seamlessly into modern SOC operations.

IBM Resilient: Process-Governed, Case-Management–First SOAR

IBM Resilient stands apart from many other automation platforms because its foundation is not rapid orchestration or event driven processing but rather disciplined process governance. Resilient views every security incident as a formal and highly structured case that must move through clearly defined phases, tasks, approvals, and documentation checkpoints. This philosophy makes Resilient function much like a digital incident response binder, ensuring that every action is recorded, every requirement is met, and every step follows the organization's regulatory and procedural expectations. In environments where legal defensibility is essential, this approach is not simply helpful, it is mandatory.

Internally, Resilient organizes all cases around playbooks that mirror formal incident response frameworks. These playbooks break down the entire case lifecycle into discrete phases such as detection, analysis, containment, eradication, and recovery. Within each phase, specific tasks are assigned to roles with explicit expectations for completion. Analysts receive guided workflows that tell them what to do, when to do it, and what evidence they must collect before moving forward. This structured method removes ambiguity, ensures consistency across shifts and teams, and allows organizations to demonstrate compliance in a way that is both precise and meticulously documented.

Automation in Resilient exists to support these structured processes rather than override them. Scripts, integrations, and connectors are invoked at moments defined by the playbook. Resilient might automatically enrich a suspicious file hash, retrieve logs from an endpoint, gather identity details from a directory service, or notify legal counsel when an incident reaches a predetermined threshold. However, automation never becomes the driving force of the workflow. The governing principle is that people make decisions and the playbook defines the path, while automation steps in only to provide efficiency, evidence, or procedural validation. This design philosophy makes Resilient particularly strong in organizations where regulatory frameworks such as PCI, HIPAA, SOX, CJIS, or government standards require exact documentation of every investigative and response step. Resilient excels in financial institutions, defense agencies, insurance sectors, and other high accountability environments. It maintains detailed evidence repositories, action logs, chain of custody records, and approval histories. Every modification and every status change is preserved in a way that can stand up to legal scrutiny or internal audit requirements. This is not merely a convenience for regulated enterprises; it is a critical operational safeguard.

The same strengths that make Resilient a powerful governance tool also introduce limitations. Because processes must be defined up front, automation can be slower to implement and less adaptable to sudden changes in threat landscape or workflow expectations. Rapid experimentation, high volume enrichment, and loosely structured automation programs are more difficult to build in this model. In fast moving MSSPs or cloud native SOCs that rely heavily on massive automation pipelines, Resilient may feel restrictive compared to more flexible platforms like Tines or Cortex XSOAR. Furthermore, organizations that ingest large volumes of alerts may find that Resilient performs best as a case management system rather than an alert triage front end.

Still, for organizations that must demonstrate maturity, consistency, and procedural rigor, Resilient delivers exceptional value. It encourages disciplined operational behavior and prevents the drift that often plagues SOCs without formal process anchors.

The platform is most effective when paired with a well documented response framework, strong governance culture, and clear separation between automation and human decision making. In that context, Resilient becomes a powerful tool for strengthening accountability, improving repeatability, and elevating the overall reliability of security operations.

Microsoft Sentinel Automation Rules & Logic Apps: Cloud-Native Orchestration

Microsoft Sentinel approaches automation through a layered system built around Automation Rules and Logic Apps, both of which sit naturally inside the Azure cloud ecosystem. Automation Rules serve as Sentinel's decision layer. They evaluate every incoming alert or incident and determine whether automation should occur, what playbook should run, and under what conditions the workflow is allowed to proceed. These rules function as policy gates that help enforce structure and prevent unnecessary automation. They also allow the SOC to embed initial filtering logic, apply incident routing rules, set classification defaults, or auto assign incidents to different teams. This makes Automation Rules more than simple triggers; they become the first step in a disciplined orchestration pipeline.

Logic Apps represent the engine that carries out the work. They are serverless and event driven, designed to scale on demand without requiring the SOC to provision or maintain any infrastructure. When a Logic App is triggered by an Automation Rule, it launches a workflow built from modular actions. Each action might call an API, query Microsoft Graph, enrich an indicator through an external threat intelligence service, send investigative details to a Teams channel, open a ServiceNow ticket, disable a suspicious account in Entra ID, or isolate a compromised machine through Defender. Because Logic Apps run on top of Azure's enterprise workflow architecture, they inherit the reliability, resilience, and global scaling of the Azure platform. Workflows can run thousands of times simultaneously without resource conflicts. One of the most valuable strengths of Sentinel automation lies in its deep alignment with Microsoft's identity and endpoint ecosystem. Because Defender, Entra ID, Azure AD Conditional Access, and Office 365 feed telemetry directly into Sentinel through native connectors, Logic Apps can use that data instantly to guide automated decision making. For example, if an incident involves suspicious sign in activity, a Logic App can query the user's conditional access status, gather risk scores, collect contextual data from Entra ID Identity Protection, and make an automated determination about whether additional action is justified. The integration is seamless because all these services share the same Azure identity and resource models.

Logic Apps can be constructed visually through the designer interface or defined using JSON. The visual designer supports branching logic, loops, variable handling, retry policies, error handling, approvals, and time based waits. More complex workflows often include durable functions, which provide additional state management capabilities. Although Logic Apps themselves are stateless, they can store and pass structured data between steps, making it possible to build multi stage enrichment sequences that maintain context throughout the workflow. Approvals can also be embedded through Teams, email, or custom connectors so that analysts remain involved when high risk actions need human oversight.

With these advantages come operational and financial considerations. Every Logic App execution consumes Azure resources. In low volume environments this cost is negligible, but in large SOCs particularly MSSPs running hundreds of automations per hour monthly expenses can rise sharply if playbooks are inefficient. For example, repeated API calls, unnecessary enrichment steps, or poorly designed branching structures can lead to inflated consumption. Teams must also consider the cost of data movement. A workflow that frequently queries Log Analytics or cross workspace telemetry may produce additional consumption charges. As a result, mature Sentinel deployments treat automation design as an engineering discipline, incorporating caching strategies, optimized branching, reusable components, and thoughtful throttling to avoid waste.

Management complexity is another factor. Logic Apps live inside Azure resource groups, subject to Azure permissions, roles, and governance models. Large SOCs with many playbooks must handle version control, naming standards, change control, secure credential management through Key Vault, and monitoring through Azure Monitor. Playbooks often span multiple workloads and may require coordination with cloud engineering or identity teams. Without disciplined governance, the automation layer can become fragmented, inconsistent, or vulnerable to privilege misconfigurations.

Despite these challenges, Sentinel automation excels when deployed in environments that rely heavily on Microsoft cloud services. The combination of Automation

Rules, Logic Apps, and rich Microsoft telemetry allows for rapid, high fidelity orchestration tailored to identity centric security models. Automated enrichment, routine containment, user messaging, and cross system coordination happen with minimal friction. Even complex response chains can be executed in seconds across global cloud infrastructure. In organizations with mixed or multi cloud environments, Sentinel automation remains effective but requires more deliberate engineering. Third party tools must be integrated through connectors, custom APIs, or built in actions. The effort is worthwhile, but it demands more intentional design than purely Microsoft centric workflows.

For cloud forward SOCs, Sentinel's automation system is one of the strongest available. It allows teams to move beyond alert handling and into orchestrated response capabilities that are scalable, repeatable, and deeply embedded in the same ecosystem that generates the telemetry. When engineered with care, Sentinel automation becomes a strategic multiplier, reducing manual workload, increasing consistency, and accelerating decision making across the entire security program.

Comparative Automation Philosophy

Every SOAR platform embodies a distinct vision of how security operations should function. These products are not simply collections of automated tasks. They are reflections of design principles and operational assumptions about how analysts investigate incidents, how systems exchange information, and how decision making should be structured inside the SOC.

Cortex XSOAR represents a philosophy centered on state, context, and narrative. It treats every incident as a living object that evolves over time, gathering enrichment, decisions, evidence, and analyst actions into a unified case record. XSOAR imagines automation as an extension of human reasoning. It builds deep, branching workflows that adapt based on prior results. This makes it incredibly powerful for complex, multi stage investigations where memory and context matter. It also makes XSOAR ideal for large enterprises that require a forensic quality record of every decision made along the way. The tradeoff is complexity. XSOAR demands disciplined engineering, structured version control, and careful governance to prevent playbook sprawl or integration drift.

Tines approaches automation from the opposite direction. Instead of building stateful, incident centric investigations, it takes an event driven view of the world. A single message or webhook arrives and triggers a series of atomic tasks that pass JSON shaped artifacts between them. Tines workflows do not carry the burden of a long running state. They fire, execute, and complete without retaining memory. This gives Tines exceptional scalability and incredible speed. It can process thousands of parallel events with ease. This makes the platform valuable for environments with massive enrichment requirements, email security automation, or large MSSPs that cannot afford slow or heavy automation stacks. Tines shifts human oversight into the communication layer, inviting analysts to approve actions through tools they already use, such as Teams or Slack. The tradeoff is that Tines depends heavily on external systems for incident tracking because it does not provide deep case management of its own.

IBM Resilient takes a very different path. Its automation philosophy is rooted in governance, compliance, and procedural rigor. Resilient assumes that incidents are not simply technical events but legal and regulatory matters requiring documentation, chain of custody, and defined phases of response. Its workflow engine mirrors formal response frameworks and breaks cases into assigned tasks, approvals, and structured evidence submissions. Automation exists primarily to support human decision making and ensure that each step adheres to policy. This model is invaluable in highly regulated industries that must present response records to auditors or legal teams. The tradeoff is reduced speed and flexibility. Resilient is methodical by design, and high volume alert environments may find the approach too structured for rapid triage.

Microsoft Sentinel automation is built around cloud native elasticity. Sentinel assumes that detection, enrichment, and containment occur within a distributed environment where identity, endpoint, network, and cloud telemetry flow seamlessly through Azure. Automation Rules act as the governance layer and Logic Apps perform the orchestration. The model emphasizes policy enforcement, scaling on demand, and deep integration with Microsoft security controls. Sentinel's automation philosophy is not built around narrative or case state. Instead, it focuses on rapid, event driven response across cloud services. It excels where organizations rely heavily on Microsoft infrastructure. The primary caution is cost and complexity. Automation can become expensive if workflows generate excessive calls or if ingestion is not controlled.

Choosing a SOAR platform is not a simple technology selection. It is a reflection of the SOC's identity. A team that values deep case context may prefer XSOAR. A team that needs lightweight, high throughput processing may adopt Tines. A team constrained by regulations or formal review cycles may turn to IBM Resilient. A cloud forward organization living inside the Microsoft ecosystem often gravitates toward Sentinel because automation aligns directly with its identity and cloud strategy.

Some of the most advanced SOCs do not rely on a single platform. They combine tools intentionally. Tines or Sentinel may handle enrichment pipelines and real time orchestration. XSOAR or Resilient may serve as the case management layer for investigations. By separating fast automation from governed response, SOCs can achieve the best of both philosophies.

Understanding these internal mechanics empowers SOC leaders to design automation that is stable, predictable, and truly scalable. SOAR platforms encode institutional knowledge into executable workflows. Well engineered automation preserves expertise, reduces variance between analysts, and accelerates decisions without sacrificing oversight. The power of SOAR does not lie in replacing human analysts. It lies in amplifying them, enabling analysts to use their judgment and investigative skill while the automation layer handles the noise, the repetition, and the mechanics. This is the heart of modern SOC automation philosophy: humans decide, automation executes, and together they form a system far stronger than either alone.

Chapter 19

Deep Dive: EDR/XDR Tools

CrowdStrike Falcon: Cloud-First, Intelligence-Driven Endpoint Detection

CrowdStrike Falcon represents a profound shift in how endpoint security is conceived. Instead of relying on heavy local agents that must detect threats in isolation, Falcon moves the analytical center of gravity into a globally distributed cloud platform. The endpoint sensor becomes the eyes and ears of the system rather than its brain. This architectural choice allows Falcon to correlate activity not just within a single organization but across millions of devices worldwide. The result is a detection platform that learns continuously from global telemetry and applies those lessons instantly to all customers.

At the device level, Falcon employs an extremely lightweight sensor. Installation rarely requires a reboot and imposes almost no resource burden on user systems. Despite its small footprint, the sensor collects a remarkably broad set of behavioral indicators. It records process creation events, parent child lineage, command line arguments, thread injections, registry modifications, memory allocation patterns, credential related interactions, and detailed network metadata. This telemetry is streamed in near real time to the cloud where it becomes part of a collective intelligence model.

The heart of Falcon's detection ecosystem is the Threat Graph, a globally scaled graph database that maps relationships between billions of events. It connects identities, processes, files, IP addresses, system behaviors, registry interactions, and hundreds of other attributes into a single relational structure. When a threat actor reuses infrastructure or repeats a behavioral pattern seen elsewhere in the world, the Threat Graph notices. This gives Falcon a tremendous advantage over purely local

EDR systems. A novel loader observed in one region may trigger detections worldwide minutes later. Falcon customers effectively share a distributed early warning system.

CrowdStrike's detection philosophy is fundamentally behavioral. Instead of relying on static signatures or hash matching, Falcon evaluates sequences of events. A single command may not be suspicious, but a command executed in the wrong context, with the wrong parent process, at the wrong time, or in a pattern that resembles known adversary tradecraft becomes highly meaningful. Falcon excels at identifying these behavioral chains. An encoded PowerShell command spawning credential dumping activity, followed by unexpected lateral movement attempts, and then a suspicious scheduled task creation is a pattern the system recognizes quickly. It does not matter whether the adversary uses known tooling or invents something new. The behaviors themselves tell the story.

A defining feature of Falcon is its adversary attribution capability. CrowdStrike associates specific clusters of activity with known threat groups, such as COZY BEAR, WIZARD SPIDER, AQUATIC PANDA, or SILENT CHOLLIMA. These associations are grounded in years of intelligence analysis and observed behavioral patterns. For SOC analysts, attribution provides immediate context. When a detection explicitly links to a threat group known for ransomware operations, credential theft campaigns, or espionage, the response posture changes instantly.

Detection is only half the equation. Falcon's response capabilities are centralized through a cloud based console that allows analysts to contain and remediate threats from anywhere. The platform supports process termination, file quarantine, network isolation, and host level containment while preserving communication with the sensor. During active intrusions, analysts can use Real Time Response to issue remote commands, inspect directories, gather forensic evidence, remove persistence mechanisms, or even pull memory samples. These capabilities turn Falcon into a full scale incident response platform rather than merely an alerting tool.

The breadth of Falcon's telemetry supports powerful investigations, but its investigation interface often requires analysts to pivot through several views. Process graphs, event timelines, detection summaries, and network flow details each reveal part of the story. Falcon favors a federated intelligence model that prioritizes depth of insight over a single, unified pane of glass. While this may require additional clicks, it also allows analysts to explore the data from multiple angles and reconstruct complex attack sequences with precision.

Falcon's cloud centered architecture comes with important tradeoffs. Because detection logic lives in the cloud, SOC teams do not have deep visibility into the exact models or rules behind many detections. The interpretability is limited to behavior descriptions, MITRE ATT and CK mappings, and contextual metadata. For most organizations this is acceptable, especially considering Falcon's extremely high detection accuracy, but environments that demand fine tuned custom rules may find the platform less flexible than open frameworks such as Elastic.

Even with these limitations, Falcon continues to lead the industry in intelligence driven endpoint detection. Its global telemetry advantage, behavioral analysis engine, adversary attribution capabilities, and remote response tools provide a comprehensive solution for both detection and containment. Falcon's greatest strength is that it delivers high fidelity security outcomes without requiring complex on premises infrastructure or extensive tuning teams. Organizations that adopt Falcon gain not only a powerful EDR, but an intelligence platform that grows smarter with every new threat observed anywhere in the world.

In practice, this means Falcon often identifies sophisticated intrusions earlier than competing tools. It reduces the cognitive burden on analysts by surfacing only meaningful behavioral signals rather than drowning them in noise. It empowers rapid response without physical access to the endpoint. And most importantly, it embodies a modern, cloud informed vision of security. Falcon's design philosophy is clear: centralize intelligence, distribute telemetry, and let the cloud reason at global scale.

Microsoft Defender: Deep OS Integration and Identity-Aware Detection

Microsoft Defender for Endpoint represents a very different school of endpoint protection compared to platforms that operate as external agents layered onto the operating system. Defender is woven directly into the fabric of Windows itself. It observes the system from the inside rather than from the outside, giving it a level of visibility and introspection that few other tools can match. Defender does not bolt itself onto Windows; it is part of Windows. This design philosophy allows Defender to see the operating system at a depth that external EDR tools can only approximate.

At the telemetry level, Defender collects an enormous amount of granular information from across Windows internals. It draws from kernel level signals, thread and process execution, PowerShell invocation pipelines, the Antimalware Scan Interface, Event Tracing for Windows providers, registry activity, file system behavior, authentication subsystems, and memory operations. One of Defender's defining advantages is its insight into PowerShell activity. It can view both invocation metadata and script content, even when obfuscated. Defender pairs this information with AMSI which extracts code from memory before execution, revealing malicious content that traditional signature based engines would miss entirely.

Defender also has unusually strong identity awareness. Because it is tightly integrated with Azure Active Directory and the broader Microsoft identity ecosystem, it can blend endpoint activity with authentication behavior in real time. A suspicious process running on a device may be a mild concern, but if the same device also shows abnormal sign in patterns, risky login behavior, or conditional access policy triggers, the detection gains far more weight. Defender is designed to treat identity and endpoint as inseparable components of modern attacks. This makes it especially effective at detecting credential abuse, lateral movement techniques, and token manipulation.

Detection within Defender arises from multiple layers of logic. Local heuristics provide fast, lightweight behavioral checks on the device itself. Cloud analytics perform deeper reasoning across massive datasets, identifying activity that deviates from normal patterns across millions of endpoints. Microsoft threat intelligence teams continuously feed both static intelligence and emerging tradecraft insights into the detection engine. Defender also benefits from cross domain correlation. Signals from Azure AD, Office 365, Intune, Conditional Access, and Microsoft Defender for Cloud are aggregated to produce more accurate alerts with stronger investigative context.

Because Defender operates inside the operating system, it detects many forms of living off the land activity that are easy for adversaries to hide from less integrated EDR tools. Techniques involving WMI, scheduled tasks, remote management tools, credential dumping, or malicious use of built in system binaries often stand out clearly in Defender's telemetry. It recognizes unexpected parent child process relationships, anomalous command sequences, and subtle deviations from normal user behavior. This capability is one of Defender's strongest attributes in enterprise environments where attackers frequently rely on native tooling to avoid detection.

Defender's telemetry flows natively into Microsoft Sentinel, forming a seamless connection between endpoint data and the organization's cloud native SIEM. This pipeline requires no custom engineering, no complex parsing rules, and no additional agents. For SOC teams already operating in the Microsoft ecosystem, the result is an extremely efficient monitoring workflow. Incidents created by Defender appear instantly in Sentinel with enriched context, MITRE ATT and CK mappings, risk scores, and correlated alerts across identity, endpoint, cloud resources, and SaaS applications.

However, Defender's effectiveness depends heavily on configuration maturity. A surprisingly large number of deployments rely only on default settings which provide partial visibility. To unlock Defender's full capability, organizations must enable advanced auditing, configure attack surface reduction rules, tune cloud delivered protection, enforce strict configuration baselines, and pair the sensor with strong identity governance. Without these steps, Defender leaves significant blind spots and does not collect the depth of information required for high fidelity detection.

When configured correctly, Microsoft Defender becomes an exceptionally powerful detection and response platform. It provides deep insight into operating system behavior, natural correlation with identity events, automated investigation features, and rapid containment actions such as device isolation, process termination, or forensic package collection. It aligns naturally with modern enterprise environments where identity is often the new perimeter and where living off the land attacks dominate the threat landscape.

Defender is at its best in organizations that are already invested in Azure AD, Office 365, and the Microsoft security suite. In those ecosystems it becomes more than just an EDR. It becomes a unified security fabric where endpoint activity, identity signals, cloud telemetry, and administrative policies all intersect. This gives SOC teams a coherent picture of attacker behavior, tying together signals that other tools would treat separately. Defender's value grows as more Microsoft services are connected to it.

In a world where adversaries increasingly exploit legitimate tools, blend into normal activity, and target identity as the primary attack vector, Defender's inside out visibility offers a critical advantage. It does not merely observe the operating system; it understands the operating system. It does not simply detect malicious binaries; it detects malicious behavior. And when paired with a mature configuration and a well trained SOC, Microsoft Defender for Endpoint becomes a cornerstone of resilient and intelligence driven enterprise security.

Cortex XDR: Cross-Domain, Analytics-Driven XDR

Cortex XDR offered by Palo Alto Networks represents a major shift in how detection and response is conceptualized. Rather than treating endpoints, networks, users, and cloud platforms as separate islands that must each be monitored in isolation, Cortex XDR views the enterprise as a single interconnected nervous system. Every signal from every domain feeds into a shared analytic brain. This allows the platform to detect attacks that would remain invisible when any single telemetry source is viewed alone. Cortex XDR is not simply an endpoint tool. It is a cross domain detection engine designed to reconstruct entire attack chains with clarity.

At the endpoint level, Cortex XDR collects detailed telemetry similar to advanced detection platforms. It monitors process launches, command lines, thread injections, DLL usage, kernel transitions, registry operations, file system changes, and memory interactions. But the strength of Cortex XDR does not come from endpoint telemetry alone. It comes from the fusion of that telemetry with the rich dataset provided by Palo Alto firewalls, DNS logs, SaaS identity logs, cloud audit streams, and network flow data. When these sources are integrated fully, Cortex XDR gains an unusually wide field of view into how users, systems, and workloads behave across the entire enterprise.

This integration produces powerful outcomes during threat detection. A suspicious script on an endpoint may appear benign in isolation, but Cortex XDR does not view it in isolation. It compares that script activity with outbound network connections, user authentication history, file access patterns, firewall traffic, and recent cloud changes to determine whether the behavior fits a known benign pattern or suggests a coordinated attack. In this way, Cortex XDR favors pattern recognition over point in time anomalies. It looks for attack sequences rather than single indicators.

Machine learning plays a central role in Cortex XDR. Models analyze baseline behavior for hosts, users, and network flows. These models learn what normal looks like inside the environment and then flag deviations that may indicate compromise. This includes rare process chain sequences, unusual host to host communication patterns, sudden changes in user behavior, or unexpected cloud resource modifications. Because these models draw from multiple domains of telemetry, the behavioral insights they generate are far more contextual than those of traditional endpoint detection tools.

One of the most valuable features in Cortex XDR is its incident timeline. The platform translates raw telemetry into a rich narrative that visualizes how an attack unfolded step by step. Analysts can see where execution began, how the adversary escalated privileges, how they moved laterally, what connections they attempted, and what persistence mechanisms they deployed. This single timeline weaves together signals from endpoints, firewalls, identity sources, and cloud infrastructure. It eliminates guesswork and gives analysts a comprehensive understanding of what really happened rather than a fragmented view based on isolated alerts.

Response actions take advantage of the same cross domain approach. Cortex XDR is not limited to isolating endpoints or removing files. It allows analysts to block malicious traffic at the firewall, revoke cloud resource permissions, disable compromised accounts, terminate sessions, prevent lateral movement, or execute remote cleanup scripts. These actions can be coordinated from a single console. When an enterprise uses Palo Alto firewalls, Prisma Cloud, and Cortex Data Lake together, the response becomes enterprise wide rather than device focused. Attackers are not stopped in one location. They are stopped across every layer of the environment simultaneously.

However, the advantages of Cortex XDR depend on full ecosystem integration. To unlock its true power, organizations must feed it consistent network logs, firewall data, identity signals, cloud audit records, and endpoint telemetry. Environments that rely on a fragmented toolset often need additional engineering effort to achieve the level of visibility that Cortex XDR expects. The platform becomes significantly more effective when the entire Palo Alto ecosystem is in place and well configured. Without that maturity, the cross domain engine has fewer threads to tie together and may not reach its full detection potential.

Cortex XDR also requires analysts to think differently. Investigations are no longer confined to host level analysis. Analysts must understand identity behavior, cloud activity, network signals, and endpoint telemetry as a unified system. The platform rewards SOCs with strong analytical maturity and a willingness to adopt a systems level perspective.

For organizations working toward a consolidated and integrated security ecosystem, Cortex XDR delivers exceptional value. It detects attacks through their relationships, not their symptoms. It reconstructs adversary behavior with remarkable clarity. It correlates identity, network, and endpoint signals into a single investigative lens. And it enables rapid, coordinated response actions across every layer of the enterprise.

Cortex XDR is one of the most complete XDR architectures available for enterprises that desire unified visibility, behavioral detection, and an analytics engine that truly understands how attackers move across modern environments. When an organization commits to that integrated model, Cortex XDR becomes a powerful instrument that transforms scattered data points into coherent security intelligence.

Detection Behaviors and Telemetry Differences

Although these platforms serve similar purposes, their detection behaviors differ significantly. SentinelOne emphasizes rapid, autonomous local detection. CrowdStrike emphasizes intelligence-driven, cloud-correlated detection. Microsoft Defender emphasizes OS-native visibility and identity integration. Cortex XDR emphasizes correlated multi-domain analytics.

These differences directly affect SOC workflows. SentinelOne often produces high-confidence, low-noise alerts but may lack broader context without integration. CrowdStrike alerts are rich in adversary intelligence but may require additional investigation pivots. Defender alerts are deeply detailed but can be noisy if improperly configured. Cortex XDR incidents are comprehensive but require mature analysts to interpret multi-domain correlations.

Understanding these tradeoffs allows SOCs to tune workflows appropriately, design better enrichment pipelines, and avoid misinterpreting alerts outside their detection philosophy. EDR and XDR platforms are not interchangeable commodities; they are fundamentally different detection engines shaped by architectural philosophy. By understanding how SentinelOne, CrowdStrike, Microsoft Defender, and Cortex XDR collect telemetry, detect behavior, and trigger response, SOC teams gain the insight needed to investigate efficiently, tune detections effectively, and design resilient security operations. Mastery of these tools transforms endpoint data from raw telemetry into decisive defensive advantage.

Chapter 20

Deep Dive: Threat Intelligence Tools

Threat intelligence is the connective tissue between raw telemetry and informed decision-making. In a modern SOC, intelligence tools do not exist to provide curiosity-driven data; they exist to reduce uncertainty, accelerate triage, improve detection quality, and inform containment decisions. Understanding how major threat intelligence platforms work internally and how to integrate them programmatically is essential for building scalable, automated SOC operations. This chapter examines VirusTotal, AbuseIPDB, GreyNoise, Shodan, Recorded Future, and MISP through an operational lens, focusing on internal mechanics, data provenance, and API-driven integration patterns.

VirusTotal: Multi-Engine Reputation and Behavioral Intelligence

VirusTotal has become one of the most influential intelligence platforms in modern security operations. It is not an antivirus engine in the traditional sense, nor is it a simple lookup database. Instead, VirusTotal is a vast reputation and behavioral analysis ecosystem that blends data from antivirus vendors, sandbox technologies, machine learning engines, reverse engineers, and a global community of researchers. It is a clearinghouse of collective intelligence, where hundreds of analytical signals converge to create a multidimensional portrait of suspicious artifacts. For SOC analysts, VirusTotal offers both speed and depth. It accelerates triage while providing enough context to guide meaningful investigative decisions.

At its foundation, VirusTotal accepts a wide range of submissions. These include file binaries, URLs, IP addresses, domains, and cryptographic hashes. Once an artifact enters the system, it undergoes layered analysis. Antivirus engines apply static signatures that detect known malware families or patterns. Behavioral sandboxes execute the file inside controlled environments and record system changes, process activity, network connections, privilege modifications, and attempts at persistence. Metadata such as file entropy, packer signatures, embedded strings, import tables, and compilation timestamps add additional analytic value. A rich community of contributors also participates. Researchers annotate samples, upload YARA rules, comment on variants, and flag suspicious traits they have observed in the wild.

VirusTotal's power is not in a single verdict. Its power comes from the aggregation of intelligence signals. SOC analysts use VirusTotal not as an absolute judge but as a barometer of confidence. A file flagged by many engines carries meaning, but the pattern of which engines flag it and how they categorize it often matters more. A newly submitted hash that appears only once in the database may signal novel malware or targeted activity. Meanwhile, a hash that appears thousands of times may indicate commodity malware or widespread opportunistic attacks. VirusTotal also provides historical context. Analysts can examine first seen and last seen dates, frequency of submissions, changes in detection over time, and relationships between samples. These insights help distinguish a new threat from a well known campaign.

In automated SOC environments, VirusTotal frequently acts as a first line of enrichment. When a SIEM or EDR raises an alert that contains a hash or URL, SOAR workflows often query VirusTotal immediately. The returned data detection ratios, confidence scores, family names, sandbox behavior tags, mutexes, C two indicators, and clusters of related artifacts are then parsed automatically. Enrichment like this allows the SOC to sort genuine threats from routine noise at remarkable speed. A SOAR workflow may escalate a finding automatically if VirusTotal reports associations with high risk families such as Emotet, QakBot, Kryptik, RedLine, or Cobalt Strike loaders. Analysts begin their investigation already armed with global context.

The VirusTotal API is intentionally simple, enabling rapid integration into any platform that handles structured data. A single query can return antivirus verdicts, behavioral findings, MITRE ATT and CK mappings provided by some engines, network indicators extracted in sandboxes, and relationships drawn from previous submissions. This wealth of information becomes a decision support tool. Analysts are not expected to rely entirely on VirusTotal, but they use it to calibrate their suspicion. It turns raw indicators into meaningful intelligence.

However, VirusTotal must be approached thoughtfully. High detection ratios can occasionally mislead, especially for legitimate administrative tools that resemble hacker utilities. Likewise, a clean scan in VirusTotal does not guarantee safety. Advanced adversaries often deploy custom binaries that appear nowhere in public databases. Fileless attacks, macro based malware, scripts executed directly in memory, and adversary tools designed for single use rarely leave signatures that VirusTotal can observe. SOC teams must therefore treat VirusTotal as a confidence amplifier, not a decision engine. It strengthens suspicion when other clues exist but should not serve as the sole source of truth.

One of the platform's most powerful features is its relationship mapping. VirusTotal creates clusters of similar samples using structural, behavioral, and static similarities. Analysts can pivot from one artifact to dozens of related ones. A suspicious document may reveal the domains it connects to, the URLs embedded within it, and the hash values of macros extracted during analysis. These relationships help uncover the scope of a threat beyond a single alert. Detection engineers rely on this same relational intelligence to build YARA rules that match families of related samples or identify packers and obfuscation techniques used across multiple campaigns.

As powerful as it is, VirusTotal also requires operational discipline. Files uploaded to VirusTotal are shared within the broader intelligence community. They may be analyzed, clustered, stored, and reviewed by vendors and researchers. For this reason, SOC teams must not upload sensitive documents, confidential source code, proprietary binaries, or materials that may contain regulated data. Mature SOCs implement internal policies that dictate what can and cannot be submitted. When necessary, isolated private sandboxes are used for sensitive analysis.

When applied responsibly, VirusTotal becomes one of the most effective force multipliers available to a SOC. It accelerates triage, enriches investigations, supports threat intelligence programs, enhances malware research, and improves detection engineering. During a fast moving incident, VirusTotal often becomes the first confirmation that a suspicious artifact is associated with a known malware family or active campaign. This confirmation allows analysts to escalate quickly and decisively. VirusTotal stands as a living knowledge base of global adversary activity, constantly evolving as new samples arrive and researchers contribute insights. For SOC teams that understand how to interpret its signals and use its intelligence in context, it is an indispensable tool that transforms isolated indicators into actionable understanding.

AbuseIPDB: Community-Driven IP Reputation

AbuseIPDB has become one of the most practical and immediately useful reputation platforms for SOC teams because it focuses on a single objective: identifying malicious IP activity with clarity and speed. Instead of tracking malware families or adversary groups, AbuseIPDB concentrates entirely on the behavior of IP addresses as observed across the global internet. Its strength comes from community scale. Thousands of researchers, security teams, hosting providers, and automated systems submit verified abuse reports every day, creating a constantly updated reputation ecosystem. This crowd sourced intelligence gives SOC analysts a real time snapshot of hostile activity that is grounded in observable behavior rather than theoretical risk.

At the center of the platform is a confidence score generated from several inputs. These include the number of reports submitted about an IP, the severity of the reported behavior, the diversity of reporters involved, and the recency of the events. Time matters greatly in the scoring model. An IP that attempted brute force attacks moments ago is far more important to an investigator than an IP that sent spam a year earlier. AbuseIPDB therefore prioritizes fresh, active threats that correlate directly with the type of activity most SOCs encounter every day such as credential stuffing, unauthorized login attempts, forced browsing, and opportunistic exploitation of internet facing systems.

AbuseIPDB enriches every IP with valuable metadata. Analysts can immediately see the associated autonomous system, the service provider, the country, the number of historical reports, and the specific incident categories that apply. Categories reveal the nature of the threat whether repeated SSH attempts, SQL injection tests, phishing distribution, or participation in distributed denial of service activity. This contextual view allows analysts to validate their instincts quickly. For example, if a firewall logs repeated failed SSH attempts from an unfamiliar IP, AbuseIPDB often reveals whether that same address has been targeting systems worldwide with identical behavior. The ability to merge local evidence with global intelligence dramatically reduces triage time and lifts the quality of investigative decisions.

Most SOC teams integrate AbuseIPDB into SIEM and SOAR workflows so reputation checks run automatically. When an alert contains an external IP address whether it comes from an authentication event, a firewall detection, endpoint network telemetry, or an intrusion signature the enrichment pipeline triggers an API lookup. The returned data is parsed and evaluated through automated logic that examines the confidence score, the most recent report date, the related categories, and the variety of contributors. These values become decision inputs. An IP with a very high confidence score and recent signs of brute force behavior might be escalated or even blocked automatically. A low score with old or unrelated categories may support deprioritization.

AbuseIPDB also helps SOCs distinguish between real threats and noisy but harmless services. Some cloud platforms run scanners or uptime monitors that mimic hostile patterns. These services occasionally generate abuse reports, but the metadata usually reveals their true nature. Mature SOCs often build allowlists for well known scanning services to prevent constant false alarms. This type of clarity makes AbuseIPDB an essential tool for avoiding wasted analyst effort.

The platform becomes even more powerful when analysts correlate its data with endpoint context, firewall flows, cloud access logs, or identity events. A high score combined with suspicious user activity or unusual process behavior may indicate genuine intrusion attempts. Conversely, an IP that generates unusual traffic but has no reputation history may signal targeted reconnaissance that automated systems would otherwise overlook. AbuseIPDB gives analysts a faster way to differentiate random scanning from adversaries who are studying the environment deliberately.

The community driven model behind AbuseIPDB ensures that every participant benefits from the observations of others. Organizations that submit accurate reports help strengthen the platform for everyone and help cultivate a living global picture of malicious activity. AbuseIPDB does not function as a verdict engine that declares absolute truth. It is a risk amplifier. When used in combination with SIEM analytics, endpoint telemetry, and human judgment, it increases confidence, accelerates triage, and reduces uncertainty in the investigative process.

GreyNoise: Contextualizing Internet Background Noise

GreyNoise solves one of the longest standing pain points in Security Operations: the overwhelming volume of internet background radiation. Every exposed service VPN, firewall, web server, SSH port, or IoT device receives constant probes from scanners, bots, researchers, cloud crawlers, and opportunistic adversaries. Most of this traffic is not targeted. It is indiscriminate activity sweeping the internet and looking for common weaknesses. Without context, however, SOC analysts cannot easily distinguish harmless background scans from meaningful reconnaissance. This is where GreyNoise becomes transformative.

At its core, GreyNoise operates by monitoring the internet at scale using a massive global network of sensors designed to attract scanning activity. When an IP engages in broad, untargeted scanning across the public internet, GreyNoise collects the activity and classifies it based on behavior, frequency, tooling, payloads, and scanning patterns. Instead of focusing on maliciousness alone, which is a difficult determination to make, GreyNoise focuses on intent and scope: is this IP scanning everyone, or is it scanning you for a reason?

This distinction is critical. A SOC alert triggered by failed SSH logins or unusual connection attempts may seem threatening, but if GreyNoise shows that the source IP is part of a well known mass scanner or benign research organization, the operational significance changes entirely. Conversely, an IP that never appears in GreyNoise data may represent truly anomalous, targeted, or emerging activity worth deeper scrutiny.

GreyNoise classifies IPs into categories such as:

- Benign scanners (research projects, academic studies, vendor telemetry collection)
- Common noise (mass-scale opportunistic scans affecting everyone on the internet)
- Malicious scanners (botnets, exploit attempts, worm propagation)
- Unknown/uncategorized (no broad scanning observed, potentially targeted activity)

The value of this classification is not just informational, it is operational. SOC teams use GreyNoise to help determine whether a firewall alert, IDS signature, or perimeter anomaly represents something that demands analyst attention or merely reflects the constant hum of automated scanning. This context dramatically reduces the number of alerts requiring manual triage and prevents analysts from wasting time on benign events that have no security impact.

GreyNoise becomes exponentially more powerful when integrated directly into SIEM and SOAR enrichment. When an alert contains an external IP address, automated workflows query GreyNoise through the API. The returned metadata is then processed according to SOC logic:

- If GreyNoise labels the IP as "benign noise", the alert may be automatically suppressed or marked informational.
- If the IP is "malicious noise" (e.g., scanning for known exploit vectors), it may be triaged but with lower priority.

- If the IP is "unknown"especially when combined with other suspicious behavior the alert is escalated for analyst review.

This automated stratification not only streamlines triage but also improves signal fidelity. Instead of drowning in predictable, low-value alerts, analysts can focus their time on unusual or high-risk activity that warrants human investigation.

GreyNoise is especially powerful in environments with exposed perimeter services, cloud infrastructure, or large-scale web presence. For these organizations, a significant portion of alerts stem from automated internet-scanning tools. Without GreyNoise context, these alerts may burden Tier 1 analysts who treat every inbound request as potentially targeted. With GreyNoise enrichment, however, the SOC develops an intelligence-driven posture in which benign background noise is quietly filtered out before it drains resources.

Perhaps the most important contribution of GreyNoise is confidence. Analysts often hesitate to close alerts early without high-quality context, fearing they may overlook real threats. GreyNoise gives them a defensible basis grounded in global data. Instead of guessing whether an IP scanning SSH is relevant, they can state confidently: "*This IP scans the entire internet regularly and is not performing targeted activity. No further action required.*"

By reframing how SOCs interpret inbound noise, GreyNoise does more than reduce alertsit enhances accuracy, improves triage confidence, and strengthens the entire detection pipeline. When embedded early in automated workflows, it helps the SOC reclaim analyst hours while preserving, and often improving, sensitivity to real threats. In short, GreyNoise is not just a filter, it is a contextual intelligence layer that separates the meaningful from the meaningless at scale.

Shodan: External Attack Surface Intelligence

Shodan is often described as "the search engine for the Internet of Things," but in reality, it is far broader and more consequential for Security Operations Centers. Shodan continuously scans large swaths of the public internet collecting metadata from exposed services, devices, cloud systems, industrial control equipment, and enterprise infrastructure. Its purpose is not to find malicious actors but to catalog what is exposed. For SOCs, this visibility is indispensable.

How Shodan Crawlers Work

Shodan deploys a distributed network of scanning nodes across multiple regions and cloud providers. These nodes perform constant, methodical scans of public IP ranges similar to how Google indexes websites, but instead of HTML content, Shodan indexes machine-level metadata. Its crawlers attempt to interact with exposed services and collect whatever information the service willingly reveals:

- Banners (e.g., SSH, FTP, SMTP, RDP, Telnet)

- HTTP headers and server responses
- TLS certificate details (issuer, expiration, subject, public key algorithms)
- Protocol handshakes (Modbus, VNC, Elasticsearch, MongoDB, etc.)
- Authentication prompts or default credential banners
- Device metadata (vendor, version, OS type, firmware)

This data is generated entirely from publicly accessible systems meaning anything Shodan can see is, by definition, visible to attackers. Shodan's scanning architecture is optimized to fingerprint devices with minimal disruption. Unlike malicious scanners, Shodan does not brute-force services or exploit weaknesses; it performs non-intrusive probing. But because attackers routinely use Shodan themselves, SOC teams must assume that any exposed asset Shodan identifies is also known to adversaries.

Why Shodan Matters for SOC Operations

Although Shodan is not a traditional threat intelligence feed because it does not identify malicious actors, it provides situational intelligence about the organization's attack surface. Most security failures originate from exposure: forgotten servers, outdated services, unpatched web applications, cloud misconfigurations, and test systems accidentally placed on the public internet. Shodan finds these exposures before an attacker weaponizes them.

For SOCs, this visibility is priceless.

1. Attack Surface Identification

Shodan reveals assets security teams often forget exist:

- Legacy VPN appliances
- Development or QA systems placed temporarily on the internet
- Orphaned cloud instances
- ATMs, cameras, printers, or IoT devices exposed inadvertently
- Databases without authentication

- Misconfigured RDP, VNC, SMB shares

A SOC can use Shodan to map external infrastructure continuously either manually or via API-driven monitoring. Any newly exposed asset becomes an investigation.

2. Exposure Validation During Incident Response

When analysts investigate suspicious outbound traffic, the destination's identity matters. If an endpoint is communicating with an unfamiliar IP, Shodan enrichment helps determine:

- What service is running on that IP
- Whether the service appears benign or suspicious
- Whether the endpoint-connected port aligns with expected protocols
- Whether the foreign system is misconfigured or malicious-looking

For instance, if a workstation contacts an IP hosting an exposed Elasticsearch database known to be abused by attackers, this raises immediate concern.

3. Threat Hunting Across the External Perimeter

Threat hunters use Shodan defensively by looking for their own organization:

- Searching for domains, ASN ranges, or IP blocks owned by the company
- Identifying accidental exposures
- Finding outdated versions of services Shodan has flagged as vulnerable
- Viewing historical exposure data

This proactive approach often discovers vulnerabilities before attackers do.

4. Compliance & Governance

Certain industries (e.g., finance, healthcare, federal contracting) require proof that internet-facing assets are inventoried and secured. Shodan provides independent verification.

API Integration for Automation and Enrichment

Shodan's API makes it easy for SOC teams to embed external exposure intelligence directly into:

- SIEM enrichment workflows
- SOAR playbooks
- Vulnerability management programs
- Attack surface monitoring pipelines

For example, a SOAR playbook investigating suspicious outbound traffic may query Shodan automatically. Returned metadata can answer questions such as:

- "What service is this IP running?"
- "Is the certificate self-signed or linked to known malware C2 infrastructure?"
- "Does the destination appear to be a honeypot, ICS device, or exposed admin panel?"

This context informs escalation decisions. If Shodan identifies the remote system as a Tor exit node, abused proxy service, or exposed IoT panel, the SOC prioritizes investigation. If the system appears to be a benign web server running standard software, risk may be lower.

Shodan as a Threat-Hunting Ally

Even though Shodan is not primarily a threat feed, it indirectly supports detection:

- Attackers frequently use Shodan to select targets.
- Exposed services are statistically more likely to be attacked.
- Shodan tags known vulnerabilities (e.g., Log4j exposure, RDP open to the world).
- Shodan historical data reveals how long an asset has been exposed.

Threat hunters often pivot from internal logs to Shodan:

"This server received scanning activity. Was it visible on Shodan beforehand? If so, how long?"

The longer something is exposed, the higher the likelihood that it has been targeted.

Shodan Is Not a Threat Detector It Is an Exposure Detector

Understanding Shodan's purpose is essential to using it effectively within a SOC. Shodan does not indicate whether an attacker is actively targeting your environment. It cannot tell you whether malicious actors have attempted intrusion, executed exploits, or engaged in credential attacks. Instead, Shodan provides something equally important but fundamentally different: a real-time reflection of what your organization exposes to the public internet.

Traditional SOC tooling SIEMs, EDR agents, firewalls, intrusion detection systems focused inward, detecting suspicious signals within network or endpoint telemetry. These tools reveal indicators of compromise, anomalous behavior, and malicious activity after it has begun. Shodan, by contrast, looks outward. It shows what attackers see when they scan the public-facing infrastructure of your organization.

And this distinction carries significant operational weight, because attackers use Shodan extensively for reconnaissance. Before scanning your network themselves, threat actors often query Shodan to locate vulnerable services, outdated systems, misconfigured ports, exposed databases, or publicly accessible admin interfaces. Ransomware groups, botnet operators, exploit kit distributors, and low-skilled script kiddies all rely on Shodan to accelerate target acquisition. In many cases, attackers initiate campaigns based on data Shodan has already indexed, meaning your exposure may be known to adversaries long before your SOC becomes aware of it.

For defenders, this creates an opportunity. Shodan becomes a mirror reflecting your attack surface exactly as a hacker would see it. If Shodan can index an exposed asset, attackers can indeed and do leverage it. This is why Shodan is best understood as an exposure detector, not a threat detector. It alerts you not to threats in progress, but to conditions that invite threats.

When SOC teams combine inward-facing detection with outward-facing exposure intelligence, they achieve a more complete defensive posture. Internal tools warn you when malicious activity occurs; Shodan warns you when you are unintentionally advertising vulnerabilities to the world. Used together, they close the visibility gap between what is happening inside the environment and what adversaries can discover from the outside. In modern cybersecurity operations, where misconfigurations and overlooked assets are among the most common root causes of breaches, that outward visibility is invaluable.

Recorded Future: Intelligence Fusion and Risk Scoring

Recorded Future occupies the top tier of commercial threat intelligence platforms, offering capabilities that extend far beyond traditional indicator-based services. Its strength lies in the ability to aggregate vast amounts of intelligence from across the open web, dark web marketplaces, criminal forums, code repositories, vulnerability disclosures, attack infrastructure tracking, and even geopolitical reporting. Recorded Future processes this information through sophisticated machine learning models that correlate disparate signals and transform them into meaningful risk scores for entities such as IP addresses, domains, malware families, vulnerabilities, and threat actors. Unlike narrow reputation services, which simply label an artifact as clean or malicious, Recorded Future explains why an indicator matters and what broader activity it is tied to. This contextual approach allows SOC analysts to prioritize investigations not by noise or frequency, but by relevance to current threat campaigns and adversary behavior.

What sets Recorded Future apart is its ability to answer investigative questions that SIEMs and traditional feeds cannot. It provides insight into who may be behind an indicator, what tools or malware families they use, what campaigns are active, and how a particular domain or address fits within a larger attack ecosystem. An IP address with minimal noise may still be strongly associated with an active ransomware group and therefore represent a far higher risk than a random scanner that triggers alerts regularly. By providing this intelligence, Recorded Future shifts the SOC from reactive triage toward informed, strategic decision-making. Analysts gain clarity not only about what they are seeing, but about why it matters in the broader threat landscape.

Most SOCs integrate Recorded Future through API-based enrichment, allowing the platform to feed risk scores, intelligence summaries, associated MITRE ATT&CK techniques, infrastructure relationships, and current campaign details directly into SIEM and SOAR workflows. This integration transforms alert triage. Instead of treating indicators in isolation, analysts immediately understand whether an artifact is part of a known adversary toolkit or connected to a widely exploited vulnerability. They can see whether similar activity has been observed targeting the same industry or region, whether an attacker is currently active, and whether escalation is warranted. This context helps SOC teams, especially MSSPs handling many clients, prioritize high-risk threats and allocate human resources more effectively.

Recorded Future also enhances reporting and executive communication. Its intelligence cards and narrative summaries translate complex technical relationships into clear, actionable insights that leaders can understand. SOC managers use Recorded Future to prepare weekly threat briefs, executive dashboards, and client summaries, often linking specific detections to broader adversary campaigns or industry-wide trends. This ability to frame incidents within a strategic context strengthens risk communication and reinforces the SOC's value as a proactive security function rather than a reactive alert handler. Recorded Future provides the connective tissue between raw indicators and strategic threat understanding. It elevates investigations by supplying context, clarifies prioritization by scoring risk intelligently, and enables organizations to align detection engineering and incident response with real-world adversary activity. For SOCs seeking to mature beyond basic monitoring into intelligence-driven operations, Recorded Future serves as an indispensable engine for insight, prioritization, and foresight.

MISP: Open Intelligence Sharing and Collaboration

MISP (Malware Information Sharing Platform) is an open-source threat intelligence sharing platform designed for structured collaboration. Internally, MISP stores indicators, attributes, events, galaxy clusters (for threat actors and malware families), and relationships between entities. Unlike commercial feeds, MISP emphasizes transparency and community-driven curation.

SOCs use MISP to both consume and contribute intelligence. Internally curated indicatorsderived from investigations or threat huntscan be published to trusted communities. Conversely, organizations ingest community intelligence relevant to their sector or geography.

API-driven integration allows MISP to feed SIEM correlation rules, enrich alerts, and support detection engineering. Because MISP data is structured, SOCs can map indicators directly into detection pipelines. The effectiveness of MISP depends on governancepoorly curated instances can introduce noise, while disciplined, scope-limited instances become powerful intelligence hubs.

Integrating Threat Intelligence via API

Integration is where threat intelligence delivers real value. Manually checking indicators does not scale. Mature SOCs integrate threat intelligence tools into SIEM and SOAR workflows through APIs, caching responses and applying logic consistently. A common integration pattern involves triggering enrichment during alert creation. The SIEM forwards an indicator to SOAR, which queries multiple sources concurrently: VirusTotal for reputation, GreyNoise for classification, AbuseIPDB for abuse history, and Recorded Future for contextual risk. Responses are normalized, scored, and presented to analysts or used to trigger automation.

Key best practices include rate-limit awareness, response caching, confidence weighting, and clear threshold policies. No single intelligence source should dictate action in isolation. Instead, SOCs combine signals to build confidence-based decisions that are auditable and repeatable.

Threat intelligence tools are not interchangeable commodities; each provides a distinct lens on risk. VirusTotal amplifies reputation confidence. AbuseIPDB tracks active

IP abuse. GreyNoise filters background noise. Shodan reveals exposure. Recorded Future adds strategic context. MISP enables collaboration. By understanding how each tool works internally and integrating them programmatically into detection and response workflows, SOCs transform intelligence into operational advantage, reducing noise, accelerating response, and improving trust in automated decisions.

Chapter 21

Deep Dive: DevOps for SOC Operations

Modern SOCs are no longer staffed solely by analysts clicking through consoles. High-performing SOCs operate as engineering organizations. They build, test, deploy, version, and continuously improve detections and automations using the same DevOps principles that power scalable software systems. This fusion often called SecOps or SOC Engineering is what enables speed without sacrificing reliability.

This chapter explains how SOC teams use APIs, micro-automations, scripting, serverless execution, source control, and CI/CD pipelines to transform security operations from manual reaction into governed, repeatable systems.

Using APIs for Enrichment

In a modern Security Operations Center, APIs function as the connective tissue that links every major security platform into one cohesive operational ecosystem. Nearly every enterprise security toolSIEMs, SOARs, EDR suites, firewalls, identity providers, threat intelligence platforms, vulnerability scanners, and ticketing systems expose functionality through APIs. What once required analysts to manually log in to multiple consoles, export logs, copy IPs into threat intelligence portals, or manually create tickets can now be orchestrated programmatically. APIs eliminate repetitive manual work and enable SOC teams to enrich alerts, execute responses, and correlate intelligence automatically and consistently.

API-driven enrichment begins the moment an alert is generated. An alert typically contains one or more artifactsan IP address, domain, hash, username, hostname, URL, or file path. Automation systems (SOAR platforms, serverless functions, or custom Python microservices) extract these artifacts and issue concurrent API queries to external and internal enrichment sources. These may include

VirusTotal for malware reputation, GreyNoise for background scanning classification, AbuseIPDB for abuse scores, Recorded Future for contextual intelligence, or Active Directory APIs for identity validation. Instead of analysts performing a dozen manual lookups, enrichment pipelines complete this work in seconds, returning structured intelligence that can be evaluated instantly.

Because enrichment is only useful when it is reliable, mature SOCs emphasize consistency and normalization. Each enrichment source produces different response formats, field names, and data structures. To prevent downstream logic from breaking, SOC engineers design standardized schemas/uniform data models into which all enrichment responses are mapped. This allows playbooks and detection rules to consume data predictably, regardless of whether the enrichment originated from a commercial CTI platform, internal asset database, or free OSINT source. With standardized structures, enrichment pipelines become reusable modules that power hundreds of playbooks, detection workflows, and automated response actions.

Error handling is another critical component of successful API automation. External tools may throttle requests, temporarily fail, or return malformed data. A mature SOC designs enrichment pipelines to degrade gracefully, timeouts must not block triage workflows, failed queries must not halt investigations, and fallback logic must ensure that even partial results can move an alert forward. Automated workflows often include retry logic, caching of recent responses, and intelligent load balancing to remain stable under heavy alert volume.

API key security is equally important. Because enrichment and automation often touch highly sensitive systems, SOC teams store API keys in encrypted secret managers with strict access controls. Keys are rotated regularly, limited to specific IP ranges, and scoped with least privilege only the permissions necessary for enrichment or response actions. This prevents automation components from becoming new attack surfaces and maintains compliance with security governance standards.

Over time, API enrichment pipelines become foundational to the SOC's overall architecture. They evolve from simple lookups into powerful data-fusion engines. Instead of manually correlating disparate signals, SOC analysts and engineers can rely on automated workflows that combine identity attributes, threat intelligence context, asset inventory data, vulnerability exposure, and historical incident patterns all before an analyst even opens the ticket. These pipelines accelerate triage, improve detection fidelity, reduce alert fatigue, and enable response actions that are both faster and more consistent than manual processes.

Ultimately, API-driven automation transforms SOC operations from a reactive, labor-intensive function into a scalable, intelligence-driven capability. API pipelines become reusable building blocks, powering automated containment, high-confidence blocking decisions, dynamic risk scoring, and enriched reporting. They are not peripheral enhancements; they are the foundation upon which modern, high-velocity SOCs are engineered.

Building Micro-Automations

In a mature SOC, automation is not delivered as large, monolithic playbooks that attempt to handle every phase of an investigation from start to finish. Such all-in-one automations tend to become brittle over time. They are difficult to update, prone to unexpected failures, and nearly impossible to test thoroughly because a single change can affect dozens of dependent steps. Instead, high-functioning SOCs adopt a micro-automation strategy building small, modular automation components that each perform one task exceptionally well. These components are then chained together in orchestrated workflows, similar to modern microservices architectures used in DevOps engineering.

A micro-automation may do something as simple as validating IP reputation through a threat intelligence API, retrieving endpoint metadata from an EDR tool, checking MFA status for a user via an identity provider, or submitting a hash to a sandbox. Each micro-automation is deliberately narrow in scope, with a clearly defined input and output. Because the automation does only one thing, its behavior is predictable, deterministic, and easy to test repeatedly. If something breaks such as an API schema, authentication method, or external service the SOC can repair or update that micro-component without disrupting entire playbooks.

This modular approach dramatically increases flexibility. When analysts or engineers identify a noisy detection, need to enrich data differently, or introduce a new threat intelligence source, they modify or create a targeted micro-automation rather than rewriting complex, multi-page workflows. Micro-automations can be reused across dozens of playbooks, reducing duplication and ensuring consistent behavior across all alert-handling pipelines. As new tools, APIs, or methods are added to the SOC environment, engineers simply build new micro-automations that plug into the existing orchestration layer.

SOC teams commonly implement micro-automations using SOAR sub-playbooks, serverless functions (such as AWS Lambda, Azure Functions, or Google Cloud Functions), containers, or small Python scripts triggered by SIEM events. These lightweight automation units form the building blocks of larger workflows. For example, an alert triage playbook may call four independent micro-automations one for IP reputation, one for endpoint context, one for identity verification, and one for asset classification before passing the enriched alert to a decision engine. If any component needs tuning or replacement, the rest of the pipeline remains unaffected.

Over time, a mature SOC develops an internal "automation library," a curated set of reusable micro-automations that form an internal automation framework. Analysts and engineers can then assemble complex workflows from these building blocks without writing new logic for every alert type or platform integration. This results in faster development cycles, safer code, higher stability, and a more scalable automation ecosystem.

Micro-automations also enhance auditability and compliance. Because each unit is limited in scope, documenting behavior and proving operational integrity becomes far simpler. Auditors and SOC managers can review specific components rather than tracing logic across massive monolithic playbooks. This reduces the risk of undocumented logic, hidden dependencies, or unexpected playbook branching that often plagues large automation designs.

Ultimately, micro-automations transform SOC automation from a fragile, tangled collection of long workflows into a clean, modular, scalable engineering discipline. They enable rapid adaptation, minimize operational risk, and ensure automation becomes a force multiplier rather than a maintenance burden.

Python Scripting for SOC Operations

Python has effectively become the primary language of SOC engineering. Its readability, massive ecosystem of libraries, and natural fit for HTTP APIs make it ideal for building the "glue" that binds disparate security tools into a cohesive detection and response ecosystem. While SOAR platforms and SIEMs provide native integrations, real-world operations frequently outgrow the capabilities of those connectors. Python fills that gap by enabling custom enrichment, correlation, orchestration, and reporting logic that would otherwise require manual analyst effort.

In most mature SOCs, Python is used wherever native tooling stops short. Analysts and engineers write scripts to query APIs that lack native SOAR connectors, normalize inconsistent JSON responses, correlate results from multiple sources, and push structured findings back into SIEMs, EDR tools, ticketing systems, or chat platforms. A Python script might pull fresh indicators from a threat feed, enrich them with context from VirusTotal and AbuseIPDB, push them into a SIEM watchlist, and then notify the SOC via Slack or Teamsall without manual intervention. Over time, these scripts evolve from quick utilities into core automation components that the SOC relies on daily.

A well-designed SOC Python script should look and behave much more like a small service than a one-off hack. It uses modular functions for clarity and reuse; structured logging so that output can be ingested by the SIEM for monitoring; clear exception handling to avoid silent failures; and configuration files or environment variables instead of hard-coded secrets and parameters. Scripts should also support a dry-run mode, allowing engineers to validate logic without actually blocking IPs, closing tickets, or disabling accounts.

Example: Simple IP Enrichment Micro-Automation

This script queries a mock IP reputation API (easily adapted for AbuseIPDB, GreyNoise, etc.), normalizes the result, and prints a JSON payload suitable for a SOAR or SIEM.

```
#!/usr/bin/env python3
import os
import json
import logging
import requests
from typing import Dict, Any

logging.basicConfig(
    level=logging.INFO,
    format="%(asctime)s [%(levelname)s]
%(message)s"
)

API_KEY = os.getenv("IP_REP_API_KEY")  # store
in env or secret manager
API_URL =
"https://api.example.com/v1/ip-reputation"


def get_ip_reputation(ip: str) -> Dict[str,
Any]:
    """Query IP reputation provider and return
raw JSON."""
    headers = {"Authorization": f"Bearer
{API_KEY}"}
    params = {"ip": ip}

    try:
```

```
        response = requests.get(API_URL,
headers=headers, params=params, timeout=5)
        response.raise_for_status()
        return response.json()
    except
requests.exceptions.RequestException as e:
        logging.error(f"Error querying
reputation API for {ip}: {e}")
        return {"error": str(e), "ip": ip}


def normalize_reputation(raw: Dict[str, Any])
-> Dict[str, Any]:
    """Normalize vendor-specific JSON into a
standard schema."""
    if "error" in raw:
        return {
            "ip": raw.get("ip"),
            "status": "error",
            "reason": raw["error"]
        }

    return {
        "ip": raw.get("ip"),
        "status": "ok",
        "score": raw.get("score"),
        "category": raw.get("category"),
        "last_seen": raw.get("last_seen"),
        "source": "example_ip_rep"
    }


if __name__ == "__main__":
    import argparse

    parser =
argparse.ArgumentParser(description="IP
reputation enrichment micro-automation")
    parser.add_argument("ip", help="IP address
to enrich")
    parser.add_argument("--dry-run",
action="store_true", help="Don't exit with
non-zero on error")
    args = parser.parse_args()
```

```
    raw = get_ip_reputation(args.ip)
    enriched = normalize_reputation(raw)

    logging.info("Enrichment result:")
    print(json.dumps(enriched, indent=2))

    if not args.dry_run and
enriched.get("status") == "error":
        exit(1)
```

This script demonstrates key best practices such as:

- Configuration via environment variables
- Dedicated functions for API calls and normalization
- Structured logging
- A `--dry-run` option
- A normalized output schema ready for ingestion by a SOAR or SIEM

Lambda Functions and Serverless Execution

Serverless computing such as AWS Lambda, Azure Functions, or Google Cloud Functions allows SOC teams to execute logic without managing servers. This aligns perfectly with event-driven security workflows.

In serverless models, a function is triggered by an event: a SIEM alert, webhook, message queue entry, or scheduled task. The function executes, performs its logic, and exits. This model provides automatic scaling, high availability, and cost efficiency functions that consume resources only when invoked.

SOC use cases include real-time enrichment, indicator validation, automated containment checks, and scheduled hygiene tasks such as stale indicator cleanup. Serverless functions are ideal for micro-automations because they enforce stateless design and clear input/output contracts.

The key considerations are security and observability. Functions must have tightly scoped permissions, structured logging, and monitoring to ensure failures are visible. Versioning is essential, as serverless functions often change rapidly during SOC tuning cycles.

Using GitHub and GitLab for Playbooks and Code

Version control is one of the most important engineering disciplines a SOC can adopt, and platforms like GitHub and GitLab provide the structure required to maintain reliable, auditable, and scalable operations. Any

SOC that stores detection logic, playbooks, or automation scripts outside of a version-controlled repository eventually encounters chaos: undocumented changes, broken workflows, overwritten scripts, missing revisions, or logic drift across environments. By contrast, a SOC that manages its engineering artifacts through GitHub or GitLab gains a predictable, controlled, and collaborative development lifecycle.

In a mature SOC, every piece of operational logicSOAR playbooks, detection rules, API integration code, enrichment modules, Python utilities, incident response templates, and infrastructure-as-code files are stored in repositories with organized structures. Playbooks are typically exported as JSON or YAML; detections are stored as KQL, SPL, or ECS-aligned YAML; and automations are maintained as Python modules. These repositories form the SOC's internal "source of truth," ensuring that any analyst or engineer can see exactly how logic has evolved, when changes were made, who made them, and why.

Repositories are usually structured by functional domains. For example, a SOC may maintain separate folders for *detections*, *automations*, *enrichment modules*, *IR workflows*, *tooling utilities*, or *CI/CD configuration files*. This arrangement makes it easy to search, maintain, and audit the collection of artifacts. A typical repository structure might look like:

```
/soc-automation-framework
  /detections
    sentinel/
    splunk/
    elastic/
  /playbooks
    soar/
    sub-playbooks/
  /python-modules
    enrichment/
    containment/
    correlation/
  /infrastructure
    terraform/
    ansible/
  /docs
    SOPs/
    runbooks/
    IR-templates/
```

Once code and configuration live in Git, the SOC begins adopting modern software engineering practices. Changes are introduced through pull requests, where team members submit modifications that must be reviewed by peers before merging. This process enforces quality control, prevents accidental errors, and encourages collaborative improvement. A SOC analyst proposing a new detection rule, for example, must document the rule, its purpose, and any associated false-positive risks. A detection engineer reviews the logic, hunters validate test cases, and the SOC manager provides final approval. Each commit is timestamped and tracked, preserving a forensic trail that is invaluable during audits or post-incident reviews.

Testing becomes another essential step. Before merging into the main branch, new playbooks or scripts are tested in non-production environments such as staging SOAR instances, sandbox SIEM workspaces, or isolated EDR tenants. GitHub Actions or GitLab CI/CD pipelines can automate linting, schema validation, unit tests, or simulated workflow executions. This shifts the SOC from console-driven changes to a predictable deployment pipeline where logic is validated before it impacts active investigations.

Tagging and branching strategies strengthen this model further. Branches such as feature/new-detection, bugfix/playbook-loop, or hotfix/credential-rotation allow concurrent development without disrupting stable operations. Taggingsuch as v1.0.3 or 2025-Q2-releaseenables teams to align logic versions with incident timelines. If an incident occurs on March 10, the SOC can reference the exact detection or playbook version in effect on that date, creating clarity for forensic analysis, reporting, and post-incident improvement. By using GitHub or GitLab, the SOC transitions from reactive console edits to disciplined engineering practices. Every change becomes intentional, peer-reviewed, traceable, and reversible. This dramatically reduces operational risk. It also enables new capabilities such as automated deployments, scheduled content updates, cross-team collaboration, and compliance-friendly documentation.

Pull Request Checklist for SOC Changes

```
SOC Engineering Pull Request Checklist

    ☐ Description of change provided
    ☐ Associated detection / alert /
      ticket referenced
    ☐ Test results included (staging
      SIEM or SOAR validation)
    ☐ Backward compatibility confirmed
    ☐ Documentation updated
    ☐ Security review completed (API
      keys, secrets, permissions)
    ☐ Peer review completed by:
      __________
    ☐ Ready for merge
```

SOC Repository README.md Structure

```
# SOC Automation & Detection
Repository
```

```
## Purpose
This repository serves as the source
of truth for SOC detections,
automation playbooks,
IR workflows, and engineering
utilities.

## Directory Overview
- detections/ : SIEM analytics rules
for Sentinel, Splunk, Elastic
- playbooks/  : SOAR playbooks
(YAML/JSON)
- python-modules/ : Python automation
scripts and enrichment services
- infrastructure/ : Terraform,
Ansible, and pipeline configs
- docs/ : SOPs, runbooks, templates,
IR artifacts

## Contribution Process
1. Create feature branch
2. Submit pull request
3. Obtain peer review
4. Validate in staging
5. Merge into main
6. Automated pipeline deploys to
production environment
```

CI/CD for Detections

Continuous Integration and Continuous Deployment are not just for applications they are critical for SOC detection engineering. CI/CD pipelines ensure that detection changes are validated consistently and deployed safely.

In CI/CD-enabled SOCs, detection rules are written as code and often declarative files describing logic, thresholds, and metadata. When a change is committed, automated pipelines run syntax checks, validate required fields, test queries against staging data, and ensure naming and severity standards are met. Failed checks prevent deployment Once validated, detections are promoted through environments: development, staging, and production. Canary deployment strategies allow new detections or tuned thresholds to run in limited mode before full activation. Rollbacks are simple because previous versions are always preserved.

CI/CD enforces discipline. It prevents ad-hoc rule changes that introduce noise or risk. Over time, it gives SOC leaders confidence that detection quality is improving systematically rather than unpredictably.

DevOps principles are no longer optional for modern SOCsthey are the difference between fragile operations and resilient, scalable defense. By leveraging APIs, micro-automations, Python scripting, serverless execution, source control, and CI/CD pipelines, SOC teams evolve into high-performance engineering organizations. This chapter provides the blueprint for integrating DevOps into SOC operations, ensuring that security keeps pace with both attackers and technology.

SECTION VII

THE BUSINESS OF SOCs

Chapter 22

Building an MSSP SOC Offering

Building a SOC for internal use and building a SOC as a commercial service are fundamentally different challenges. An MSSP SOC is not just a security functionit is a product, governed by contracts, expectations, liability, and scalability. Technical excellence alone is insufficient. Successful MSSPs design SOC offerings that are clearly defined, priced sustainably, operationally repeatable, legally defensible, and scalable across multiple clients simultaneously.

This chapter provides a complete operational blueprint for creating an MSSP-grade SOC offering, from service packaging and pricing to delivery models, SLAs, legal constraints, and multi-tenant architecture.

Packaging SOC Services

The first step in building an MSSP SOC is defining *what you actually sell*. Vague descriptions like "24/7 monitoring" lead to mismatched expectations, scope creep, and contractual risk. Mature MSSPs package SOC services into clearly defined tiers, each with explicit inclusions and exclusions.

Service packages are typically built around core SOC capabilities: monitoring, alert triage, incident response support, threat intelligence, reporting, and tuning. Entry-level packages may include detection and notification only, بينما advanced packages include enrichment, response coordination, threat hunting, and advisory services. The key is consistency, every client in a tier receives the same baseline service so operations remain repeatable.

Packaging must also define *boundaries*. Does the SOC take response actions or only recommend them? Is incident response included or billable separately? Are investigations limited by time or scope? Clear boundaries protect both the MSSP and the client. Packaging decisions should align with operational maturity. Promising advanced response without the staffing, tooling, or automation to deliver it will damage credibility quickly.

Pricing Models: From Cost Reality to Sustainable Security

Pricing is one of the most misunderstood and most dangerous aspects of SOC operations. It is where otherwise capable security teams fail, either by underpricing services until analysts burn out and margins collapse, or by overpricing without clearly communicating value, driving customer attrition or executive resistance. Effective SOC pricing is neither arbitrary nor reactive; it is a disciplined exercise in cost modeling, risk translation, and value justification.

Whether you are proposing an in-house SOC to executive leadership or designing a commercial MSSP offering, the fundamentals are the same: pricing must reflect what the SOC costs to operate, what risks it reduces, and what outcomes it enables.

In-House SOC Pricing: From Security Proposal to Board Approval

Funding an internal SOC is not a simple matter of requesting tools or headcount, it is a structured, multi-stage budgeting process that begins with technical pain points and ends in a boardroom where executives evaluate risk, cost, and organizational priorities. The process functions as both a financial justification and a narrative exercise: leadership must understand not only what the SOC will do, but why failing to build one exposes the organization to unacceptable business risk.

Step 1: Security & IT Identify the Need

The journey typically begins within the technical team's security operations, incident response, IT infrastructure who begin observing patterns that indicate the current security posture cannot scale. Alert volumes increase beyond the team's capacity to investigate, incidents are discovered through luck or after damage is done, and cloud environments expand without corresponding monitoring. Regulatory pressures often intensify at the same time, introducing mandatory requirements that cannot be met with manual processes or part-time monitoring. During this early phase, teams do *not* request a SOC directly; instead, they frame the issue in terms of unmanaged operational risk. They communicate that the organization is already *bearing the cost* of lacking a SOCthrough slow detection, incomplete visibility, and rising threat exposure.

This reframing is crucial. Executives rarely respond to technical arguments alone, but they respond quickly to operational, financial, and reputational risk. By emphasizing what gaps exist rather than what solution they want the technical teams build momentum for leadership to explore options, including the creation of an internal SOC.

Step 2: The CISO Builds the SOC Business Case

Once the need is identified, the CISO becomes the architect of the SOC proposal. The role of the CISO is not merely to present a shopping list of tools and roles but to translate highly technical risk into language that executive leadership and the board can weigh alongside other strategic initiatives. A strong SOC business case begins with measurable risk. The CISO outlines current detection times, recent near-miss incidents, audit findings, and gaps in visibility across endpoints, identity, cloud, and network. They then project how these risks will compound as the organization grows, adopts new technologies, or enters new regulatory landscapes.

From there, the CISO maps these risks to operational consequences: downtime, business disruption, financial penalties, legal exposure, loss of data integrity, or compromise of customer trust. The most effective proposals highlight the cost of inaction. The board must understand that doing nothing is not cost-neutral; it increases the likelihood of a breach and magnifies the impact of one when it occurs.

The formal SOC budget is then constructed, typically broken into key operational domains: personnel (analysts, engineers, SOC leadership), technology (SIEM, EDR, SOAR, threat intelligence), infrastructure (cloud storage, ingestion pipelines, retention tiers), and ongoing operations (training, certifications, reporting, shift coverage). This budget is framed not as a technical wish list but as a risk-mitigation investment. A CISO might summarize: *"A $3.2M annual SOC investment reduces mean time to detect from 21 days to under 15 minutes, lowers breach likelihood significantly, and materially reduces regulatory and financial* *exposure."* This positions the SOC as both a defensive shield and a business enabler.

At this stage, the CISO also outlines coverage models, business hours, follow-the-sun, hybrid staffing, or full 24/7and presents cost differentials. These models help executives understand the operational trade-offs between cost, capability, and risk tolerance.

Step 3: Board and Executive Review

When the proposal reaches the CEO, CFO, COO, or Board, it undergoes the same rigorous evaluation as any other strategic investment. Executives assess the SOC in terms of cost predictability, long-term sustainability, and measurable reductions in organizational risk. They also evaluate alignment with regulatory frameworksPCI, HIPAA, SOX, GLBA, FedRAMP, or industry-specific mandates which often require proof of continuous monitoring and incident response capabilities.

Importantly, the SOC proposal does not compete only with other security initiatives; it competes with *all* enterprise investments. The CISO must therefore articulate how a SOC protects revenue, preserves business continuity, and enhances brand trust. Rather than portraying the SOC as a "security expense," successful CISOs frame it as insurance and operational resilience, a necessary part of sustaining the enterprise in the face of increasing digital threats.

When approved, the SOC budget becomes a predictable operational expense rather than a discretionary spend. It is absorbed into annual planning cycles, reviewed during quarterly business reviews, and used as the foundation for future capability expansion. The decision to fund a SOC is often accompanied by a multi-year roadmap that includes staffing phases, technology rollouts, detection engineering milestones, and maturity targets.

MSSP SOC Pricing: Turning Operations into a Product

When offering SOC services commercially, pricing must achieve everything an internal SOC budget does plus margin, scalability, and contractual defensibility. This is where many MSSPs fail.

Unlike internal SOCs, MSSPs cannot subsidize inefficiency. Every alert, investigation, and overnight incident has a direct revenue impact.

Common MSSP Pricing Models

Per-Endpoint Pricing

Per-endpoint pricing is the most common and simplest model. Clients pay a fixed monthly amount per monitored device.

This model works well when:

- EDR is central to detection
- Endpoint count correlates with analyst workload
- Clients want cost predictability

However, it breaks down when:

- High-logging servers generate disproportionate SIEM costs
- Cloud workloads explode telemetry volume
- Endpoint-based pricing ignores identity and SaaS risk

Per-endpoint pricing must be modeled carefully to avoid ingestion-driven margin erosion.

Per-User Pricing

Per-user pricing is often used where identity monitoring is central. It aligns well with SaaS-heavy and zero-trust environments but can underestimate workloads in organizations with shared infrastructure or privileged accounts.

Per-Log-Volume Pricing

Log-volume pricing aligns most closely with actual SOC cost structure, especially SIEM licensing and storage. However, clients often struggle to understand it, and unpredictable spikes can create billing disputes.

This model works best when paired with:

- Clear ingestion caps
- Overage controls
- Transparent dashboards

Hybrid Pricing (Recommended)

Most mature MSSPs adopt a hybrid pricing model, combining:

- A base platform fee (covers staffing, infrastructure, reporting)
- A variable component (endpoints, users, or log volume)

This balances predictability for the client with sustainability for the MSSP.

True Cost Components MSSPs Must Price In

Effective MSSP pricing accounts for full life-cycle cost, not just analyst salaries.

This includes:

- Tier 1–3 analyst coverage
- SOC management and QA
- SIEM ingestion and retention
- SOAR execution costs
- EDR licensing
- Threat intelligence subscriptions

- Ticketing and reporting platforms
- After-hours staffing premiums
- Account management and client communications
- Training, certifications, and turnover

Critically, pricing must model worst-case scenarios, such as prolonged incidents requiring sustained analyst attention. If pricing only works on "average" days, the model is broken.

Discounting Strategy and Risk

Discounting is not inherently bad, but it must be intentional and time-bound.

Bad discounting:

- Permanent underpricing to win deals
- Discounting without scope reduction
- Discounting without exit clauses

Good discounting:

- Introductory pricing with clear reversion
- Proof-of-value pilots
- Strategic reference accounts

Once a client is anchored to an unsustainable price, correcting it often requires renegotiation or churn. Strong MSSPs avoid this by pricing for longevity, not acquisition speed.

Whether internal or commercial, pricing is not about being cheaper, rather, it is about being viable. Internal SOC budgets must survive executive scrutiny and deliver measurable risk reduction. MSSP pricing must absorb volatility, scale cleanly, and protect analysts from burnout. The strongest SOCs, whether internal or outsourced, are priced to endure pressure, not just to win approval.

Deliverables

Deliverables are how clients perceive value. While SOC work happens continuously, clients experience it through outputs: alerts, tickets, reports, briefings, and recommendations. MSSPs must standardize deliverables to ensure consistency across the customer base.

Core deliverables typically include real-time alert notifications, incident summaries, periodic reports, SLA performance metrics, and recommendations. These outputs must be timely, understandable, and tailored to the audience. Executive-facing reports focus on risk and impact, while technical appendices support internal IT and security teams. MSSPs must also define deliverable cadence. Daily notifications, weekly summaries, and monthly reports should be predictable. Deliverables that arrive inconsistently erode trust even if technical performance is strong. Documentation of deliverables should be referenced explicitly in contracts and service descriptions, eliminating ambiguity around what the client will receive.

Service Level Agreements (SLAs) Designing Enforceable, Scalable SOC Commitments

Service Level Agreements occupy a uniquely important place in the MSSP ecosystem. They are one of the few documents that both the technical team and the client leadership will read closely, and they shape the psychological and operational foundation of the entire security relationship. A well crafted SLA does not simply outline expectations. It creates a shared language for performance, a mutual understanding of responsibilities, and a structure for how the SOC and the client will navigate moments of urgency, uncertainty, and risk. Without this clarity, the SOC becomes a black box in the eyes of the client. Every delayed response, every ambiguous alert, and every unclear escalation creates frustration and erodes trust. With a proper SLA, however, the SOC becomes predictable, accountable, and aligned with the business outcomes the client values most.

In many organizations, SLAs are treated as an afterthought or a marketing checkbox. Sales teams frequently push for aggressive commitments to win contracts, promising five minute triage windows, guaranteed containment, or unrealistic remediation timelines that sound attractive in a proposal but cannot be delivered consistently in real operations. This is how MSSPs unintentionally create their own failures. An SLA that is too ambitious does not impress clients for long. Instead, it becomes the contractual basis for receiving complaints, service credits, or even legal disputes. SOC leaders therefore must approach SLAs with the same engineering discipline applied to detection tuning, IR playbook design, or log pipeline architecture. SLAs are not sales tools. They are operational documents that must reflect the true capability of the SOC.

At their core, SLAs serve four fundamental purposes. First, they define what actions the SOC commits to perform, whether triage, enrichment, investigation, escalation, or communication. Second, they define how quickly those actions will occur, often specifying initial response times for different alert severities as well as expectations for investigation updates and client notifications. Third, SLAs define the conditions under which the SLA clock begins, pauses, and ends. This is an area where vague definitions can create significant problems. If the SLA clock begins at the moment a log arrives rather than when a correlated alert is generated, the SOC is already behind before an analyst even sees the event. Fourth, SLAs establish what the MSSP is not responsible for. Boundary setting protects the SOC from being held accountable for client side failures such as misconfigured endpoints, unpatched servers, unavailable staff, or missing log sources.

The most important principle to understand is that SLAs do not and must not guarantee outcomes. No SLA should promise that breaches will be prevented, that malware will be eradicated within a fixed number of minutes, or that an attacker's behavior can be controlled. Any wording that implies a guaranteed security outcome exposes the MSSP to unnecessary legal and financial risk. The SOC does not control the attacker's timeline, the client's patching discipline, or the inherent vulnerabilities in legacy applications. What the SOC can guarantee is its own performance: timely detection, prompt response, disciplined communication, and execution of documented processes. These are the pillars of an enforceable SLA.

Strong SLAs go further by describing the operational reality behind each commitment. For example, a well written SLA will not simply say "High severity alerts will be triaged within fifteen minutes." It will define what qualifies as a high severity alert, which detection sources feed that category, and whether automated enrichment occurs before analyst triage. It will clarify whether the SLA applies only to alerts the SOC receives during staffed hours, whether after hours triage is performed by an on-call analyst, or whether certain services are strictly best effort outside business hours. The more precisely these conditions are defined, the fewer points of ambiguity will arise during incidents.

Another critical function of SLAs is managing client expectations during ongoing investigations. Clients often assume that once an alert is acknowledged, the SOC immediately begins containing the threat. In reality, triage, enrichment, and validation must occur before containment decisions can be made. An effective SLA explains this investigative sequence and sets clear expectations for communication cadences. Update intervals, escalation paths, and decision checkpoints should all be defined explicitly. This reduces emotional escalation during crises and ensures the client understands what the SOC is doing even when the situation is evolving rapidly.

A well structured SLA also protects the MSSP from absorbing responsibility for client side operational failures. If a client disables logging on an endpoint, delays installing the EDR agent on new systems, or ignores repeated vulnerability notifications, the SOC cannot be blamed when a breach is discovered. Effective SLAs include sections specifying customer responsibilities, such as maintaining supported operating systems, preserving sensor integrity, responding to escalation attempts, and granting required permissions. These responsibilities ensure that the SOC can perform its work effectively, and they provide legal protection should the client fail to uphold their side of the agreement.

Ultimately, SLAs are not merely contractual formalities. They are instruments of clarity, alignment, and operational discipline. They guide analysts, protect the MSSP, and establish a shared understanding of how the SOC will act when threats emerge. In a mature

SOC, the SLA becomes part of the operational rhythm. It shapes triage priorities, staffing decisions, escalation procedures, and communication workflows. It calibrates client expectations so the SOC can perform consistently under pressure. And perhaps most importantly, it offers a foundation of trust upon which long term partnership is built.

Foundational SLA Metrics

In any mature MSSP SOC, Service Level Agreements form the backbone of operational accountability. They establish clear expectations between the SOC and its clients, define measurable performance targets, and protect both sides from ambiguity. SLAs are not arbitrary timeframes; they are engineered around analyst workload, alert volume, risk tolerance, and the realities of detection and response. Four core SLA categories appear in virtually every professional SOC contract: Time-to-Triage (TTT), Time-to-Notification (TTN), Time-to-Escalation (TTE), and Reporting Delivery timelines. Each provides structure and predictability to the incident management lifecycle.

Time-to-Triage (TTT)

Time-to-Triage is the most fundamental SLA in an MSSP environment because it governs how quickly a human will review each alert. TTT is defined as the time between an alert entering the MSSP's monitoring platform and the moment an analyst begins investigation, assigns an initial classification, and determines whether the alert is benign, suspicious, or malicious. The objective of this SLA is not to require a full investigation at first touch but to ensure that alerts do not backlog or go unnoticed for extended periods. TTT protects clients from slow detection while simultaneously protecting the MSSP from being expected to deliver full forensic analysis within the first few minutes of an alert's creation. It provides a predictable operational rhythm that aligns SOC staffing with alert volume, helping ensure clients receive prompt initial attention even during peak activity.

Time-to-Notification (TTN)

Time-to-Notification governs how quickly the SOC will notify the client once mandatory reporting criteria have been met. TTN begins when an analyst confirms that an alert represents reportable activity, typically suspicious or malicious behavior requiring client awareness or action and ends when the client is notified through the agreed-upon channel, such as phone, email, ticketing system, or a formal bridge call. This SLA focuses solely on *notification*, not containment or remediation. It ensures that clients receive timely, actionable information without delay, while preventing unrealistic expectations that complex investigative or IR steps should be completed before communication. TTN is especially important in regulated industries where disclosure timeframes matter, and where delayed communication can exacerbate damage or compliance exposure.

Time-to-Escalation (TTE)

Time-to-Escalation defines how quickly high-severity or time-sensitive events must be elevated either to higher-tier analysts within the SOC or to the client's internal escalation paths. TTE begins when escalation criteria are met such as confirmation of credential compromise, lateral movement, malware execution, or exploitation of a critical system and ends when the incident is transferred to Tier 2, Tier 3, or the Incident Response lead. For MSSPs, TTE ensures that serious threats move through the SOC hierarchy without bottleneck or ambiguity. Escalation is not simply a notification it is a handoff to more specialized resources with authority to initiate containment or deeper investigation. strong TTE discipline prevents lower-tier analysts from becoming overwhelmed by incidents beyond their scope and ensures clients are engaged promptly when decisions or approvals are required.

Reporting Delivery SLAs

Reporting is the final pillar of MSSP accountability. Every client expects written documentation of what occurred, when it happened, what actions were taken, and what the outcome was. Reporting SLAs govern delivery timelines for multiple report types, including initial incident summaries, full IR reports, daily updates during active events, and monthly or quarterly security summaries. These timelines ensure that clients remain informed throughout the incident lifecycle and receive structured, evidence-backed artifacts for compliance, insurance claims, regulatory review, or internal audit purposes. For example, an MSSP might commit to delivering an initial incident summary within four hours of containment, a full IR report within three business days, daily updates for ongoing incidents, and monthly summary reports that outline trends, SLA adherence, tuning recommendations, and threat landscape insights. Reporting SLAs reinforce transparency, demonstrate operational maturity, and help build client trust by ensuring communication continues beyond the initial response.

Severity-Based SLA Examples

SLA timing should always be tied to severity, not alert type alone.

Example Severity Model

Severity	Description
Critical (P1)	Active confirmed compromise, ransomware behavior, lateral movement, data exfiltration
High (P2)	High-confidence malicious activity with no confirmed impact
Medium (P3)	Suspicious activity requiring investigation

Low (P4)	Benign, informational, or policy violation

Example SLA Table (24/7 SOC)

Severity	Time-to-Triage	Time-to-Notification	Escalation
Critical	*≤ 15 minutes*	*≤ 30 minutes*	*Immediate*
High	*≤ 30 minutes*	*≤ 1 hour*	*≤ 2 hours*
Medium	*≤ 4 hours*	*As needed*	*Tier 1*

Low	*≤ 1 business day*	*Optional*	*None*

SLAs by Incident Type

While severity classifications provide a useful starting point for defining response expectations, severity alone is not enough to create meaningful or realistic Service Level Agreements. Different categories of security incidents impose unique operational, technical, and communication requirements, and mature MSSP tailors SLAs accordingly. Treating all "high-severity" events as equal ignores the fact that ransomware demands immediate containment, credential compromise requires identity provider coordination, and malware infections vary widely in complexity. Category-specific SLAs allow MSSPs to match their obligations to the real-world demands of each incident type while giving clients precise expectations for how the SOC will respond.

Incident-type modifiers also protect the MSSP. Without them, a client may expect instantaneous ransomware response and the same for a routine malware alert even though the operational workflows, tooling, authorization requirements, and forensic steps are fundamentally different. By defining tailored SLAs, the MSSP ensures clarity, avoids disputes, and aligns response processes with the unique risks each threat category poses.

Ransomware Incidents

Ransomware is treated as its own category because of its extraordinary operational and financial impact. When signs of ransomware appear such as mass file encryption, unauthorized privilege escalation, or indicators of human-operated intrusion, the SOC must abandon standard triage queues and engage immediately. For that reason, ransomware-related SLAs typically require instant triage and immediate client notification regardless of the time of day. This ensures that containment actions begin as rapidly as possible before encryption spreads across systems or lateral movement accelerates.

Host isolation, however, may require explicit client authorization unless the MSSP has pre-approved emergency containment rights. Isolation can disrupt critical operations, so many clients want executive or IT-operations sign-off before pulling machines off the network. Ransomware SLAs also mandate continuous status updates, often every 60 minutes, because ransomware events escalate quickly and require synchronized action across SOC, IT, legal, and executive teams. The goal is high-tempo communication paired with rapid containment to limit spread and preserve forensic evidence.

Credential Compromise

Suspected or confirmed credential compromise presents a different challenge. Unlike ransomware, the danger is not immediate encryption but unauthorized access, which may already be active or may occur later if action is delayed. SLAs for credential compromise focus on rapid investigation of authentication logs to determine the scope of misuse, including failed and successful logins, federated authentication patterns, MFA events, and unusual geolocations.

Password resets or credential revocation are generally not performed automatically by the MSSP; they require explicit approval from the client or identity provider administrators. This ensures proper change-control and prevents accidental service disruption, especially where privileged accounts or service accounts are involved. Identity logsAzure AD, Okta, on-prem AD, or SSO providers are often the client's responsibility to maintain. MSSP SLAs clarify that credential compromise investigations depend on timely access to these logs, and delays may pause SLA countdowns. These distinctions allow the SOC to act quickly while respecting identity governance frameworks.

Malware Detection

Malware alerts encompass a wide range from trivial adware to trojans, worms, implants, or rootkits so SLAs for this category emphasize structured enrichment and controlled containment. When malware indicators emerge, SOC analysts are expected to enrich the alert by submitting samples or hashes to sandboxes, extracting IOCs, correlating telemetry with EDR process trees, and reviewing persistence mechanisms. These steps must occur within a defined SLA window to ensure clients receive actionable insight while the infection is still contained.

Host containment for malware follows predefined client rules. Some organizations authorize automatic EDR isolation for all malware alerts, while others restrict isolation to confirmed malicious activity only. The SLA clarifies under what conditions the SOC can isolate a host without client approval and when escalation is required first. By defining these boundaries, the MSSP avoids accidental outages while still providing rapid containment for genuinely harmful threats.

Defining Client Responsibilities

This is the most frequently omittedand most importantsection in SOC SLAs. SLAs must pause when MSSP progress is blocked by the client.

Client Responsibility Examples

Among all the components that make up a strong Service Level Agreement, none is more frequently overlooked or more essential than the clear definition of client responsibilities. Many MSSPs learn this lesson only after encountering disputes, missed expectations, or investigations that stall because the client failed to take necessary action. A SOC cannot operate in a vacuum. It requires access, information, cooperation, and timely decision making from the client. When these elements are missing, the MSSP cannot meaningfully progress, yet without proper contractual language the MSSP may still be held accountable for delays it did not cause. This is why mature SOCs treat client responsibility definitions not as optional content but as a fundamental pillar of the SLA.

A surprising number of organizations sign SOC agreements without understanding that the client plays an active role in the security process. For example, the SOC cannot notify the correct individuals during an incident if the client does not maintain an updated escalation contact list. In many cases, the SOC is forced to chase outdated phone numbers, disconnected email addresses, or personnel who have left the company entirely. When such delays occur, the MSSP must not be blamed for failing to meet communication SLAs. Likewise, the SOC cannot perform containment actions that require client approval if the client's leadership does not respond. Actions like host isolation, identity disablement, password resets, or firewall modifications often require explicit authorization. If the SOC is waiting for the client to approve the action, the SLA clock must pause. Without this protection the MSSP becomes exposed to unfair complaints and even legal or financial penalties for circumstances beyond its control.

Another major area of shared responsibility involves the client's obligation to maintain the technical foundations that support SOC operations. The SOC cannot investigate an alert related to a host that does not have an EDR agent installed, nor can it meet detection SLAs if the client fails to onboard critical log sources such as firewalls, domain controllers, cloud audit logs, or VPN servers. These are common real world scenarios. Clients forget to install agents on new devices, fail to renew licenses, disable logging to reduce storage costs, or misconfigure systems that feed the SIEM. When this happens, the MSSP cannot be faulted for missing detections or delayed investigations. A well written SLA therefore must specify that the client is responsible for maintaining coverage and that SLA obligations apply only to assets and log sources that have been properly onboarded.

Remediation responsibilities must also be spelled out clearly. Many MSSPs focus on detection and initial response but do not provide full hands-on remediation unless contracted separately. In such cases, system patching, reimaging, firewall rule changes, vulnerability resolution, and credential rotation fall to the client's internal IT or security teams. When a client delays these actions, the SOC may see repeated alerts or prolonged exposure windows. Without contractual boundaries the client may incorrectly assume that the MSSP is responsible for resolving every downstream issue, even when those tasks were never included in the service scope. A mature SLA therefore describes exactly which party owns which remediation steps and clarifies that delays caused by the client do not constitute MSSP underperformance.

To ensure fairness, SLAs must contain explicit pause conditions. A pause clause protects the MSSP by freezing the SLA countdown whenever progress is blocked by client inaction. This clause typically states that SLA timers stop when the MSSP requires client approval, information, access, credentials, resources, or technical remediation. These clauses are not only reasonable but absolutely necessary. Without them the MSSP could be penalized for delays entirely outside its influence. Pause clauses also provide transparency. They show the client exactly where delays are occurring and place accountability where it belongs. They encourage clients to engage actively and respond promptly during investigations, knowing their own responsiveness affects SLA outcomes.

Over time, client responsibility definitions become as important to the relationship as the SOC's own commitments. They reinforce that security is a shared effort requiring participation from both sides. Mature MSSPs review these client responsibilities during onboarding, validate them during quarterly business reviews, and even reflect them in reporting dashboards to show how client delays affect operational performance. This shared clarity prevents blame shifting, establishes realistic expectations, and protects the MSSP from being judged by conditions it does not control. More importantly, it ensures that the SOC can operate effectively, respond quickly, and deliver value without unnecessary friction.

Automation & SLA Measurement

The ability to measure Service Level Agreements accurately rests entirely on the presence of complete and reliable automation. Any SOC that attempts to track SLA compliance manually through spreadsheets, analyst commentary, or informal note taking eventually discovers that the process is not only fragile but fundamentally indefensible. Human recorded timing is subjective, easily misinterpreted, prone to error, and vulnerable to dispute. In contrast, automated measurement binds SLA clocks directly to system generated timestamps, creating a single authoritative record of performance. This is the standard for mature MSSPs because it eliminates interpretation and replaces it with objective, immutable evidence.

In a well engineered SOC, an SLA timer does not begin when an analyst notices an alert. It begins at the moment the alert enters the environment. The SIEM logs the creation time or ingestion time, and that timestamp becomes the baseline from which all calculations flow.

The SOC cannot modify this timestamp, nor should it be able to. It serves as the definitive record of when the SOC became responsible for the event. Once the first triage action occurs, the system transitions the alert into a different state and the SLA engine adjusts its calculations accordingly. If an analyst delays triage, the numbers reflect that delay. If the SOC reacts promptly, the record demonstrates that performance clearly. Automation therefore gives an honest picture of reality and allows leaders to understand not only whether SLAs were met, but how efficiently the SOC is operating.

One of the most valuable components of automated SLA management is the ability to pause and resume timers based on dependency conditions. SOC analysts frequently require client approvals or access before continuing an investigation. For example, they may need permission to isolate a device, reset a privileged account, or run administrative queries on a cloud resource. When such approval is requested, the timer must stop automatically. Without an automated pause function, the MSSP would appear to miss SLAs simply because the client did not answer an email or phone call. Automation protects the MSSP by enforcing fairness and also provides transparency for the client, who can clearly see where the process halted and why.

Because multiple platforms participate in the SOC workflow, strict synchronization is essential. The SIEM provides the initial event timestamp. The SOAR system applies enrichment and action based timing. The ticketing system displays the progressing SLA window, warns analysts of anticipated breaches, and generates audit ready summaries. All three systems must agree on timing or the SLA record becomes inconsistent. Modern platforms integrate these layers so that the SOC never relies on parallel clocks or disconnected systems. Instead, there is one authoritative timeline, composed of event creation, enrichment, triage, escalation, approval, containment, and closure. Each state transition is recorded automatically with a time, an actor, and a reason, forming an auditable chain of custody for the alert lifecycle.

Immutability is a core requirement of this system. No analyst should ever be allowed to adjust timestamps manually. Any platform that enables such behavior undermines both the reliability of the SLA and the legal protection of the MSSP. Immutable logs act as a shield. During quarterly reviews, audits, or disputes, the MSSP can present a clear, tamper resistant record of exactly when each action occurred. This preserves trust and prevents the perception that timing was altered to meet or avoid SLA penalties.

Automation also provides a deeper operational benefit. Once SLA timing becomes measurable at scale, leaders gain insight into performance patterns that previously remained hidden. They can see which alert types take the longest to triage, which shifts encounter the most bottlenecks, or which client environments consistently cause delays. They can identify analysts who excel at rapid triage and those who may need additional training. They can observe where automation reduces workload and where new playbooks might be needed. SLA measurement therefore becomes both a compliance tool and a strategic instrument for continuous improvement.

For the client, automation eliminates ambiguity. Instead of relying on subjective status updates, the client receives a clear, objective record of SOC performance. They can see when the SOC acted, when their own teams caused delays, and how the alert moved through the lifecycle. This improves trust, strengthens communication, and reduces friction during escalation. Both parties benefit from the clarity and fairness that automation provides.

Without automation, SLA tracking becomes an approximation, often inaccurate and easily challenged. With automation, SLA tracking becomes a discipline grounded in clear evidence and supported by the entire SOC technology stack. This is how mature MSSPs manage SLA commitments, and it is the only sustainable approach in environments where accuracy, transparency, and accountability are essential.

SLA Reporting & Transparency

SLA reporting is one of the most important instruments of trust in the relationship between an MSSP and its clients. A mature SOC does not wait for clients to request performance data or demand explanations. Instead, it surfaces SLA information proactively and at predictable intervals, signaling confidence in its operations and a commitment to full accountability. In this way, SLA reporting is far more than a contractual obligation. It becomes a strategic communication practice that reinforces the stability, responsiveness, and discipline of the SOC.

Internally, SLA reporting begins long before the client sees the results. Strong SOCs conduct weekly internal SLA reviews to maintain operational oversight. These internal sessions allow managers and senior engineers to identify early signs of strain such as longer triage times, excessive escalation delays, recurring tool errors, or workflow steps that consistently cause slowdowns. By reviewing SLA data every week, leadership can intervene before these issues expand into systemic inefficiencies. Weekly monitoring also helps identify training needs. If a particular analyst routinely approaches or misses triage times, the SOC can provide coaching, workflow refinements, or improved automation support long before the issue becomes a client concern.

Externally, clients typically receive monthly SLA summaries, and these summaries function as both an operational scorecard and a transparency report. Monthly SLA reporting must speak the language of business. Clients should not need deep technical knowledge to understand the performance of their SOC. Instead, the report must focus on clarity, outcome, and reliability. Monthly reports often include triage time compliance, response time adherence, containment responsiveness, and the number of alerts handled for the month. When an SLA is missed, the report must include a clear explanation of what happened and what corrective actions were taken to prevent recurrence. This level of honesty builds trust and signals that the SOC is not hiding performance shortcomings but addressing them openly and professionally.

Beyond monthly summaries, quarterly trend analysis provides the long view that executives and senior stakeholders require. Quarterly observations reveal whether SOC performance is improving, holding steady, or declining over time. These trend reports often appear in quarterly business reviews, where they serve as the foundation for discussions about automation expansion, detection tuning, staffing adjustments, or client side improvements such as improved log coverage or faster approval paths. Quarterly trends help clients understand not just how the SOC performed in isolated moments, but how the entire security operation is evolving in resilience and responsiveness.

Regardless of reporting cadence, all SLA documents must include certain core informational elements. They must display overall SLA compliance percentages, broken down by categories such as triage, notification, containment, and escalation. Where breaches occur, the report must identify the root cause with precision. Some breaches originate within the MSSP because of unexpected alert surges, tool outages, or delayed analyst actions. Others are caused by client delays, missing log sources, unreachable stakeholders, or systems that the client failed to maintain. A credible SLA report must attribute each root cause accurately and support the explanation with system recorded timestamps. It must also list corrective actions that were taken or planned, whether those involve tuning improvements, increased automation, policy adjustments, or workflow redesign. These corrective actions demonstrate forward motion rather than passive acknowledgment.

A mature SOC understands that SLA reporting is as much about relationships as it is about numbers. When clients consistently observe timely reporting, honest explanations, and evidence based performance metrics, they approach SLA governance cooperatively rather than adversarially. The SOC becomes a partner in strengthening the client environment rather than a service vendor who must be policed. In this context, transparency becomes the foundation of long term retention. Clients trust what they can see. Regular, structured, accurate, and candid SLA reporting ensures they always see the full picture.

Avoiding Dangerous SLA Pitfalls

SOC SLAs are deceptively difficult to design well. Many MSSPs and internal SOCs unintentionally create SLAs that are impossible to meet, too vague to enforce, or so poorly scoped that they guarantee disputes and operational strain. The most common pitfall is promising aggressive response times without conducting a realistic staffing analysis. An MSSP may declare a five-minute triage SLA because it sounds competitive, yet without 24/7 staffing, automated enrichment, and workload controls, that commitment will collapse the first time alert volume spikes. This type of mistake erodes client trust and damages the SOC's credibility, sometimes irreparably.

Another recurring problem is treating all alerts or incidents as equal. When SLAs are uniform across all severity levels, the SOC is forced to respond to minor hygiene alerts as urgently as critical ransomware activity. Not only does this waste resources, but it also increases the likelihood that true high-risk events will be buried in noise. Mature SOCs tailor SLAs by severity category and incident type, ensuring that the most dangerous threats receive the fastest human attention. A flat, one-size-fits-all SLA model is not a sign of simplicity, it is a sign of poor engineering.

Equally dangerous is the tendency to guarantee outcomes rather than actions. An SLA can promise to review, notify, escalate, or contain within a defined time window; it cannot promise to prevent breaches, stop all lateral movement, or ensure no data exposure occurs. Such guarantees are not only unrealistic, they are legally dangerous. When SLAs imply outcomes that no SOC can control, they expose the MSSP to financial liability and undermine the defensibility of the service. Action-based

SLAs, grounded in operational steps, are the only sustainable model.

Many SOCs also fail to document after-hours expectations. If the SLA does not explicitly state whether triage, containment, or client notifications occur during nights, weekends, or holidays, misunderstandings are inevitable. Clients may assume 24/7 coverage even when they only purchased business-hours monitoring. This gap often surfaces during a crisis when it is too late to clarify. Therefore, SLAs must explicitly define coverage windows, including holidays, after-hours contact procedures, and emergency escalation pathways. Another dangerous oversight is neglecting to define escalation dependencies. Even the most responsive SOC cannot progress during an incident if client approvals, identity provider access, firewall permissions, or endpoint management controls are unavailable. Without clear language that SLA timers pause when the SOC is blocked by client action or missing access, the MSSP becomes responsible for delays outside its control. Mature contracts prevent this by documenting escalation dependencies upfront and codifying pause conditions.

All of these mistakes point to a single overarching principle: If the SOC cannot consistently meet an SLA during peak incident conditions, the SLA is invalid. SLAs must be designed for high-stress, high-volume conditions, not for ideal days when alert volume is low and staffing is full. If an SLA only works when the SOC is having a "good day," it is not a real SLAit is a marketing promise masquerading as an operational guarantee.

This leads directly to the final design truth of SOC SLAs: SLAs are not marketing tools; they are engineering contracts. When designed properly, they establish stable expectations, unify SOC and client responsibilities, and minimize ambiguity during incidents. Clients know exactly what they are entitled to. SOC analysts know exactly what they must deliver. Escalations and disputes become matters of data rather than emotion. And most importantly, the MSSP scales sustainably, because it has not overpromised in ways that require heroics to fulfill.

A well-engineered SLA protects people, process, profit, and trust simultaneously. Poorly engineered SLAs do the opposite. This chapter exists so your SOC will never fall into that trap.

Legal Considerations

Operating an MSSP SOC is not simply a matter of deploying technical tools or building efficient detection pipelines. It is a legally consequential business activity that requires careful thought about liability, confidentiality, regulatory compliance, and contractual authority. Every alert reviewed, every log stored, every containment action executed has the potential to create legal obligations. Many new MSSPs overlook this reality and treat SOC operations as though they exist in a purely technical space. In truth, SOCs operate at the intersection of law, privacy, cybersecurity, and business risk, and failure to acknowledge this intersection exposes both the MSSP and the client to unnecessary danger.

A foundational principle for any SOC leader is understanding the nature of shared liability. The moment a client grants the MSSP access to logs, tickets, or telemetry, the MSSP becomes a custodian of sensitive information. This places strict responsibilities on how that information is handled, stored, accessed, and transmitted. A poorly secured SIEM, an analyst using an unapproved device, or a misconfigured storage bucket can result in unauthorized disclosure of internal business operations or personal information. Such incidents quickly escalate into regulatory violations or breach notification events. The law does not differentiate between malicious breaches and negligent mishandling. From a regulator's perspective, improper log storage can be just as serious as an external intrusion.

Service contracts must therefore draw clear boundaries around what the SOC is authorized to do. One of the most common legal mistakes in the MSSP industry is the use of marketing language in contractual documents. Promises such as preventing breaches or eliminating threats create false expectations and enormous legal exposure. Security providers reduce risk, but cannot eliminate it. A properly written contract defines actions and expectations, not guaranteed outcomes. It should state, for example, that the SOC will monitor specific log sources, investigate alerts within agreed upon time frames, notify stakeholders when incidents are confirmed, and provide remediation recommendations. The SOC cannot promise results beyond its control, and the contract must reflect this reality.

Data privacy regulations introduce additional layers of responsibility. Depending on the client's industry, location, or user base, the SOC may be subject to frameworks such as the General Data Protection Regulation, Health Insurance Portability and Accountability Act, Payment Card Industry Data Security Standard, Sarbanes Oxley Act, Criminal Justice Information Services standards, or state and national breach notification laws. Each of these regimes places strict requirements on access control, log retention, encryption, auditability, and acceptable use. Failure to implement these controls correctly can cause indirect violations for the client. Regulators and auditors expect MSSPs to understand the relevant standards and design workflows accordingly. Claims of ignorance do not protect an MSSP from legal consequences.

Contracts serve as the backbone of legal defensibility. The Master Service Agreement and supporting Statements of Work must define the operational scope in precise detail. This includes what systems are monitored, what actions the SOC may take autonomously, when escalation is required, and what responsibilities remain with the client. Some clients expect the SOC to perform direct remediation. Others strictly prohibit containment without explicit approval. If these expectations are not spelled out clearly, the MSSP may be accused of negligence for failing to act or overreach for acting too aggressively. Clear language protects both parties.

Data retention and destruction policies must also be established. SOC investigations generate screenshots, packet captures, evidence notes, malware samples, and timeline reconstructions. These artifacts often contain highly sensitive client information. The SOC must define how long such material is stored, where it is stored, who can access it, and under what conditions it is destroyed. Retaining data longer than necessary may violate privacy regulations. Destroying it too soon may interfere with investigations or legal proceedings. Retention policies should therefore be crafted in collaboration with legal counsel and aligned with regulatory frameworks.

Confidentiality obligations extend not only to systems but to people. SOC analysts frequently observe internal employee behavior, business processes, privileged accounts, and occasionally evidence of unrelated policy violations or personnel issues. SOC staff must be bound by strict confidentiality agreements, and the MSSP must enforce clear rules regarding internal communication. Unauthorized sharing, careless conversation, or public disclosure about incidents can have serious legal implications. Every SOC must implement access controls, multi factor authentication, audit trails, and internal logging of who viewed what and when. These measures protect the client, the analysts, and the MSSP itself.

One area often overlooked in legal planning is breach notification responsibility. In most jurisdictions, the entity that owns the data is legally required to notify regulators and affected individuals. The MSSP, however, is typically the first to observe signs of compromise and may possess critical forensic artifacts needed for the notification process. The contract must clarify who notifies whom, what timelines govern disclosure, and what support the MSSP must provide. Without these boundaries, confusion during a live incident can delay mandatory reporting and lead directly to regulatory fines.

Legal clarity is ultimately a form of operational protection. It ensures that technical processes align with contractual authority, regulatory constraints, and defensible record keeping. When the MSSP, the client, and the contract all reflect the same expectations, the SOC can operate with confidence and precision. The goal is not to avoid risk entirely, which is impossible, but to structure operations so that risk is known, managed, and reduced to acceptable levels. A well designed legal framework is not an administrative burden. It is the safety net that allows the SOC to perform its work without fear of stepping beyond its mandate.

Multi-Tenant Architecture

Multi-tenancy is the foundation of scalable, profitable MSSP operations. Without it, every new client increases workload linearly and forces the SOC to reinvent tools, workflows, and configurations on a per-customer basis. A properly engineered multi-tenant architecture allows a single SOC platform to securely support dozens or hundreds of clients while maintaining strict isolation of data, identity, alerts, and workflows. It creates leverage, standardization, and predictable operations, enabling the MSSP to grow without overwhelming its analysts or infrastructure.

The first principle of multi-tenancy is logical separation. Every client's telemetry whether logs, alerts, evidence, enrichment results, or incident records must be fully isolated at the data layer. This is not optional; it is the backbone of regulatory compliance and contractual trust. SIEMs, SOAR platforms, ticketing systems, and EDR consoles must enforce tenant boundaries either through native features or meticulous architectural design. In a SIEM, this typically means isolating data via separate workspaces, indexes, ingestion keys, or access control lists. In a SOAR platform, it may require tenant-specific playbook variables, restricted folders, or context-store segmentation. In ticketing systems, tenant-specific queues ensure that analysts only access cases for the clients they are authorized to support.

Access control is equally important. Role-Based Access Control (RBAC) must map analysts to specific clients, tools, and environments. Analysts with access to Client A should not be able to see or search logs for Client

Bever. Privilege allocation must be granular: Tier 1 may receive read-only access to alerts, Tier 2 may receive investigative permissions, and IR Leads may have authority to execute containment actions. Least privilege is not merely a best practice; it protects the MSSP from accidental cross-client data exposure, one of the most damaging events an MSSP can suffer.

The second principle is shared infrastructure for efficiency. Multi-tenancy is not separate instances per client, it is one shared platform with reusable components. Detection rules, correlation logic, enrichment pipelines, reporting templates, dashboards, and automated playbooks should all be engineered once and applied everywhere. The platform injects client-specific metadata dynamically, such as asset tags, user directories, network ranges, severity mappings, or escalation contacts. This creates a consistent experience while allowing customization where needed. The MSSP benefits from economies of scale: tuning a detection rule once improves signal quality for every client; fixing a SOAR workflow once eliminates an error for the entire SOC.

The third principle is performance isolation. Multi-tenancy fails if a surge from one client, such as a malware outbreak or misconfigured device causes delays or outages for others. A mature MSSP designs queueing and load management systems that isolate workload spikes. This may include per-tenant ingestion throttles, priority-based routing, partitioned message queues, and horizontal scaling of SIEM ingestion nodes or SOAR workers. Alert storms in one tenant must not degrade triage times across the SOC. SOCs that fail at performance isolation quickly encounter SLA violations, analyst burnout, and reputational damage.

Finally, multi-tenant platforms must include tenant-level auditability. Every action queries, containment steps, playbook executions, evidence downloads must be tied to a specific analyst and client. This is essential for compliance (GDPR, HIPAA, PCI), forensic defensibility, and contractual transparency. Audit logs should allow MSSP leadership and clients to review who accessed what data, when, and why. Without tenant-level audit logging, the MSSP lacks the ability to prove proper data handling in legal or regulatory inquiries.

A successful multi-tenant architecture blends separation with shared efficiency, security with scalability, and customization with standardization. When executed properly, it becomes the engine that allows an MSSP SOC to onboard new clients quickly, improve detection quality across all environments simultaneously, and maintain operational excellence even as the client base grows.

Building an MSSP SOC offering requires more than technical skillit requires disciplined product design, financial modeling, legal awareness, and scalable architecture. By packaging services clearly, pricing sustainably, defining deliverables, enforcing SLAs, managing legal exposure, and implementing true multi-tenancy, MSSPs transform SOC operations into a reliable, defensible business. This chapter provides the blueprint for turning SOC expertise into a successful managed security service.

Chapter 23 Common SOC Pitfalls & How to Avoid Them

Most SOC failures do not result from a lack of tools, budget, or intelligence. They result from predictable operational mistakes that compound silently over time. These pitfalls rarely appear suddenly; instead, they emerge gradually as alert volume increases, environments grow more complex, and operational discipline erodes. Mature SOC leaders recognize these warning signs early and intervene decisively.

This chapter identifies the most common SOC failure modes, alert overload, tool sprawl, incomplete telemetry, escalation breakdowns, analyst burnout, and poor ROI communication and provides practical methods to prevent or reverse them.

Alert Overload (Fatigue)

Alert overload is one of the most damaging yet frequently underestimated threats to SOC performance. It does not break systems the way a misconfigured SIEM might or cripple operations the way a failed containment script could. Instead, it erodes capability quietly by overwhelming analysts with a constant barrage of low value alerts. When this happens, the SOC suffers not a technical outage but a cognitive one. Analysts forced to sift through hundreds or even thousands of irrelevant alerts each day inevitably lose focus and clarity. Their mental workload increases, their decision quality declines, and their ability to distinguish a meaningful threat from background noise deteriorates. This is not a matter of talent or training. It is simply a reflection of human limits. No individual can maintain high level vigilance when every minute brings another interruption demanding attention but offering little insight.

The danger accumulates slowly. At first, analysts treat the noise as a nuisance. Over time, they begin to dismiss minor alerts automatically just to stay afloat. Eventually, they experience a form of psychological desensitization where even high severity alerts struggle to stand out. The SOC does not realize it has drifted into complacency until an actual adversary slips through the cracks and an incident reveals that the detection pipeline has been drowning in meaningless signals for months. The tragedy is that in most cases, the analysts are blamed when in reality the structural design of the alerting system was flawed from the start.

Alert overload nearly always stems from deeper engineering and operational issues. One of the most common failures is the uncritical deployment of vendor provided detections. These rules are intentionally broad so they apply to every customer on earth. They are not tuned to reflect local baselines, business processes, administrative behavior, or environmental quirks. When a SOC enables them without modification, the result is predictable. A flood of alerts triggers for activities that are technically unusual but operationally harmless. A PowerShell script used by the IT department becomes a daily alert. A vulnerability scanner running scheduled jobs trips firewall detections repeatedly. A cloud automation process appears as privilege escalation. Alert queues fill not because the environment is under attack but because the SOC is listening to the wrong signals.

Another major cause is insufficient context at alert time. When an alert fires without enrichment from identity systems, asset inventories, EDR process lineage, or threat intelligence, analysts must reconstruct the missing context manually. They pivot back and forth between tools to determine whether the event is worth investigating. This effort is multiplied across every alert. The absence of correlation makes the problem worse. A ten step attack chain might generate ten separate alerts instead of a single correlated incident. Each one appears independent, increasing load and making it harder for analysts to recognize attack sequences.

Threshold decay also plays a significant role. A rule that once fired appropriately may become noisy when the environment changes. Workflows evolve, cloud workloads grow, user behavior shifts, and authentication patterns change. Yet many detections remain frozen in time. As months pass, thresholds drift far from real world baselines. A SOC may not notice until alert counts double or triple. Without a disciplined tuning process, detections degrade predictably, creating noise that analysts must absorb manually.

Preventing alert overload requires intentional engineering. A SOC must adopt a fundamental principle: alerts are decisions, not data. A log event is merely an observation. An alert must represent a conclusion that a human should take action. When alerts serve as notifications instead of judgments, the SOC becomes flooded with raw signals that should never reach an analyst. High quality alerts incorporate enrichment, correlation, and behavioral baselines before they are assigned. For example, a single failed login should remain a log entry. Only a clustering of failed logins combined with unusual location patterns, suspicious device fingerprints, or concurrent privilege misuse should escalate to an alert.

Mature SOCs treat alert quality as a measurable discipline. They track false positive rates per rule, analyst workload distribution, alert to incident conversion ratios, and cognitive load indicators such as alert fatigue complaints or repetitive closure patterns. They treat an excessive number of closed as benign alerts not as evidence that analysts are working hard but as evidence that detections are failing. This change in mindset transforms SOC engineering. Noise becomes a problem to solve, not an unavoidable condition of monitoring.

High performing SOCs institutionalize governance mechanisms to prevent overload from returning. They implement detection review councils that examine rules monthly. They run tuning sprints where engineers adjust thresholds, remove outdated rules, and replace simplistic detections with behaviorally rich alternatives. They create rule promotion processes where new detections must pass peer review before entering production. Automated retrospective audits identify rules with poor performance metrics or declining signal quality. These practices ensure that detection does not decay silently but evolves with the environment.

Alert overload is often misinterpreted as an analyst performance issue, but in truth it is an engineering failure. Analysts cannot compensate for flawed detection pipelines indefinitely. The solution lies not in asking analysts to work harder but in designing systems that ask less of them. When alerts are precise, enriched, and meaningful, analysts regain the cognitive capacity to think critically, investigate deeply, and respond effectively. When alerts are noisy and aimless, even the strongest SOC will struggle.

Overcoming alert overload requires a cultural shift as much as a technical one. SOC leaders must reject the belief that large alert volumes reflect strong detection coverage. In reality, the highest performing SOCs generate fewer alerts, not more, because their detections are efficient, contextual, and intentional. Noise is not a sign of vigilance. It is a sign of misalignment. A SOC that engineers out noise creates room for analysts to excel and gives the organization a far better chance of detecting the adversaries who genuinely matter.

Tool Sprawl

Tool sprawl is one of the most insidious forms of operational decline inside a SOC. It rarely appears suddenly or in dramatic fashion. Instead, it creeps in slowly and quietly, growing one procurement decision at a time. A new tool is purchased to satisfy a compliance requirement. Another is acquired in the aftermath of an incident. A third enters the environment because a vendor insisted it "closes a critical gap." A fourth arrives when an enthusiastic engineer champions a specialized capability. Years later, the SOC is no longer a cohesive system but a patchwork of disconnected platforms, half-configured deployments, and consoles that nobody has logged into for months. The ecosystem becomes fragile. Knowledge becomes tribal. And as people leave the organization, tools lose owners, configuration decays, and the original rationale for adopting them vanishes entirely.

The dangerous thing about tool sprawl is that it often masquerades as progress.

Leadership sees a long inventory of tools and assumes the SOC must be gaining visibility, improving coverage, or becoming more sophisticated. Vendors reinforce this misconception by relentlessly marketing point solutions that promise detection of specific TTPs or threat actors. But more tools do not create more security. In fact, the opposite is far more common. Every additional platform introduces its own alert feed, its own data schema, its own dashboard, and its own maintenance overhead. Analysts are forced to split their attention across multiple interfaces, each with different workflows, search languages, and authentication requirements. Investigations that should take minutes stretch into half-hour pivots as analysts gather telemetry from disparate systems. Instead of enabling detection and response, the tooling environment becomes a labyrinth that analysts must navigate before they can even begin to understand what happened.

The fragmentation of visibility may be the most harmful consequence of uncontrolled tool acquisition. When endpoint detection, identity telemetry, threat intelligence feeds, network analytics, vulnerability data, and cloud logs all live in separate platforms with no meaningful integration, the SOC loses its operational center of gravity. Analysts are forced to reconstruct context manually, stitching together what should have been correlated automatically. Duplicate or conflicting alerts begin to surface. SIEM and EDR generate overlapping signals. A cloud security tool fires alerts that the SOAR cannot parse properly. Vulnerability findings appear in four different interfaces. Before long, analysts cannot tell which tool is authoritative for which type of signal. The SOC becomes reactive and fragmented. Situational awareness suffers, and adversaries exploit these seams.

As the number of tools grows, the maintenance burden grows even faster. Each platform demands onboarding, authentication management, tuning, license tracking, patching, health monitoring, and integration upkeep. The SOC slowly becomes dependent on "tool stewards" or individuals who alone understand the quirks of a particular system. When one of those individuals resigns, takes vacation, or moves into a new role, the SOC often loses access to critical institutional knowledge. Tools break. Integrations fail silently. Alerts stop flowing. And, because no one fully understands how the tool was wired into the environment, the issue may go unnoticed until an incident exposes the gap. Tool sprawl creates technical debt that compounds over time, spreading operational risk across the entire detection pipeline.

Avoiding tool sprawl requires intentional governance, not accidental restraint. A mature SOC treats tooling as an architectural decision, not an emotional or reactionary one. Every tool must have a defined owner responsible for configuration, documentation, tuning, and integration. Its purpose must be documented in plain terms: which outcomes it enables, which workflows it supports, and which alerts or data sources depend on it. A tool that is not integrated into response workflows is not a tool, it is a liability. A tool that produces alerts but is not mapped to containment actions wastes analyst time. A tool that replicates capabilities already provided elsewhere drains budget without delivering value. Decisions must be deliberate, not driven by marketing promises or impulse purchases.

Regular tooling reviews are essential to maintaining clarity. These reviews examine utilization patterns, noise-to-signal ratios, costs, operational load, and integration depth. Some tools may prove indispensable. Others reveal themselves as expensive redundancies. Tools used by only one engineer require documentation or retirement. Threat intelligence feeds that overlap by 90 percent should be consolidated. Detection modules that generate minimal value should be disabled, tuned, or removed outright. A SOC that never prunes tools inevitably becomes unmanageable.

Purple teaming offers a direct, honest test of tool effectiveness. When offensive and defensive teams simulate attacks, they expose which tools genuinely contribute useful telemetry and which tools produce noise, miss critical behaviors, or fail to integrate meaningfully with response. Many SOCs discover during these exercises that tools they believed to be essential provide little operational value, while others unexpectedly prove themselves foundational. Purple teaming provides clarity grounded in empirical evidence rather than vendor claims, and that clarity should inform tooling decisions going forward.

At the end of the day, the SOC's strength comes not from the number of tools it deploys but from the cohesion of its architecture. A small, well-integrated set of platforms — each fulfilling a clearly defined purpose — empowers analysts to work quickly and confidently. Investigations become smoother. Automation becomes reliable. Detections become more consistent. And the SOC's mental bandwidth shifts away from tool management and back toward adversary defense, where it belongs. Tool sprawl is not inevitable. It is a sign of poor governance, rushed decisions, and a lack of architectural discipline. The SOCs that excel are those willing to retire tools, consolidate capabilities, and enforce intentional design. In those environments, security grows stronger not through accumulation but through clarity.

Incomplete Telemetry

Visibility gaps are one of the most dangerous weaknesses in a security operations program because they create false confidence. A SOC can generate beautiful dashboards and show impressive alert counts, yet still miss the events that matter most simply because the logs required to expose them were never collected in the first place. Partial visibility is more deceptive than no visibility at all. It presents the appearance of understanding while hiding the most critical parts of the story. Attackers thrive in these blind spots. They live between the alerts, in the unmonitored spaces, and in the systems that someone assumed were out of scope or not worth collecting data from. Many security failures begin not with missed alerts but with missing telemetry.

The only real solution is intentional design. Telemetry must be prioritized with the same seriousness as incident response planning or SIEM engineering. The SOC must formally identify the assets that represent the highest operational and business impact. These are the crown jewels, the systems whose compromise would have immediate and severe consequences. Around these assets, visibility must be complete. This includes detailed authentication records, administrative activity, cloud and application programming interface actions, endpoint process data, network flow information, and any logs that capture configuration changes or privilege escalation. If the SOC cannot see what is happening around its most important systems, then no amount of tuning or detection engineering can compensate.

Log onboarding must follow a structured intake process rather than ad hoc ingestion. Too many organizations point a device at the SIEM and assume the work is done. Raw logs are collected, but they arrive in unparsed formats that cannot be searched or correlated. The SOC believes it has visibility, but in reality, it has only collected noise. Proper onboarding includes format validation, parsing checks, field mapping, timestamp normalization, and verification that each data source produces usable events. A log that is collected but not parsed is the same as a camera that records static. It exists, but it cannot help you see.

Visibility should never be considered a one time project. Environments change, cloud workloads move, new applications appear, and legacy systems retire. The SOC must review telemetry coverage on a routine basis with reference to current threat models and established frameworks such as the MITRE ATT&CK knowledge base. If a technique cannot be detected because the required logs are missing, that gap is a risk that must be documented and addressed. Some gaps may be temporary and others may require architectural change, but none should be ignored. Treating visibility issues as minor inconveniences is one of the fastest ways to allow an attacker to operate unnoticed.

In mature security programs, telemetry is not accidental. It is engineered. It is measured. It is reviewed, refined, and verified. When visibility is intentional, the SOC gains the ability to understand adversary behavior clearly. When visibility is neglected, the SOC sees only fragments of the truth and attackers flourish in the spaces that nobody is watching.

Failure to Escalate

Escalation failures are often invisible until serious damage occurs. An analyst may misclassify an alert, delay escalation, or fail to recognize incident severity. While individual errors happen, systemic escalation failure indicates unclear criteria, weak training, or fear of being wrong. SOCs avoid escalation failures by defining explicit escalation thresholds. Analysts should never guess whether to escalate; SOPs should specify when and how escalation occurs. Severity definitions must be aligned across SIEMs, ticketing systems, and reporting.

Equally important is psychological safety. Analysts must be encouraged to escalate uncertainty rather than suppress it. A SOC culture that penalizes escalation mistakes teaches analysts to stay silent creating catastrophic delays Escalation drills, scenario-based training, and regular review of closed incidents help reinforce correct judgment.

Poor ROI Reporting

Poor return on investment reporting is one of the quietest yet most destructive weaknesses in a security operations program. A SOC can operate smoothly, detect real threats, and deliver strong technical performance, yet still lose funding simply because it cannot communicate its value in terms that resonate with leadership. When executives do not understand what the SOC achieves, security becomes an abstract cost rather than a strategic investment. Budget cuts begin not with dissatisfaction, but with misunderstanding. In many organizations, the root of that misunderstanding is weak or ineffective reporting.

ROI reporting fails most often when it focuses on volume instead of significance. Executives do not care how many alerts the SOC processed last month. Raw numbers are meaningless without context. What they want to know is how many incidents were contained before spreading, how response times have improved, what kinds of risks were reduced, and where the organization avoided downtime, financial loss, or regulatory exposure. They want to see how the SOC protected revenue and continuity, not how many tickets were closed. When reports emphasize only alert counts, correlation jobs, or case volumes, the message becomes lost in technical noise that does not translate into business value.

Effective reporting reframes security activity as a measurable business enabler. It connects operational outcomes to real impact. For example, a reduction in average triage time is not merely an efficiency gain. It is a reduction in adversary dwell time and therefore a reduction in the chance of successful lateral movement or data theft. Early containment of an intrusion is not just a resolved incident. It is the prevention of service disruption, reputational damage, and customer churn. Even improvements in compliance posture carry weight, because they reduce the likelihood of fines, audit failures, and regulatory findings. When a SOC shows these outcomes consistently, it demonstrates not only competence but tangible protection of business objectives.

A mature SOC does not present snapshots of activity. It tells a story of progression. Month over month, quarter over quarter, the SOC should be able to demonstrate maturing processes, improved detection fidelity, more precise automation, reduced alert volume through effective tuning, and stronger collaboration with technology and business units. Executives respond to narratives of growth and improvement far more than they respond to static tables of metrics. A SOC that learns how to communicate its progress earns trust, stability, and long term investment from leadership.

In truth, most SOC failures are not sudden implosions. They appear slowly, almost imperceptibly. Alert fatigue accumulates grain by grain. Tool sprawl grows unnoticed until it affects every workflow. Visibility gaps remain invisible until the day they no longer are. Escalation paths weaken as roles blur and assumptions accumulate. Burnout creeps in quietly, long before anyone says it aloud. Poor ROI reporting does not destroy the SOC directly, but it erodes its ability to defend itself when budgets tighten or leadership changes. These warning signs are not inevitabilities. They are signals that something must change.

This chapter, and this book as a whole, is intended to provide a corrective path. It argues that a SOC is not defined by tools or dashboards but by the quality of its engineering and the discipline of its operations. Technology amplifies what already exists. A SOC with weak processes becomes weaker with more tools. A SOC with strong processes becomes more efficient, more capable, and more resilient. Tools do not rescue a poorly structured operation. They magnify both strengths and flaws.

If there is one lesson to carry into every leadership decision, it is that process must come before technology. No SIEM, no SOAR platform, and no endpoint tool can compensate for unclear workflows or undefined responsibilities. Security operations succeed when procedures are documented, roles are clear, communication paths are established, and outcomes are measurable. Only when this foundation is in place do technical platforms evolve from noisy machinery into true force multipliers.

A SOC does not succeed because attackers are weak. It succeeds because its operations are engineered deliberately. And in the end, the ability to demonstrate that success in business language is what keeps the SOC funded, supported, and trusted.

Reinforcing the Core Lessons

A modern SOC is not a collection of tools, dashboards, or workflows. It is a living ecosystem where every function influences the next and no action exists in isolation. Detection quality shapes the pace and clarity of triage. Triage outcomes determine the accuracy and depth of investigation. Investigations reveal gaps that drive tuning and new detection engineering. Incident response produces intelligence that feeds back into threat hunting. Reporting closes the loop by validating that the SOC is not only functioning but meaningfully improving the organization's security posture. When any one of these components weakens, the entire ecosystem absorbs the impact. When each part strengthens, the system scales naturally and gracefully.

This interconnectedness is the defining reality of modern security operations. A SOC cannot rely on clever detections if triage procedures are unclear. It cannot rely on fast triage if investigations lack context. It cannot rely on advanced threat hunting if visibility gaps remain unaddressed. It cannot present credible reporting if processes are inconsistent or undocumented. Each discipline reinforces the others, and the SOC that fails to cultivate these feedback loops becomes a collection of disconnected efforts rather than a unified defensive system.

Automation plays a prominent role in this ecosystem, but automation is only as effective as the judgment encoded within it. A SOAR platform cannot fix a poorly designed workflow any more than a powerful SIEM can compensate for incomplete visibility. Automating chaos only produces chaos faster. The SOCs that thrive are the ones that treat automation as a disciplined engineering practice. Their playbooks reflect clearly defined decision paths. Their micro automations eliminate repetition without eliminating necessary human oversight. Their workflows undergo testing, version control, and continuous improvement just like any mature software system. DevOps principles have become essential for SOC sustainability. Without structured change management, reliable deployment pipelines, and source controlled logic, operational drift becomes inevitable.

Yet even with excellent tooling and automation, the SOC remains a human driven discipline. Analysts must be trained, supported, mentored, and protected. The strongest detections in the world achieve nothing if the people reviewing them are exhausted, overwhelmed, or uninformed. Emotional fatigue, unclear escalation culture, hostile communication patterns, or a lack of professional development can degrade a SOC more quickly than any technical failure. At its core, a SOC is a team of people making decisions under pressure. Organizations that understand this invest in their analysts with the same dedication they invest in their platforms. They build healthier schedules, promote knowledge sharing, standardize processes, and ensure analysts do not operate in isolation. The best leaders elevate analyst well being to a strategic priority because they know tired analysts make mistakes and supported analysts build excellence.

Finally, a SOC must learn how to tell its story. In many organizations, the technical work is strong, but the narrative is weak. If leadership cannot see the value of the SOC, funding will decline, staffing will freeze, and tooling will stagnate. Security becomes the first budget line to suffer during economic tightening because its value is often invisible unless deliberately communicated. A SOC must translate its outcomes into language the business understands. This means illustrating how risks were reduced, how incidents were contained, how downtime was avoided, and how the organization is safer today than it was last quarter. It means showing progress, maturity, growth, and strategic alignment instead of drowning executives in alert counts and dashboards. When a SOC can clearly articulate its impact, it becomes not only a defensive unit but a trusted partner in business continuity.

Taken together, these lessons define a strategic truth: a SOC is strongest when it is engineered deliberately, measured honestly, automated wisely, staffed compassionately, and represented clearly. Modern security operations succeed not through technology alone but through the careful orchestration of people, processes, and systems working in harmony. The SOC that internalizes these principles becomes resilient, adaptive, and indispensable. The SOC that does not risk becoming another cautionary tale in an industry filled with preventable failures.

An Implementation Roadmap

Translating theory into practice requires patience, sequencing, and deliberate maturity progression. A SOC cannot transform overnight, nor should it attempt to. The impulse to adopt new tools, deploy automation, or overhaul workflows all at once is both understandable and dangerous. Sustainable improvement is incremental. It comes from a structured growth path where each stage reinforces the next. What follows is not simply a checklist but a practical roadmap for SOC leaders seeking to evolve their operations with clarity and stability.

The journey begins with documentation. Before a single detection is tuned or an automation is built, the SOC must define how it intends to operate. Standard operating procedures for monitoring, triage, escalation, communication, and incident response are the foundation upon which everything else rests. These procedures must be written, reviewed, taught, and reinforced until they become the default behavior of the team. New analysts must immediately know what "right" looks like. Senior analysts must be able to challenge or refine process gaps. Without this consistency, tool investments collapse into chaos. A SOC that does not share a common operational language will never scale.

Once the procedural groundwork is stable, the next phase involves strengthening the detection pipeline and ensuring reliable telemetry. This is where most SOCs discover the hidden weaknesses in their environment: logs that arrive broken or partially parsed, alert rules that trigger on benign activity, and enrichment gaps that force analysts to perform manual context-building for every investigation. The focus here should be ruthless prioritization. Identify critical log sources and validate that they are ingested, parsed, and usable. Reduce alert noise through tuning, correlation, and contextual logic. Begin measuring alert quality rigorously, tracking false positive rates and signal-to-noise ratios until improvements become visible and repeatable.

Only after alert quality is stabilized should automation enter the picture. Automation must not be treated as a shortcut or a magic fix. It is a tool for encoding judgment and reducing repetitive cognitive load. The SOC should begin with micro automations: enrichment steps, validation checks, issuer lookups, intelligence queries, and similar low-risk tasks that assist the analyst rather than attempt full response. These early wins build trust both within the team and across leadership. As reliability increases and failure modes are understood, automation can gradually expand into conditional workflows and partial containment sequences. This measured approach prevents the common pitfall of designing overly ambitious playbooks that fail unpredictably.

With stable operations and trustworthy automation, the SOC enters its growth phase. This is where threat hunting becomes purposeful, detection engineering matures, and DevOps practices begin to reshape the SOC's technical backbone. Detections should be placed under version control. Pipelines should include testing steps to validate rule integrity before deployment. Automation should adopt CI and CD principles. Threat hunts should be informed by intelligence and telemetry, not performed ad hoc or opportunistically. This phase transforms the SOC from a reactive force into a proactive, intelligence driven capability.

The final stage involves refining the outward facing elements of the SOC: reporting, executive communication, metrics, and if the SOC supports external customers, service packaging. A SOC that has mastered internal stability can now articulate its value convincingly. It can present clear risk reduction narratives, demonstrate operational improvements over time, and provide high quality reporting that executives understand. At this level of maturity, the SOC is not merely functioning; it is flourishing. It is capable of scaling, teaching, influencing, and maturing continuously.

This roadmap is not prescriptive, nor is it rigid. It is a guide for sequencing growth in a discipline where premature complexity often leads to failure. By advancing step by step; first with documentation, then with telemetry and detection stability, then with thoughtful automation, then with engineering maturity, and finally with strategic communication, the SOC builds a structure capable of long term resilience. Strong foundations create strong operations. Strong operations create trust. And trust is the currency that allows a SOC to evolve into its full potential.

Next Steps

If you are an analyst, your next step is mastery. Learn how tools truly work, practice investigation discipline, develop communication skills, and move beyond alert closure into system improvement. If you are a SOC manager or leader, your next step is structure. Establish standards, protect analyst time, measure what matters, and lead continuous improvement intentionally. If you are building or scaling an MSSP, your next step is discipline. Package services clearly, price sustainably, enforce multi-tenant architecture, and treat your SOC as a product, not a promise. If you are an engineer, your next step is operationalization. Turn knowledge into code, logic, pipelines, and automation that others can rely on safely.

Final Thoughts

A SOC is never "finished." The threat landscape evolves, technology changes, people rotate, and businesses grow. The goal is not perfection, it is resilience. A resilient SOC adapts without collapsing, improves without burning out its people, and defends without losing clarity. This book has given you the blueprint. The next step is execution. Build deliberately. Tune relentlessly. Communicate clearly. That is what transforms a SOC into a capability and a career into mastery.

SOC & Incident Response Definitions and Acronyms

This appendix establishes shared language. Consistent terminology reduces confusion during incidents and ensures alignment across analysts, leadership, and clients.

SOC Security Operations Center

A centralized operational function responsible for the continuous monitoring, detection, investigation, containment, response, and reporting of security threats. A SOC may operate in-house or through an MSSP and functions as the nerve center for cyber defense.

SIEM Security Information and Event Management

An analytics platform that ingests logs, normalizes data, detects anomalies, correlates events, and supports investigations. SIEMs form the core of detection operations by providing searchable telemetry and actionable alerts.

SOAR Security Orchestration, Automation, and Response

A platform designed to automate repetitive SOC tasks, streamline enrichment, enforce decision logic, orchestrate multi-tool responses, and maintain case management. SOAR tools reduce analyst workload and increase consistency.

EDR / XDR Endpoint Detection & Response / Extended Detection & Response

EDR provides behavioral monitoring, telemetry collection, and automated response actions on endpoints. XDR expands visibility across multiple domainsnetwork, cloud, identity, endpoint to correlate cross-domain attacks.

IOC Indicator of Compromise

Discrete artifacts tied to malicious activity such as IP addresses, domains, URLs, file hashes, mutex names, registry keys, and process artifacts. IOCs are reactive; they identify known threats rather than novel behavior.

IOA Indicator of Attack

Behavioral indicators reflecting adversary intent, such as unusual privilege escalation, lateral movement patterns, or suspicious command execution. IOAs remain valuable even when specific IOCs change.

(TTP) Tactics, Techniques, and Procedures

Standardized descriptions of adversary behavior.

- *Tactics: the attacker's goal (e.g., persistence).*
- *Techniques: how the goal is achieved (e.g., scheduled tasks).*
- *Procedures: unique implementation details specific to a threat group.*

MITRE ATT&CK

A globally recognized framework cataloging adversary techniques, used in detection engineering, red/purple teaming, incident analysis, and coverage mapping.

MTTD / MTTR Mean Time to Detect / Mean Time to Respond

Metrics measuring detection and response efficiency.

- *MTTD measures how quickly a threat is identified.*
- *MTTR measures the time from detection to containment or remediation.*

False Positive / True Positive

- *False Positive: An alert indicating malicious behavior when none exists.*

- *True Positive: A valid alert identifying real malicious activity.*
  SOC efficiency relies on minimizing false positives and quickly validating true positives.

False Negative

A threat that occurs without triggering detection, one of the most dangerous SOC failure modes.

Containment / Eradication / Recovery

Three core incident response phases:

- *Containment: Preventing further spread or damage.*

- *Eradication: Removing adversary presence and artifacts.*

- *Recovery: Restoring systems to a trusted operational state.*

Threat Hunting

Proactive searching for hidden threats in an environment using hypotheses, behavioral analytics, and telemetry pattern analysis rather than waiting for alerts.

Telemetry

The collective system logs, events, metrics, and forensic artifacts that support monitoring and detection. Telemetry is the raw material of the SOC.

Attack Surface

The sum of all points where an adversary could attempt access. Includes:

- *External (public services, cloud assets)*
- *Internal (identity, endpoints, privileged accounts)*
- *Third-party/integrated systems*

Privilege Escalation

Adversary techniques used to gain elevated permissions such as SYSTEM, root, domain admin, or cloud admin roles.

Lateral Movement

The process by which an attacker expands access across systems after an initial compromise. Often relies on stolen credentials, SMB, RDP, SSH, or misconfigurations.

Persistence Mechanism

Any method that allows an attacker to remain in an environment after reboot, patching, or credential resets. Examples include scheduled tasks, registry run keys, WMI entries, startup scripts, and rogue cloud tokens.

C2 Command and Control

Communication channels used by attackers to remotely issue commands to compromised systems. Detection often relies on DNS patterns, beaconing behavior, or encrypted outbound traffic anomalies.

Beaconing

Regular, periodic outbound communications from infected devices to C2 servers. Often slow, stealthy, and low-volume.

Initial Access Vector

The method used to gain a foothold in the environment. Examples include phishing, credential stuffing, VPN compromise, web exploits, malware droppers, and supply-chain infiltration.

SOAR Playbook

A workflow defining automated actions, enrichment steps, decision branches, manual approvals, and notifications in response to specific alerts.

Case Management

Tracking of incident progress, evidence, notes, tasks, ownership, and communication through a SOC ticketing system.

Chain of Custody

A documented record showing who collected, handled, transferred, and stored evidence to ensure legal admissibility and forensic integrity.

Forensic Image / Memory Dump

A full, bit-for-bit snapshot of a disk or system memory used in deep forensic analysis.

Sandbox Detonation

Dynamic execution of potentially malicious files in a controlled environment to observe behavior.

Out-of-Band Communication

Communication channels separate from the compromised environment (e.g., phone calls, separate email systems) used during major incidents.

Breach Notification Window

A regulatory requirement mandating how quickly an organization must notify authorities or customers of a confirmed breach (e.g., GDPR's 72-hour rule).

Risk Score

A numerical measure assigned to entities, alerts, or vulnerabilities to rank priority based on severity, exploitability, and business impact.

Dwell Time

The length of time an attacker remains undetected inside an environment. Lowering dwell time is a primary SOC objective.

Zero Trust

A security model assuming no implicit trust inside or outside the network. Verification is required at every access point.

UEBA User and Entity Behavior Analytics

Machine-learning-driven detection focused on behavioral baselines and anomalies among users, devices, and services.

Incident Commander (IC)

The individual responsible for controlling communications, decisions, and direction during a major security incident.

Bridge Call

A coordinated communication line between SOC, IR teams, leadership, and technical stakeholders during live response operations.

Hotwash

A rapid post-incident review immediately after resolution, capturing operational lessons and areas for improvement.

Lessons Learned Report

A formalized post-incident analysis documenting root cause, detection gaps, response delays, and corrective actions.

www.ingramcontent.com/pod-product-compliance
Lightning Source LLC
LaVergne TN
LVHW052015200926
848481LV00005B/1493